I0795698

IMAGES
*of America*

# EAST HARLEM

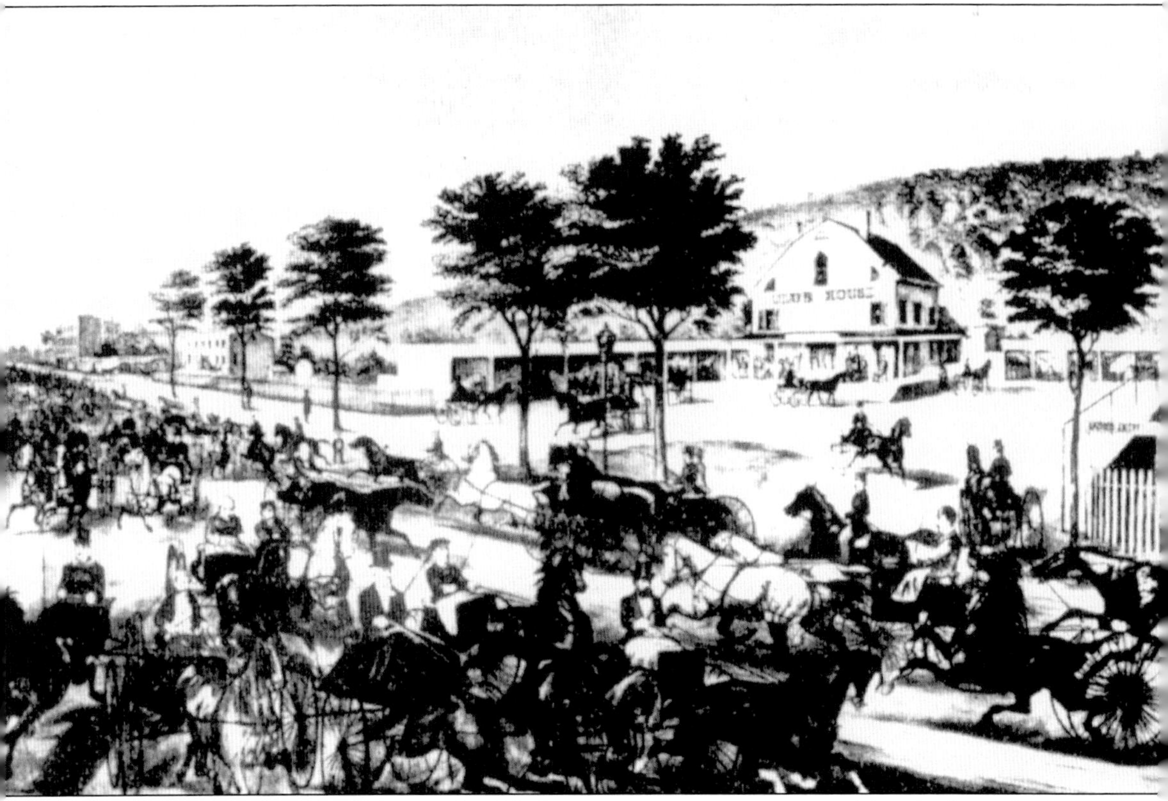

At the time of this 1850s view, East Harlem was a country resort just 11 miles from the lower tip of Manhattan. (Courtesy Pascale-Evans Photograph Archives.)

IMAGES
*of America*

# EAST HARLEM

Christopher Bell

ARCADIA
PUBLISHING

ISBN 978-0-7385-1339-3

Published by Arcadia Publishing
Charleston, South Carolina

Printed in the United States of America

Library of Congress Catalog Card Number: 2003110239

For all general information contact Arcadia Publishing at:
Telephone 843-853-2070
Fax 843-853-0044
E-mail sales@arcadiapublishing.com
For customer service and orders:
Toll-Free 1-888-313-2665

Visit us on the Internet at www.arcadiapublishing.com

*To Raphael Antonio Flores, a friend and mentor who loved East Harlem and its people.*

# Contents

# ACKNOWLEDGMENTS

I am greatly indebted to the following people for their contributions, insights, and suggestions that helped make this book a reality: Fr. Francis Skelley, St. Cecelia's Church; Fr. Alfred D'Incecco, Cardinal Hayes High School; Fr. George Stefas, St. George and St. Demitrious; Jerry and Eleanor Koffler; Raymond Rodriguez; Rev. Norman C. Eddy; Margaret McCants; Ilona Albok Vitarius; Antony Toussaint, Photographs and Prints Divisions, the Schomburg Center for Research in Black Culture; Anne Guernsey, Rights and Reproductions, the Museum of the City of New York; archivist Juan Pedro Hernandez, the Center for Puerto Rican Studies (Centro de Estudios Puertorriqueños), Hunter College, City University of New York; Stephan K. Saks, Photographic Services and Permissions, the New York Public Library; Barbara B. Sweeney; Dr. Alvin F. Poussiant, Harvard Medical School; John Blanchard; the Manhattan School of Music, Alumni Division; Ellen Perlman Simon, executive director of Union Settlement; the East Harlem Historical Society; Rose Pascale; Lois Pascale Evans; Dan Evans; Monique Flores; Denise Jones; J. Escalona; and Bruce Davidson.

Sources used for this book include *Africana: The Encyclopedia of the African and African American Experience* (1999), by Kwame Anthony Appiah and Henry Louis Gates Jr.; *The Film Encyclopedia* (2001), by Ephraim Katz; *Harlem: The Making of a Ghetto* (1963), by Gilbert Osofsky; *Memoirs of Bernardo Vega* (1984), by Cesar Andreu Iglesias; and *When Harlem Was Jewish* (1979), by Jeffrey S. Gurock.

# INTRODUCTION

East Harlem is located on the northern end of Manhattan on the East Side. Beginning at 96th Street and Fifth Avenue to the East River and ending at 142nd Street, the community is bounded by the Harlem and East Rivers and four bridges that connect East Harlem to the Bronx and Queens. For years, its neighbors have overshadowed East Harlem. To the west of the community lies Central Harlem, with its famed Harlem Renaissance, and to the south of the neighborhood lies the Upper East Side, with its opulence and wealth.

But East Harlem is significant in its own right, for its history parallels American history. As immigrants and, later, southern migrants sought the American Dream, they came to East Harlem to make their dreams a reality. Americans of every race, color, and creed at one time or another resided in East Harlem.

This continuity can be traced to the original inhabitants of the area: the Weckquaesqek Indians. The Weckquaesqeks were an offspring of the Mahican tribe related to the Algonquin Indians.

After Henry Hudson, a Hollander, arrived on the island of Manhattan in the early 1600s, the Dutch found the area ripe for cultivation. In 1626, Peter Minuit, another Dutchman, purchased Manhattan for $24, and the island was soon named New Amsterdam.

Following this transaction, 30 families left Holland and settled on the island of Manhattan. Two brothers from this group, Isaac and Henry DeForrest, along with African slaves, arrived in East Harlem and began to cultivate the area. In 1658, the area was named New Harlem (Nieuw Haerlem). Six years later, Dutch rule ended when Capt. Richard Nichols from England became the new sovereign of Manhattan and New Amsterdam became New York.

Although the Dutch would recapture New York in 1673, England regained authority the following year, and for the century following, East Harlem and the rest of Manhattan became a subject of the British Crown until the end of the Revolutionary War in 1783.

During this period, East Harlem was known for its mansions, estates, and farmland that adorned the area. In 1816, East Harlem's first school was founded. African American farmers arrived in East Harlem 14 years later and settled on 130th Street. German and Irish immigrants soon followed and built shantytowns throughout the neighborhood with jetsam and crates discarded from a nearby factory.

The first big change occurred when the New York Harlem Railroad built tracks and hotels in East Harlem. New Yorkers took advantage of these new amenities, and new arrivals to the neighborhood led to a modest population that totaled 1,500 in the middle of the 19th century.

It was the Second and Third Avenue elevated subways (built in the 1880s), which connected working families in East Harlem to the factories downtown, coupled with the Tenement House Act of 1879, that led to the burgeoning tenement construction throughout East Harlem, turning the neighborhood into a dense community seemingly overnight. These tenements housed many European immigrants from Germany and Ireland, with smaller groups from Finland. Later, immigrants arrived from eastern Europe.

The immigrants found work in the masonry, iron, stone, and rubber factories that existed throughout East Harlem, but some workers were not so lucky. Italian immigrants were exploited by the *padrone* system that allowed cheap labor for little or sometimes no wages at all. The Italians, who arrived in the late 1870s, settled east of Third Avenue from 104th to 120th Streets in an area called Little Italy.

Religion became an important part of life for East Harlemites as synagogues and churches representing many denominations were concentrated throughout the neighborhood, including Swedish, Finnish, Norwegian Lutheran, Dutch Reform, German, African Methodist, Episcopalian, Catholic, and Hungarian.

East Harlem entered the 20th century as a self-sufficient community replete with outdoor markets, theaters, movie houses, public schools, banks, hospitals, and libraries. Many African Americans from the South and Caribbeans of African descent arrived in New York during the beginning of the new century. Although many settled in Harlem, some African Americans lived at the northeast corner of East Harlem in an area called the Hill (from 99th to 102nd Streets).

Although Latinos lived in New York City since the latter half of the 19th century, by the end of World War I, some 10,000 Latinos, mostly of Puerto Rican heritage, resided in East Harlem. These new immigrants worked as *tabaqueros*, or cigar makers, in factories throughout New York City. The section in which they settled quickly became Spanish Harlem, or El Barrio.

The Latinos' arrival to East Harlem coincided with the exodus of many Europeans, mostly the Irish and Jewish, who left the community for the other neighborhoods in New York City.

Some Latinos joined the Socialist movement that took place in East Harlem during this period. One of the Socialist leaders, Morris Hillquit, a recent arrival from the Lower East Side, became involved in East Harlem politics when he ran for Congress. But Hillquit's campaigns were unsuccessful, as he lost several elections. A resident from Greenwich Village, Fiorello La Guardia, was elected to Congress from East Harlem in 1922 and would hold on to that seat until he was defeated by James Lanzetta a decade later. Vito Marcantonio, La Guardia's protégé, was elected to Congress in 1934. Although he was not reelected in 1936, Marcantonio regained his seat in 1938 and represented the neighborhood until his final defeat in 1950.

After World War II, many Puerto Ricans arrived by plane or by a boat called the *Marine Tiger* and settled in the neighborhood. During this time, public housing, which began in 1940 with the East River Houses, accelerated during the 1950s, when many tenements were razed and some neighbors and family members who lived in the same buildings for decades were displaced to other communities throughout New York City.

The high-rise housing projects replaced the tenements, and while some residents thought these conditions were better than the deteriorating tenement buildings, many detractors commented that the intimacy was gone from the community. Over 1,000 businesses were eviscerated due to the construction of public housing, and by the early 1960s, one-third of East Harlemites lived in public housing. The population, which was once over 200,000, decreased by more than 50,000. Public housing also changed the face of East Harlem as African Americans moved into the public housing projects. The Italian Americans followed the other immigrants and left East Harlem for the other boroughs in New York City. The Italian Americans who mostly remained in East Harlem resided along First or Pleasant Avenues.

Most East Harlem residents are now mostly African Americans and Latinos. But unlike the earlier immigrants who lived in East Harlem, many African Americans and Latinos found little opportunity due to racism and low-paying jobs.

For the most part, East Harlem escaped the riots that plagued other communities throughout New York City and America during the late 1960s. The community also survived New York City's fiscal crises during the 1970s and the deteriorating drug crises of the 1980s. In the late 1990s and into the 21st century, East Harlem continued its tradition of welcoming newcomers to the neighborhood as Mexican Americans and other Latinos joined the Senegalese, Asians, and whites who have become new East Harlemites.

Also, during this period, many businesses invested in the neighborhood as new franchises arrived in East Harlem. Today, East Harlemites can walk along 125th Street or along Third Avenue and purchase quality produce, merchandise, and goods as they did a century ago.

*One*

# The Early Years along 116th Street

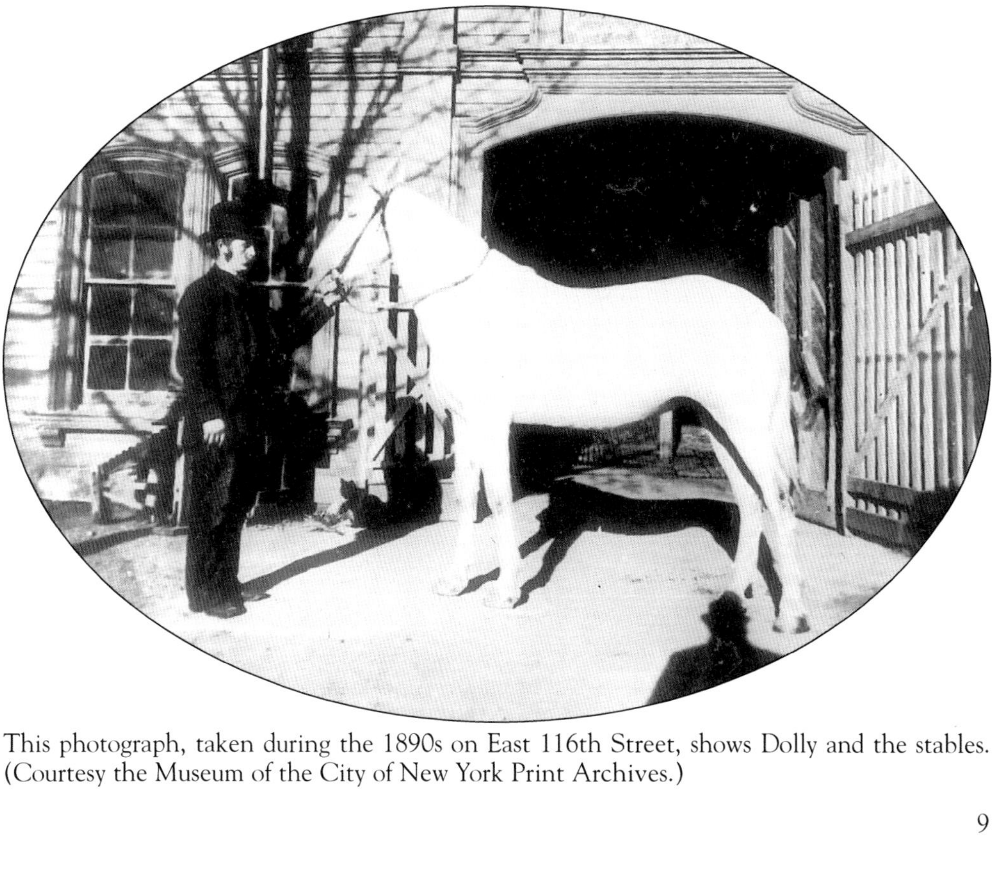

This photograph, taken during the 1890s on East 116th Street, shows Dolly and the stables. (Courtesy the Museum of the City of New York Print Archives.)

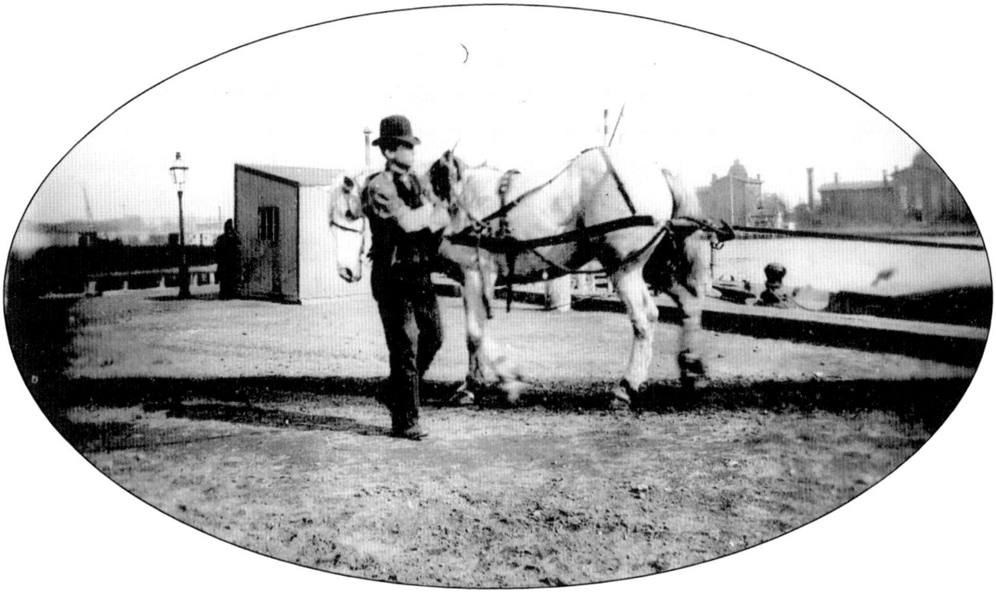

Iron, coal, lumber, and other masonry businesses were commonplace in East Harlem during the late 19th and early 20th centuries. During the 1890s, East Harlemites could be seen unloading coal on 116th Street. (Courtesy the Museum of the City of New York Print Archives.)

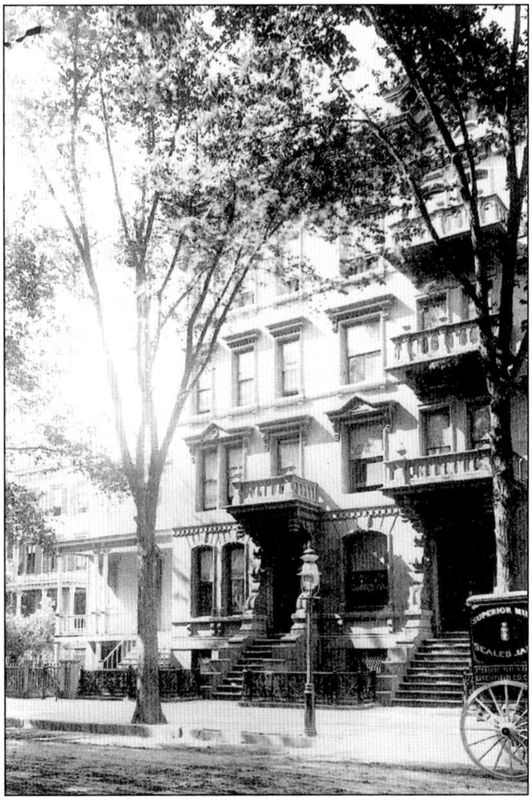

In this 1890s photograph, East Harlem is depicted as a suburban neighborhood between First and Pleasant Avenues. (Courtesy the Museum of the City of New York Print Archives.)

Rosina and Giovanni Pascale, the parents of Pete Pascale, are shown in their East Harlem backyard in the 1930s. (Courtesy Pascale-Evans Photograph Archives.)

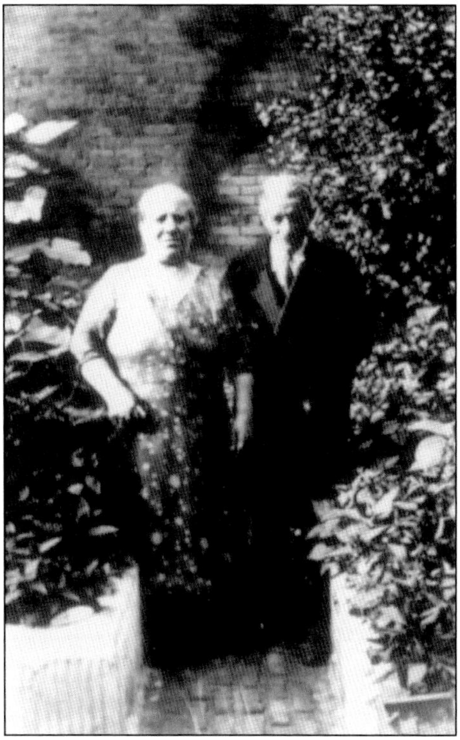

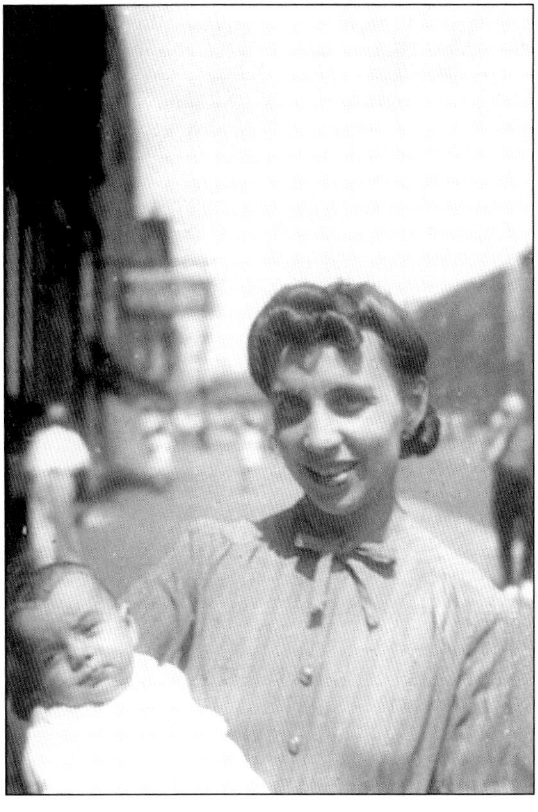

Rose Pascale is pictured in 1939 with her son John outside 326 East 116th Street. (Courtesy Pascale-Evans Photograph Archives.)

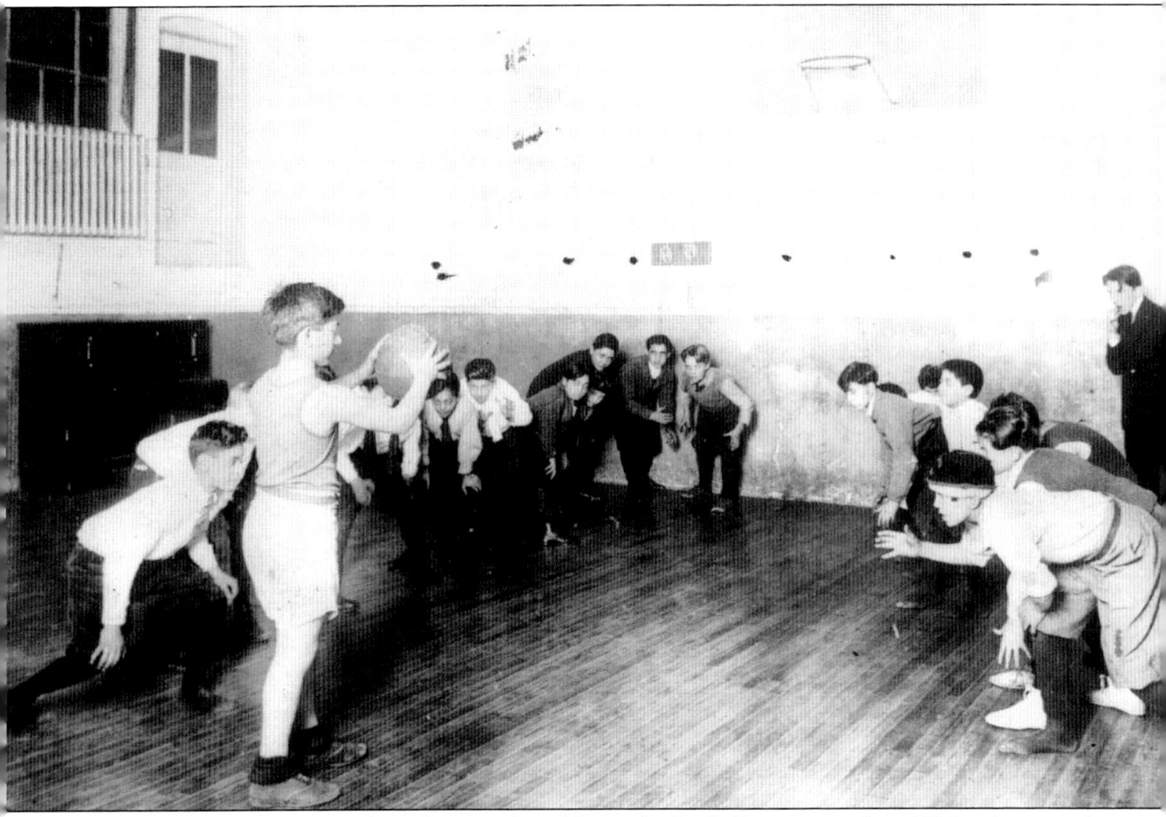

Vito Marcantonio coaches the Haarlem House basketball team in this 1920s photograph. (Courtesy Pascale-Evans Photograph Archives.)

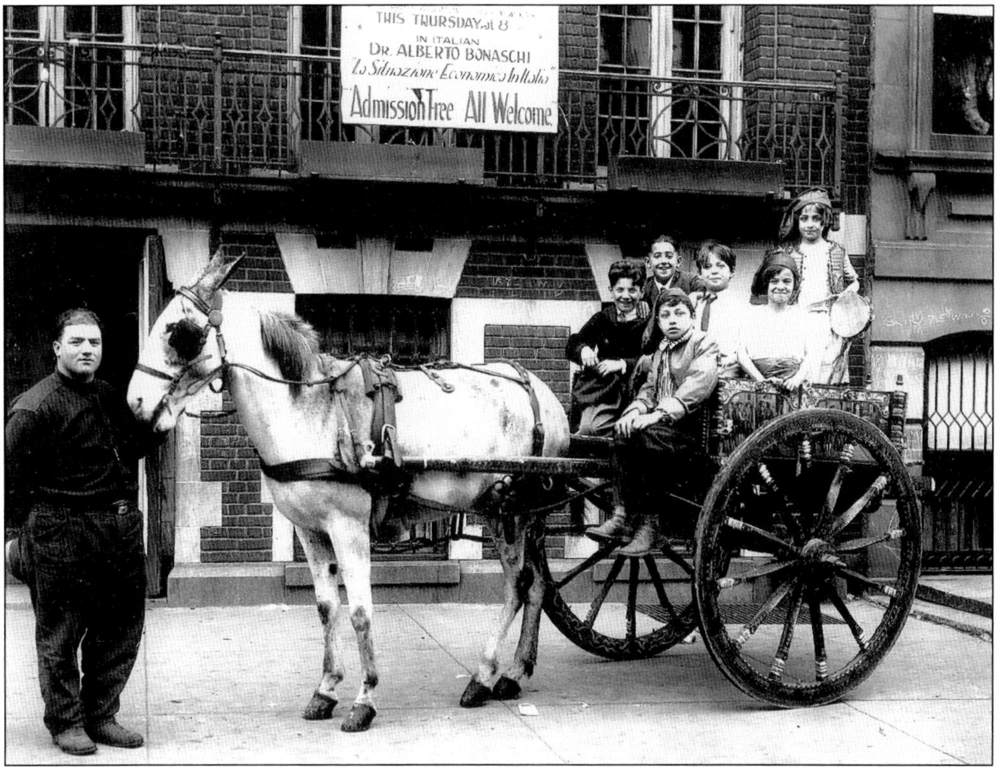


These 1930s children are seen in a Sicilian horse cart in front of Haarlem House. (Photograph by A. Tennyson Beals; courtesy Pascale-Evans Photograph Archives.)

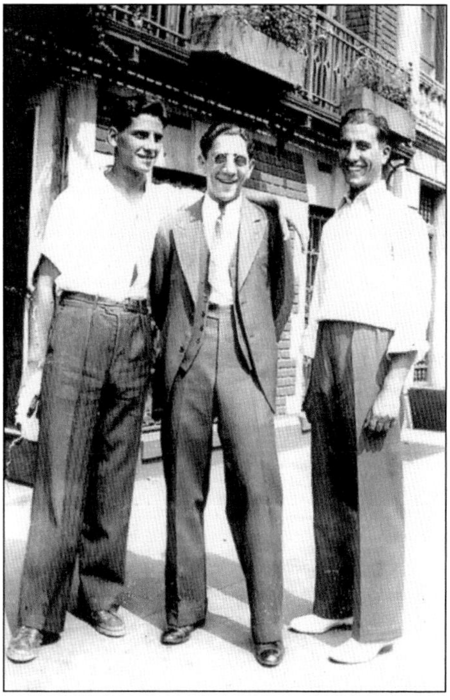

Pete Pascale (center) is seen in this 1930s view with his friends Oscar Pugliesi (left) and Louis (Murphy) Marffie in front of Haarlem House. (Courtesy Pascale-Evans Photograph Archives.)

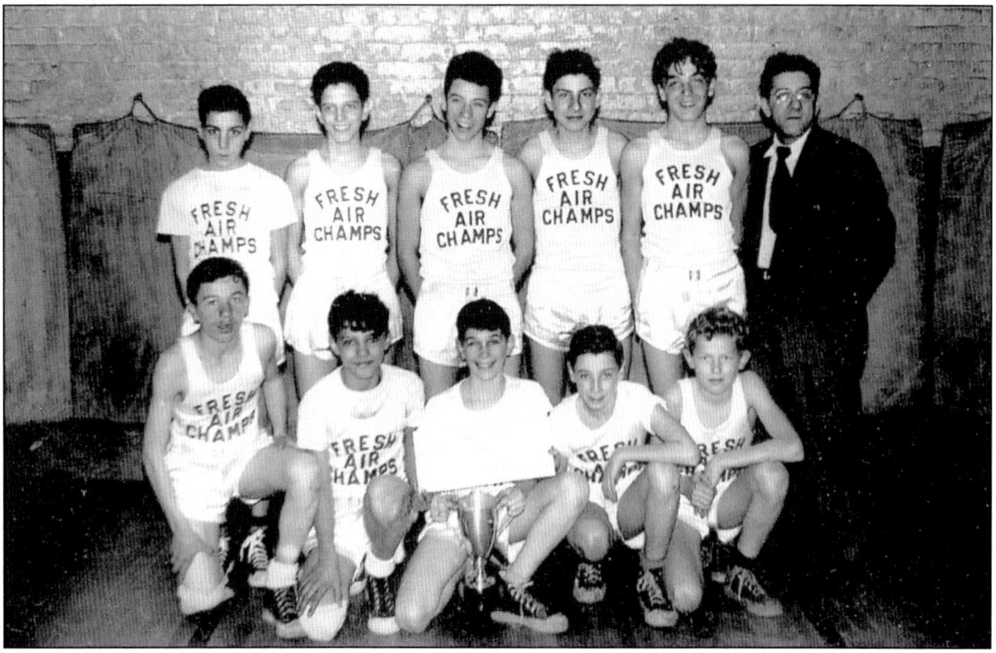


This photograph, taken inside the Haarlem House gym, shows the 1948–1949 Haarlem House Fresh Air Fund basketball team with coach Pete Pascale. Team members include Frank Sengenito, E. Vitale, J. Trimarco, J. Catlado, M. Siano, E. McCabe, A. Paglinca, Freddy Cincotti, Freddy's son Peter Cincotti (a popular composer, pianist, and singer), V. Vacco, and G. Bunzel. (Courtesy Pascale-Evans Photograph Archives.)

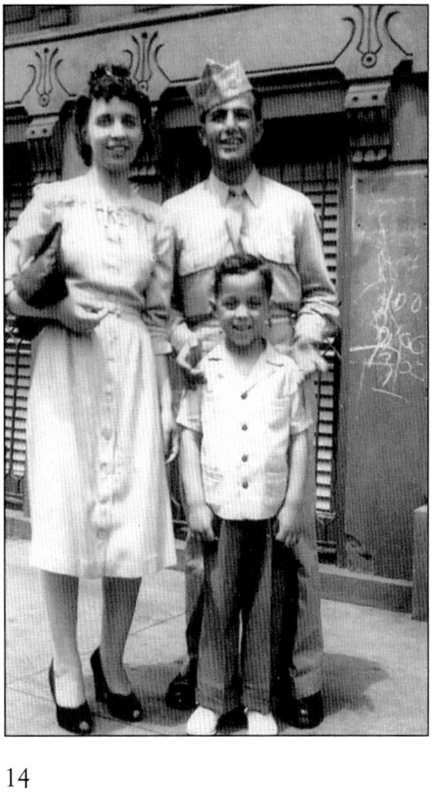

Rose Pascale, Vincent "Sonny" Capaldo (the brother of Rose Pascale), and John Pascale (the son of Rose and Pete Pascale) are seen in front of their apartment, located at 331 East 116th Street, on July 18, 1944. (Courtesy Pascale-Evans Photograph Archives.)

Elizabeth Capaldo, the mother of Rose Pascale, takes her turn in front of the building at 331 East 116th Street in the 1940s. (Courtesy Pascale-Evans Archives.)

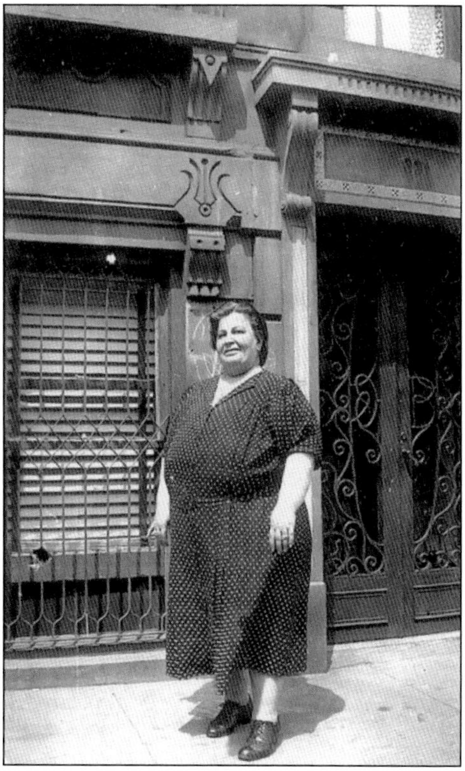

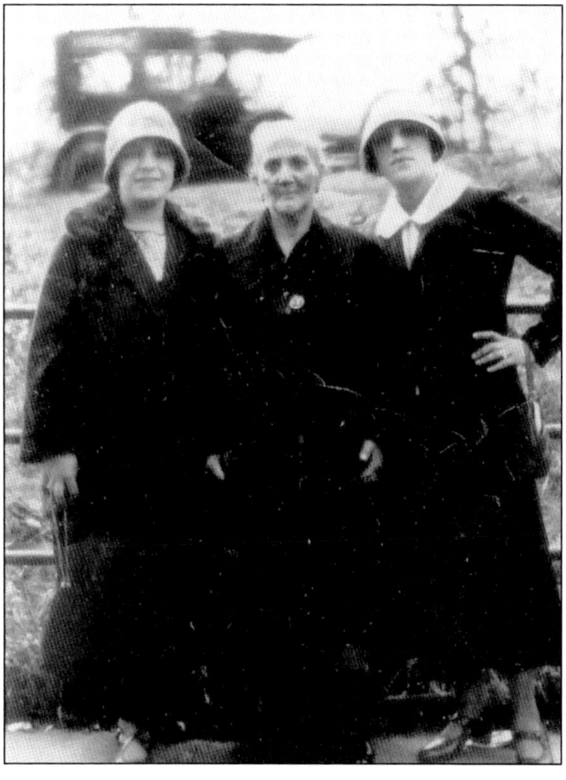

This 1920s portrait was taken at 114th Street and Jefferson Park. From left to right are Mary ?, Louisa Gamiello, and Lena Yezzo. (Courtesy Pascale-Evans Photograph Archives.)

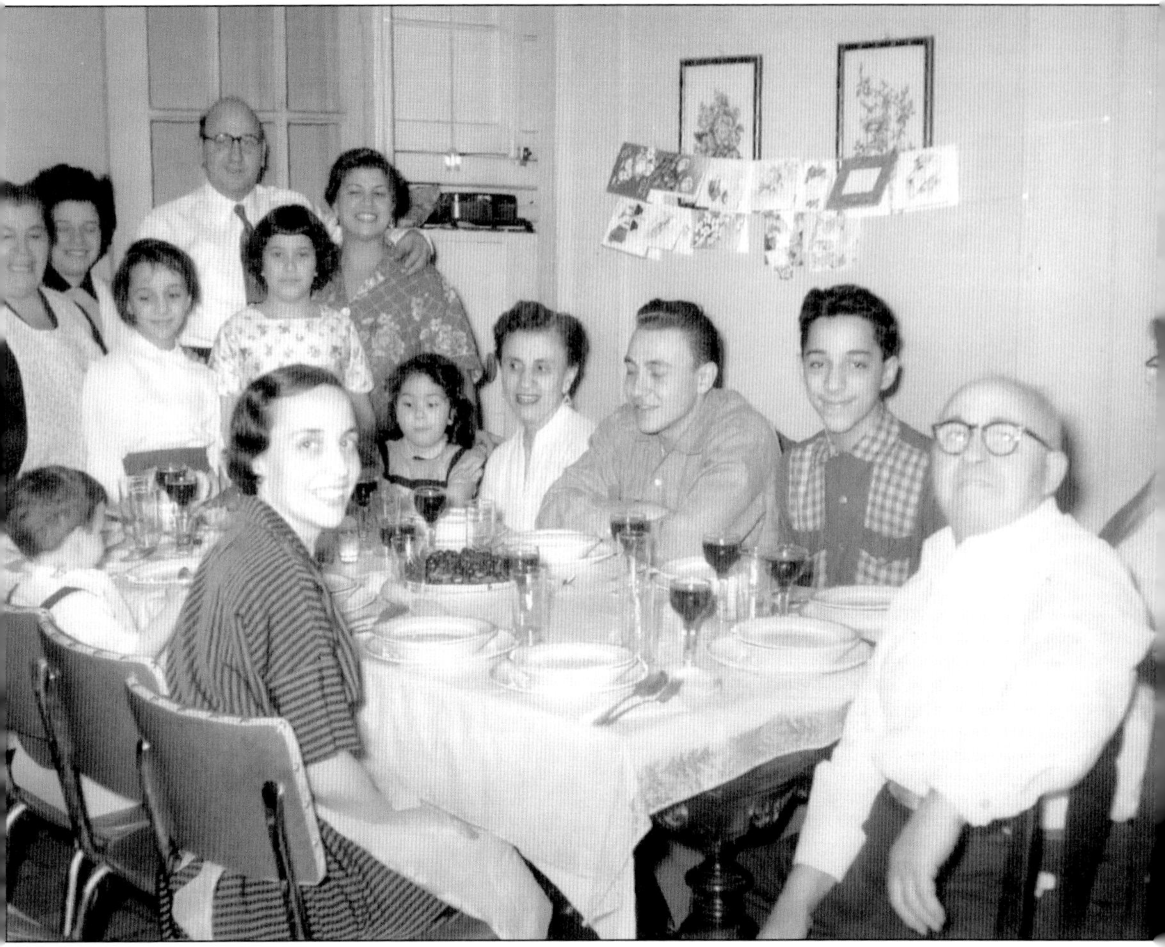

Vincent "Sonny" Capaldo took this Easter celebration photograph in 1957 at Louis and Elizabeth Capaldo's apartment at 326 East 116th Street between First and Second Avenues. The building was razed in the early 1960s. From left to right are the following: (seated) Robert Capaldo, Rose Pascale, Maria Elena Capaldo, Lena Yezzo, Tony "Cookie" Yezzo, John Pascale, Louis Capaldo, and Pete Pascale (partially visible); (standing) Elizabeth Capaldo (partially visible), Dora Capaldo, Lois Pascale, Freddy Cassotta, Leonilda Cassotta, and Dolly Cassotta. (Courtesy Pascale-Evans Photograph Archives.)

*Two*

# Prayerful People and Places

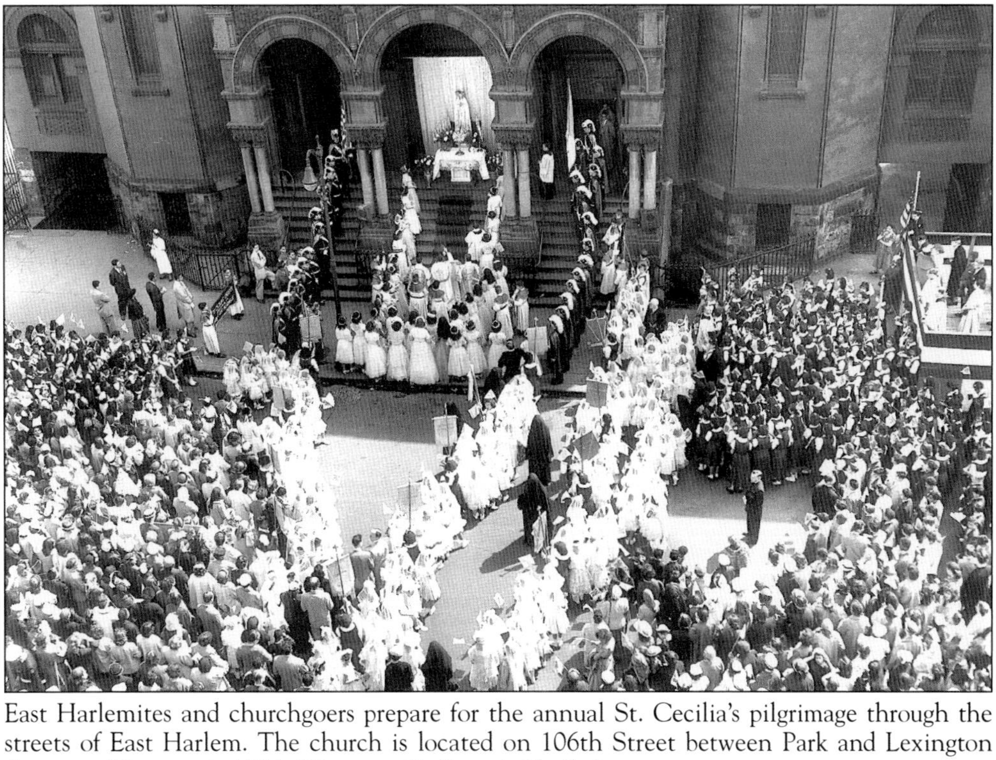

East Harlemites and churchgoers prepare for the annual St. Cecilia's pilgrimage through the streets of East Harlem. The church is located on 106th Street between Park and Lexington Avenues. The year is 1954. (Courtesy Fr. Francis Skelly.)

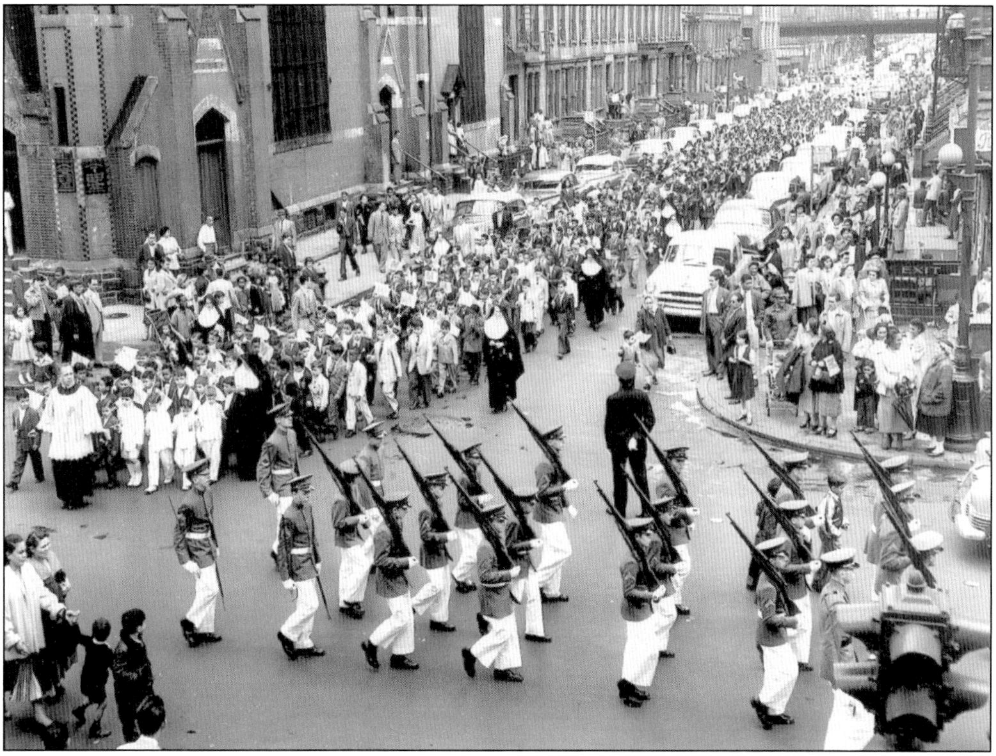

The 1954 pilgrimage makes its way to 111th Street and Lexington Avenue to the First Spanish Methodist Church before heading back to St. Cecilia's Church. The back exit to the 110th Street and Lexington Avenue station is in the right center. The Third Avenue elevated subway can be seen in the background. (Courtesy Fr. Francis Skelly.)

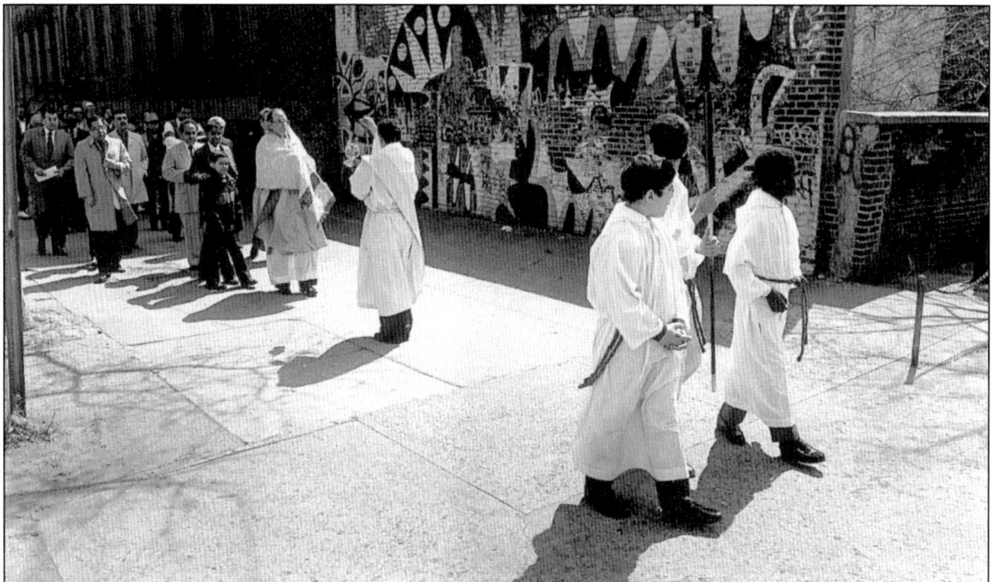

The pilgrimage is still alive in the 1980s, although the number of participants is much smaller. (Courtesy Fr. Francis Skelly.)

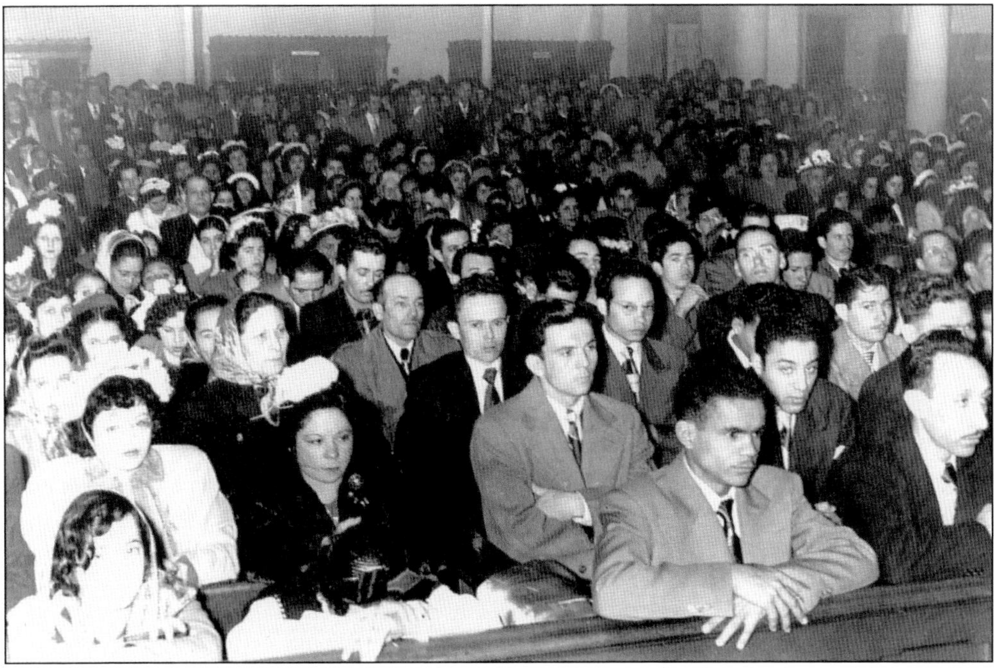

Mass was performed in Spanish for many Puerto Ricans and other Latinos at St. Cecilia's Church. This photograph was taken in 1955. (Courtesy Fr. Francis Skelly.)

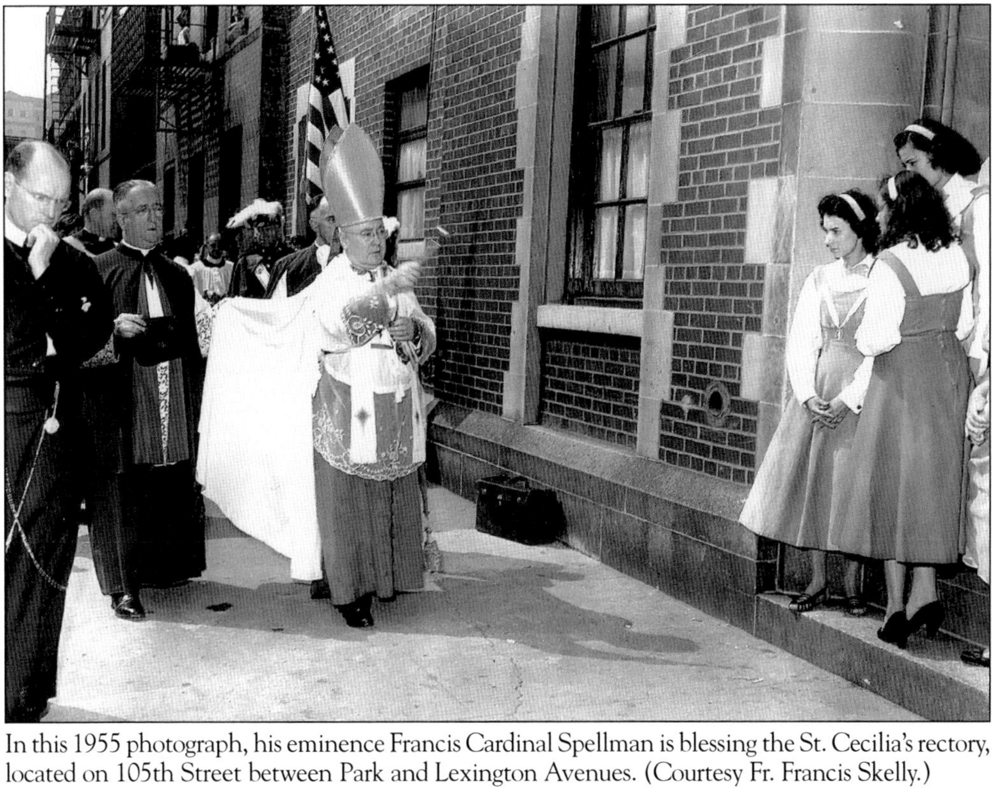

In this 1955 photograph, his eminence Francis Cardinal Spellman is blessing the St. Cecilia's rectory, located on 105th Street between Park and Lexington Avenues. (Courtesy Fr. Francis Skelly.)

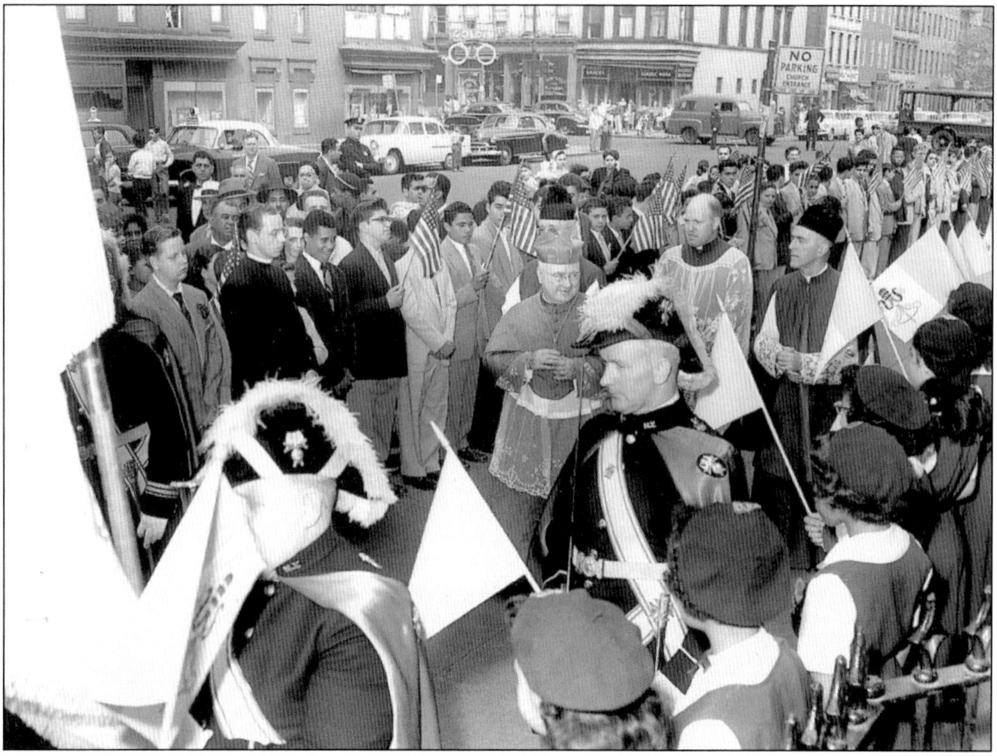


Later, well-wishers greet Cardinal Spellman as he arrives at St. Cecilia's Church. The church was built in 1887, and Fr. John Flannery was its first pastor. (Courtesy Fr. Francis Skelly.)

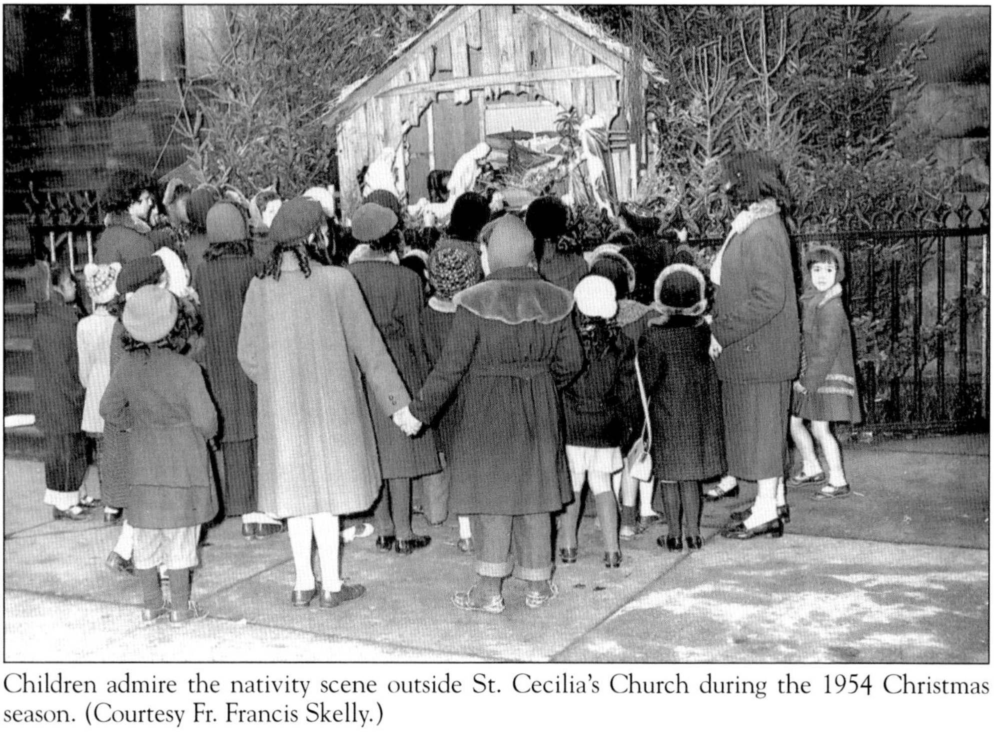

Children admire the nativity scene outside St. Cecilia's Church during the 1954 Christmas season. (Courtesy Fr. Francis Skelly.)

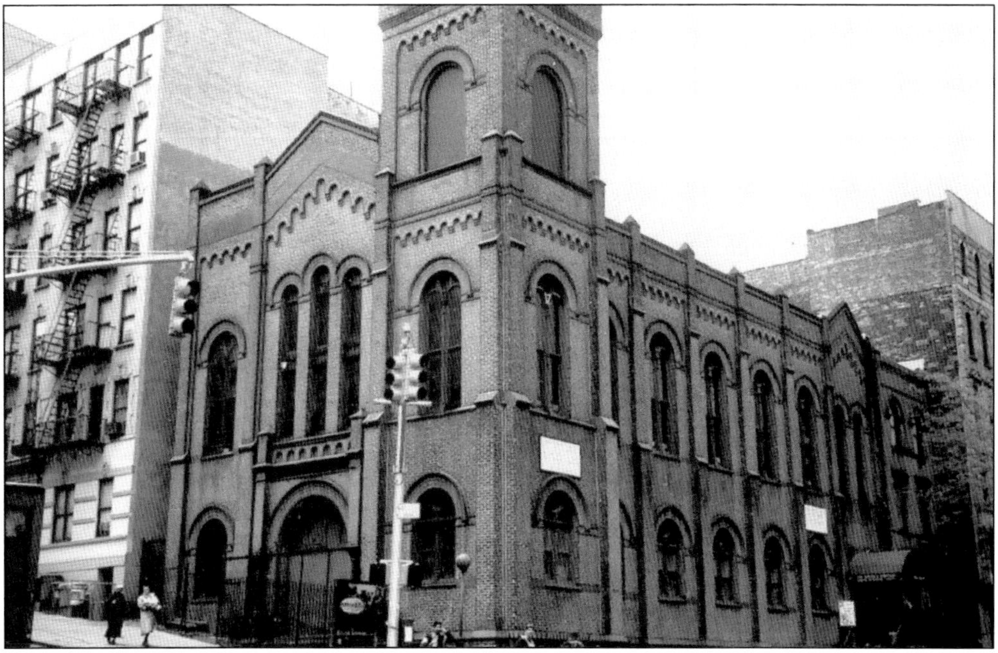

The St. George and St. Demitrious Greek Orthodox Church, located at 103rd Street and Lexington Avenue, is seen here. Originally, the St. George Church was located at 105th Street and Madison Avenue. The St. George Church merged with St. Demitrious in 1935. St. Demitrious was once located on 109th Street. Following the merger, the church moved into its present location after a Unitarian church abandoned this location. (Author's collection.)

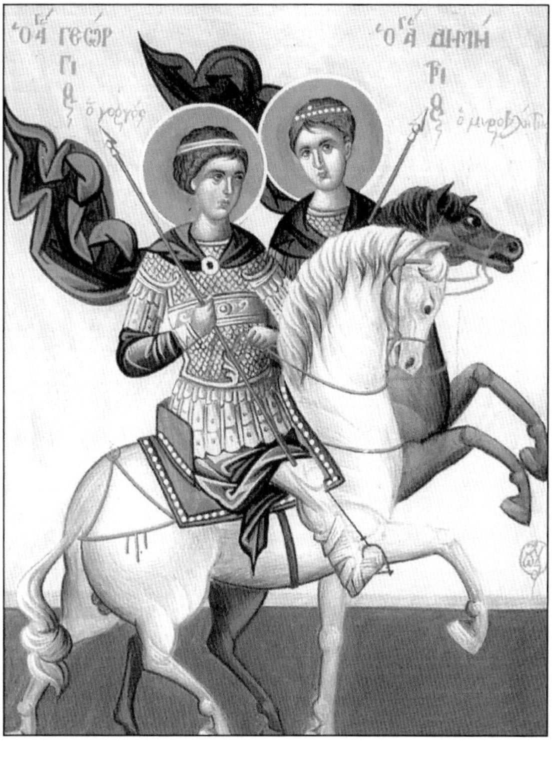

This postcard, with Greek writing, carries a blessing from the St. George and St. Demitrious Greek Orthodox Church. (Courtesy Fr. George Stefas.)

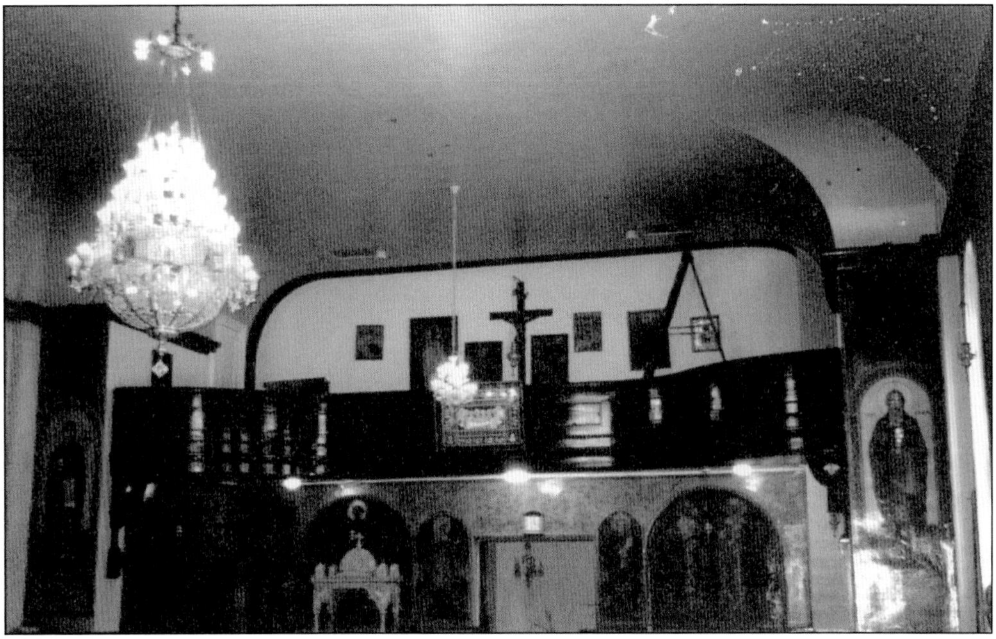

This view shows the inside of the St. George and St. Demitrious Greek Orthodox Church. (Author's collection.)

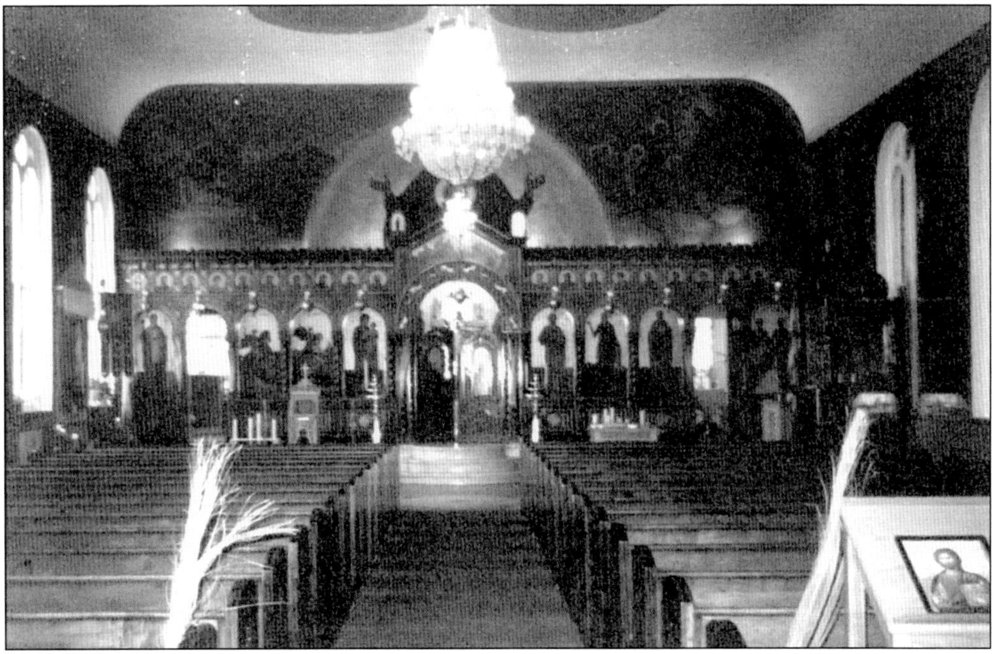

Palms indicate that the Easter service has ended, but the resplendent sight of the pews and artwork at the rear ensures that the parishioners and the curious will want to come back. (Author's collection.)

The St. Nicholas Russian Orthodox Cathedral, built in 1903, is located on 97th Street between Fifth and Madison Avenues. Recently, Russian president Vladimir Putin visited the church. (Author's collection.)

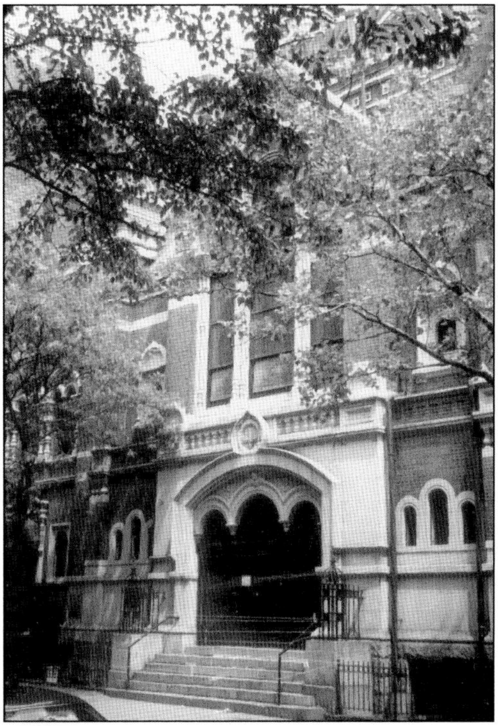

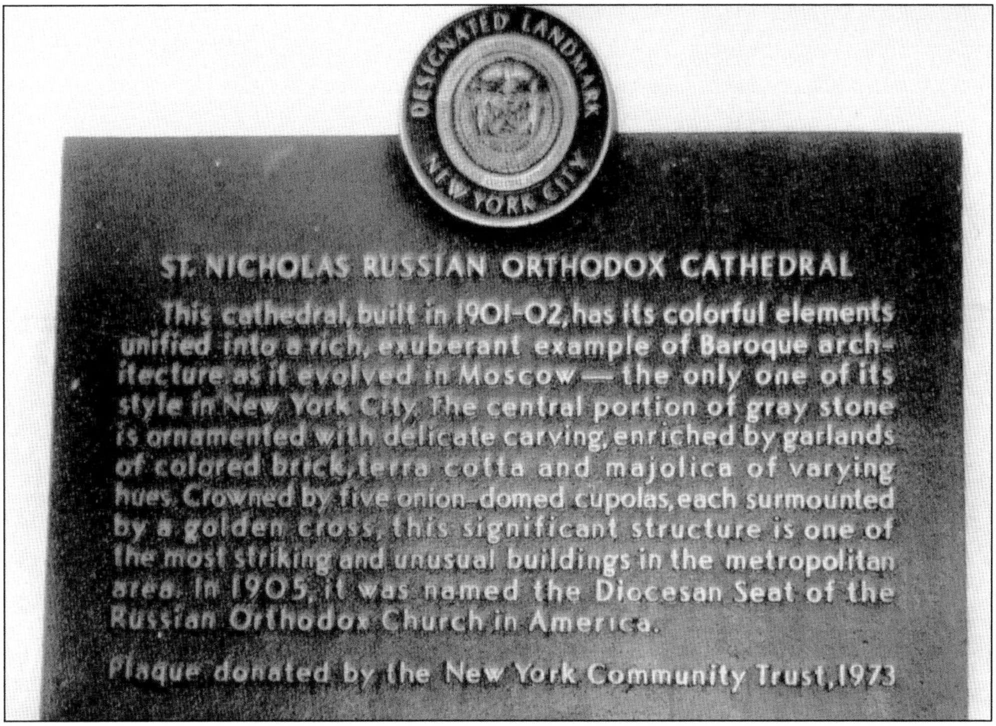


In 1973, the St. Nicholas Russian Orthodox Cathedral was named a landmark by the New York City Landmarks Preservation Committee. Seen here, a plaque commemorating the event is located adjacent to the church. (Author's collection.)

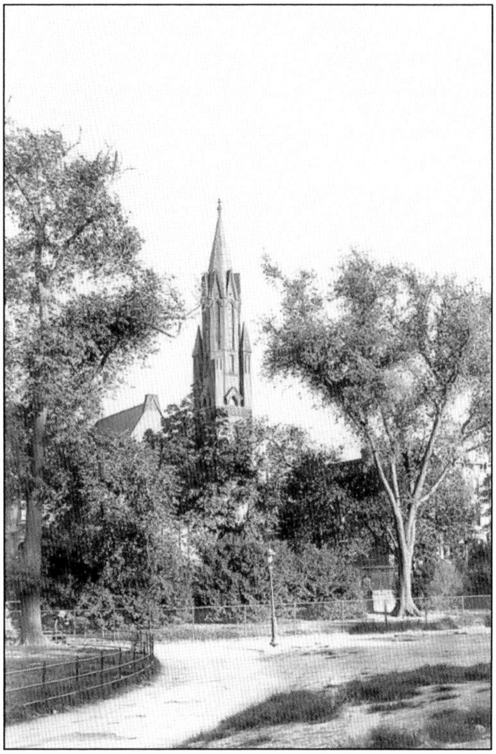

The Russian Orthodox Church was originally the Pilgrim Congregational Church, located inside Mount Morris Park. The park is located between 120th and 123rd Streets and Madison and Fifth Avenues. (Courtesy the New York Public Library.)

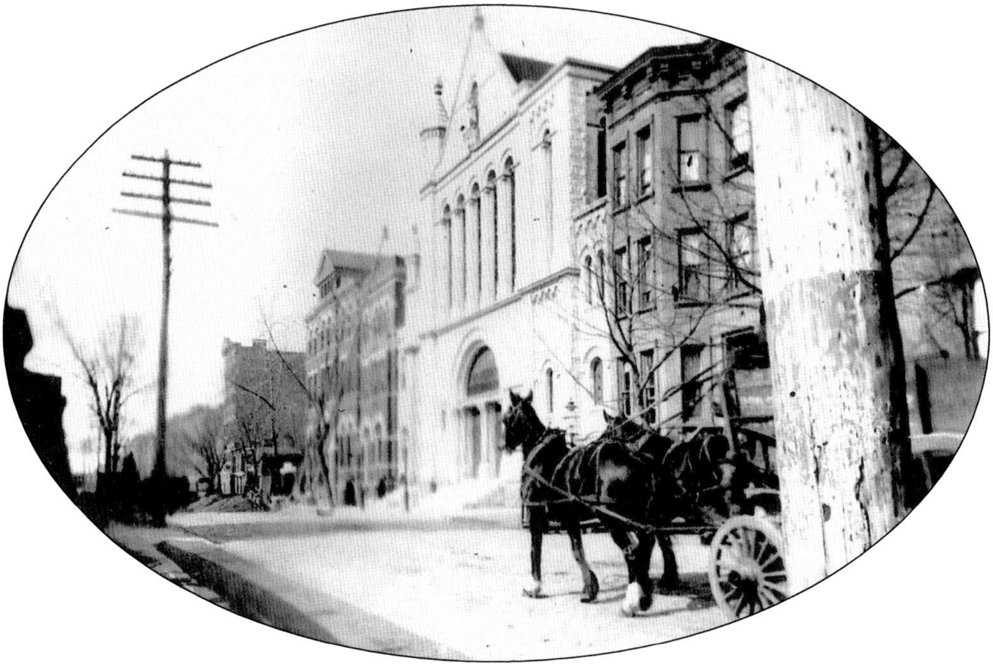

Our Lady of Mount Carmel was built in 1884. The church, seen here in the 1890s, began with the arrival of the Italian immigrants from the town of Polla, in the province of Selerno. The Pollentines viewed the Madonna as the protectress of Polla. The church's first Pollentine priest was Fr. Emiliano Kirner. (Courtesy the Museum of the City of New York.)

The Francis De Sales Church is located on 96th Street between Park and Lexington Avenues. Francis De Sales lived from the late 16th century into the 17th century. De Sales published two books on the spiritual life of Catholicism. He was canonized in 1665. Ground was broken 230 years later at the present location of the St. Francis De Sales Church. Although the church celebrated its first mass in 1896 in the church basement, it was not until 1903 that the upper section of the church was finished. (Author's collection.)

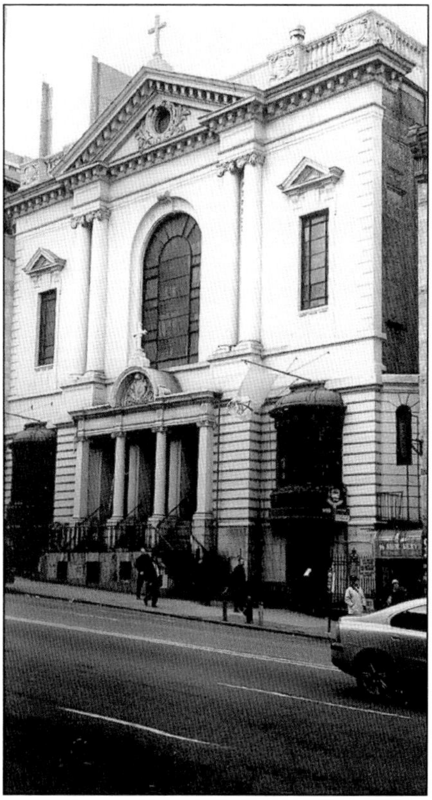

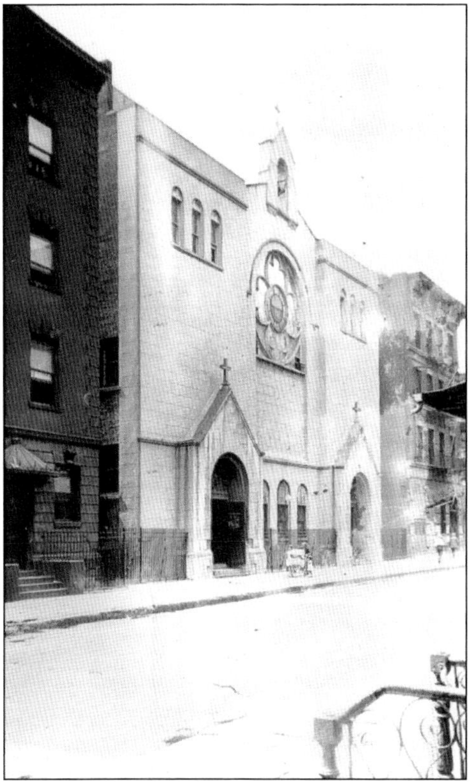

St. Lucy's parish, located on 104th Street between First and Second Avenues, is seen in this 1934 photograph. This parish is affiliated with St. Francis De Sales. (Courtesy the New York Public Library.)

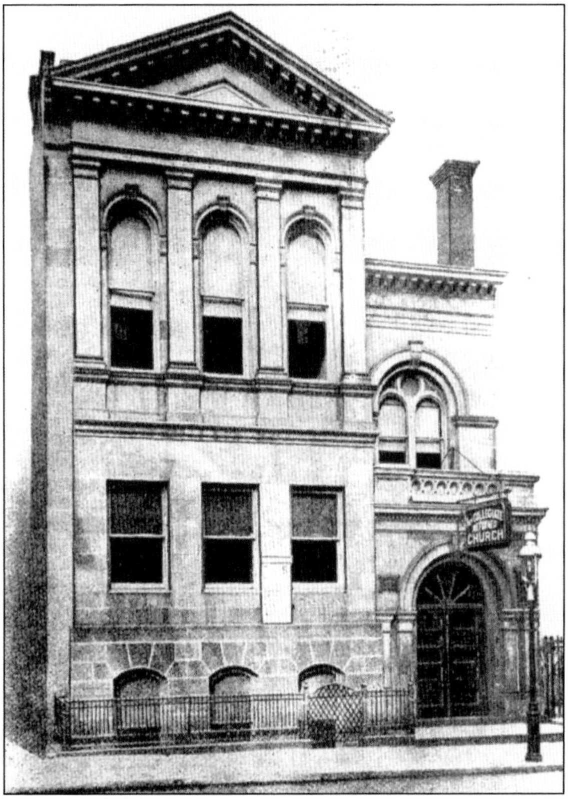

This 1908 photograph of the Collegiate Reform Church, located on 121st Street between Lexington and Park Avenues, traces its roots to the Reformed Dutch Church of Harlem, which was founded in the 1660s. Its founders were the original Dutch settlers who landed in Harlem a few decades earlier. (Courtesy the New York Public Library.)

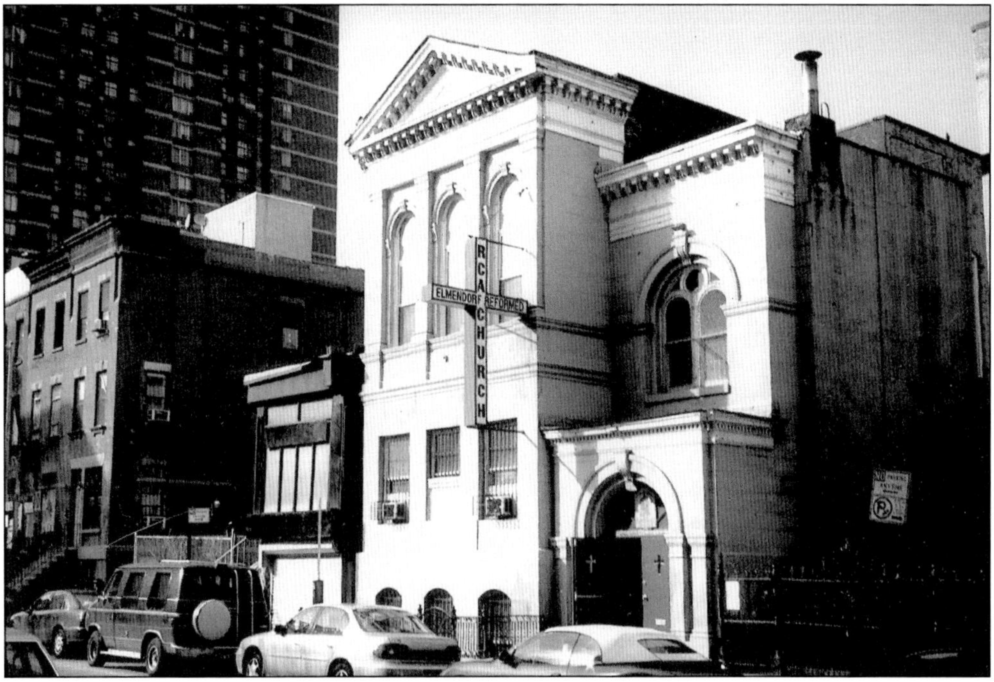


In 1910, the Collegiate Reformed Church became the Elmendorf Reformed Church, named after the Reverend Jouchim Elmendorf, who led the church from 1886 to 1898.

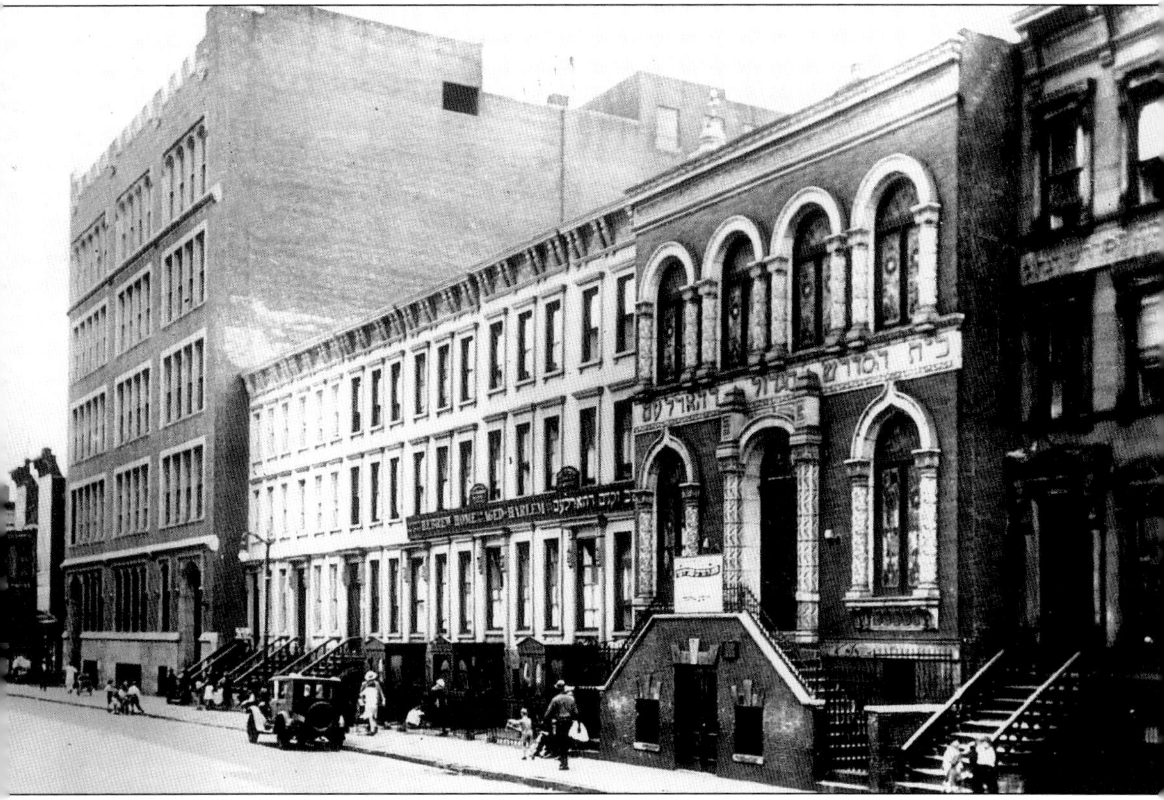

Seen on the south side of East 105th Street next to the Public School 72 Annex is Beth Hamidrash Hagodal of Harlem. On the left is the Hebrew Home for the Aged. The year of this photograph is 1929. (Courtesy the New York Public Library.)

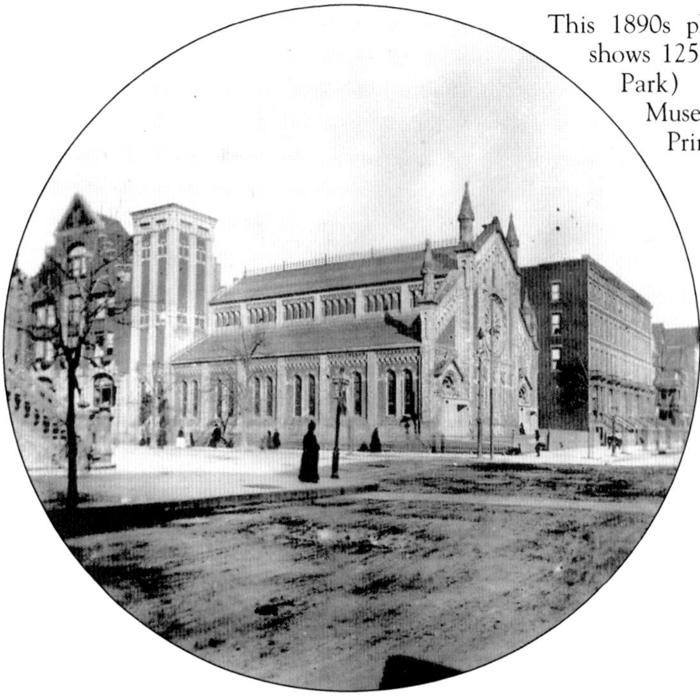

This 1890s photograph of a synagogue shows 125th Street and Fourth (now Park) Avenue. (Courtesy the Museum of the City of New York Print Archives.)

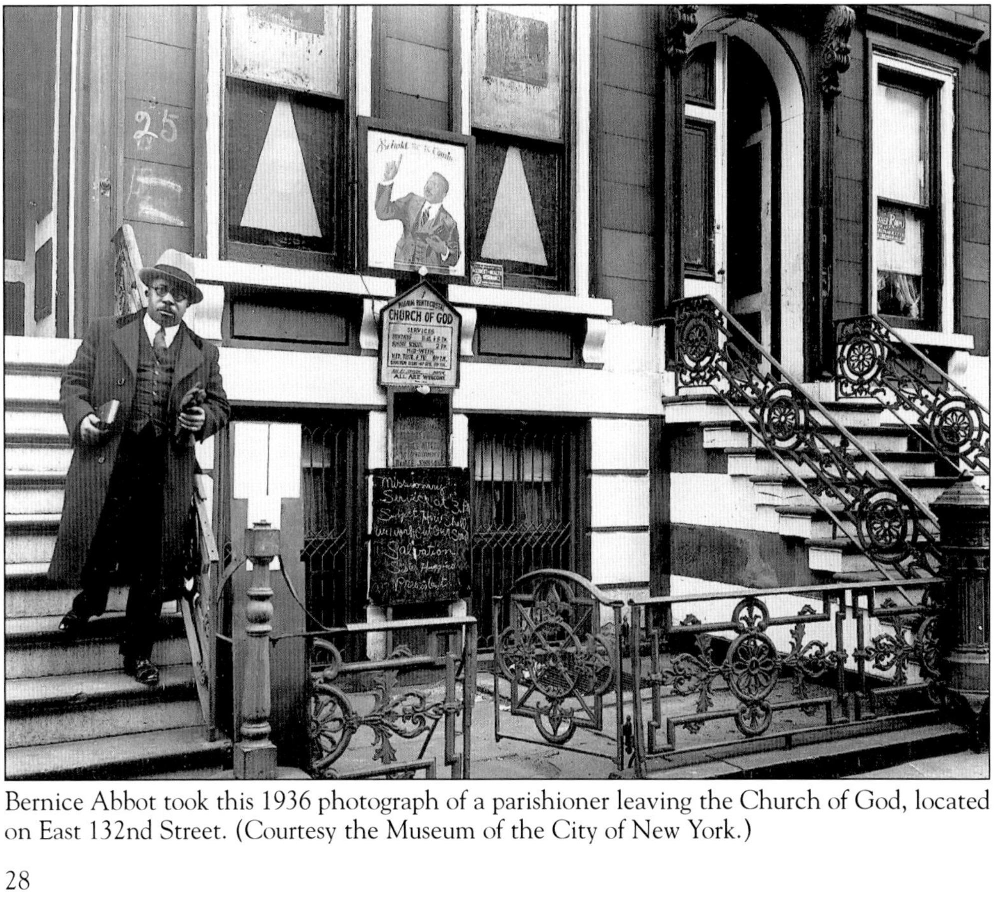


Bernice Abbot took this 1936 photograph of a parishioner leaving the Church of God, located on East 132nd Street. (Courtesy the Museum of the City of New York.)

# *Three*

# School Days

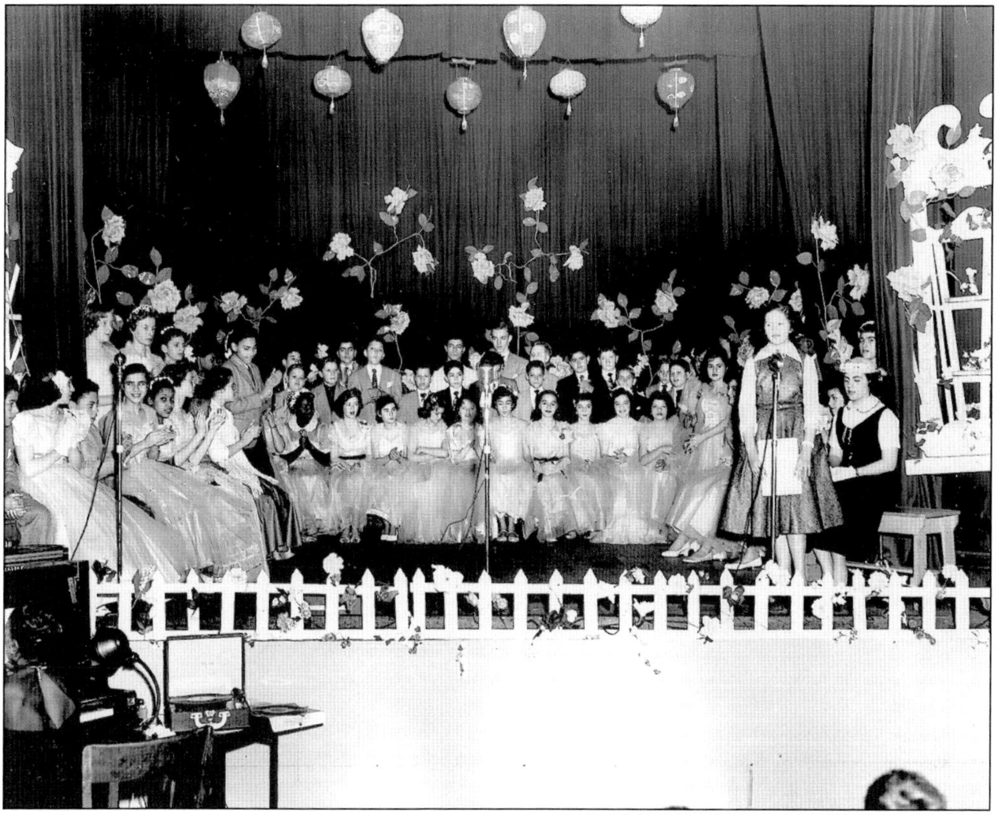

In this 1954 photograph, students play at the Commander John Shea Memorial School, located on 111th Street between Park and Lexington Avenues. The school was associated with St. Cecilia's Church. Today, the site of the Commander John Shea Memorial School is part of the Highway Church of Christ. (Courtesy Fr. Francis Skelly.)

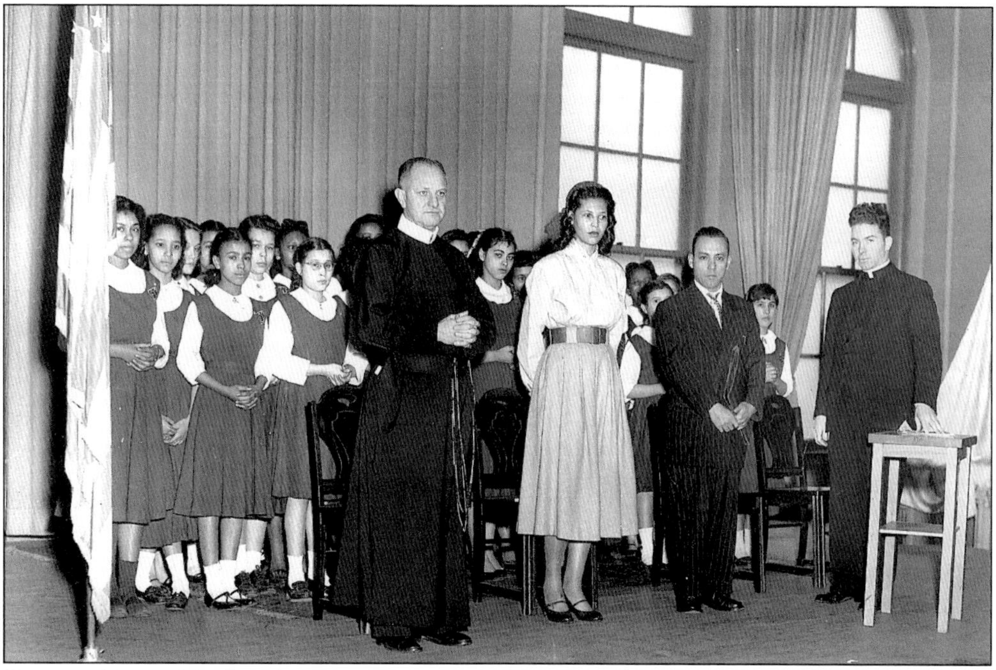

Seen is a Parent-Teacher Association meeting at Commander Shea Memorial School in 1952. (Courtesy Fr. Francis Skelly.)

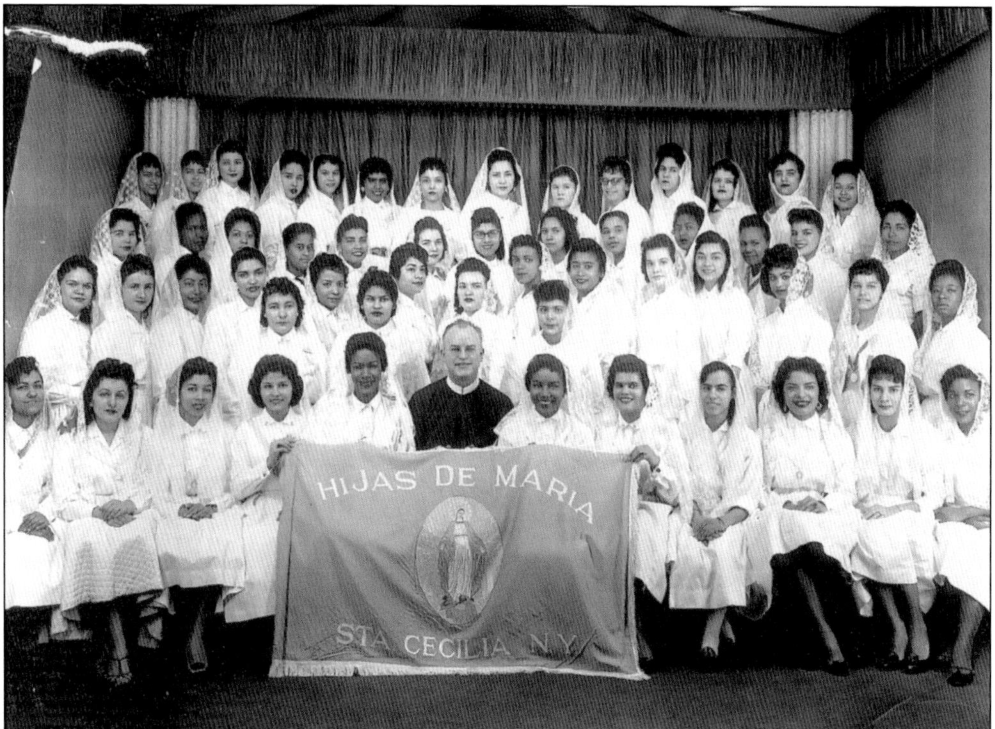


This 1948 photograph shows the Daughters of Maria (Las Hijas de Maria) girls' school. (Courtesy Fr. Francis Skelly.)

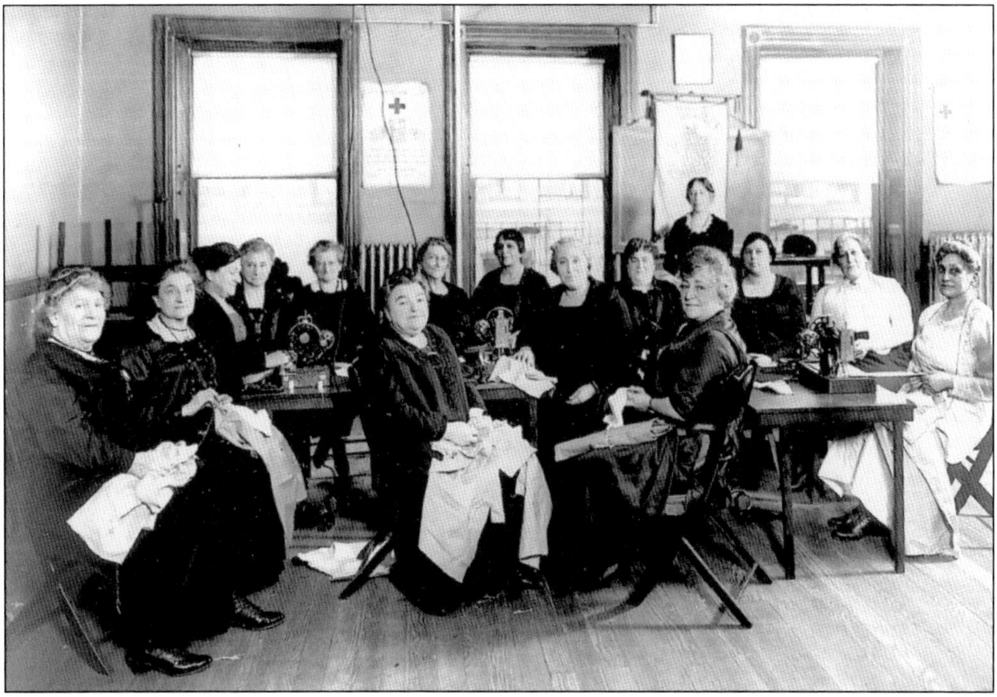

Seen in this 1920 photograph is the women's sewing circle of the Amelia Relief Society, located at 115 East 101st Street. (Courtesy the Museum of the City of New York, Byron collection.)

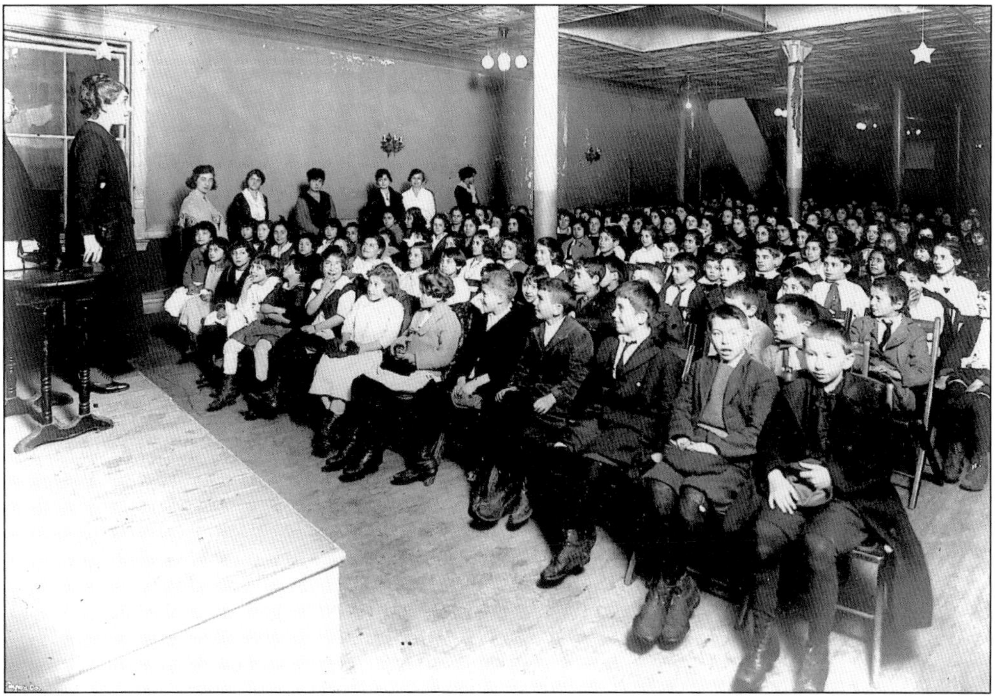

This photograph was taken in the same building as seen in the above view, but these students are attending the children's Sunday school class in 1920. (Courtesy the Museum of the City of New York, Byron collection.)

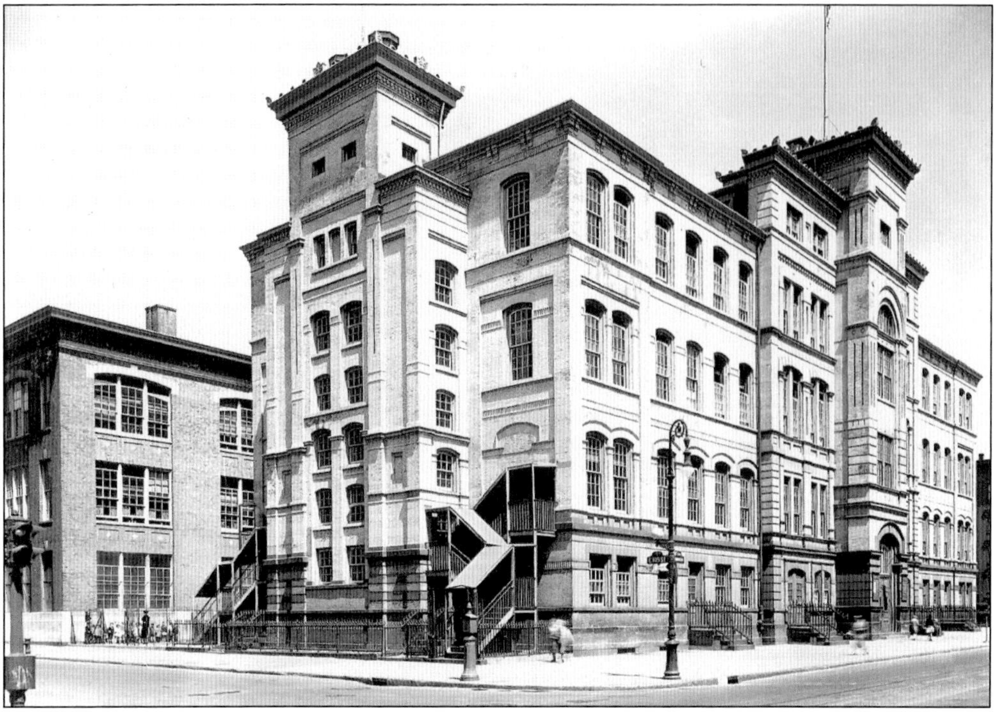

Public School 72, at 105th to 106th Streets and Lexington Avenue, is seen in this 1934 photograph. The building now houses the Julia de Burgos Cultural Center. (Courtesy the New York Public Library.)

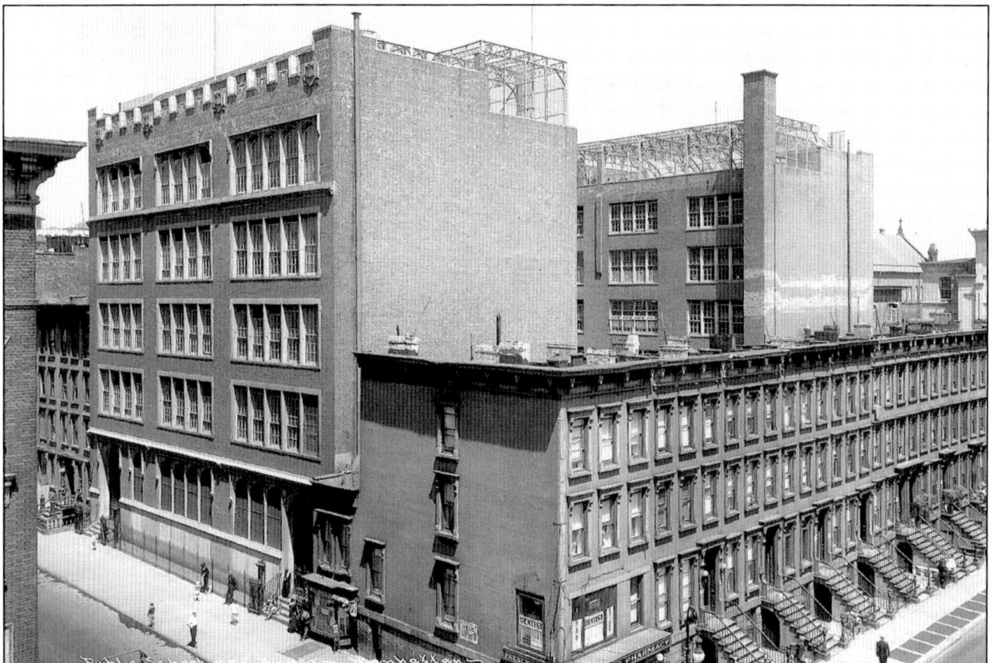

The Public School 72 Annex is located one block south of the school, from 104th to 105th Streets. Notice the brownstones in front of the school. (Courtesy the New York Public Library.)

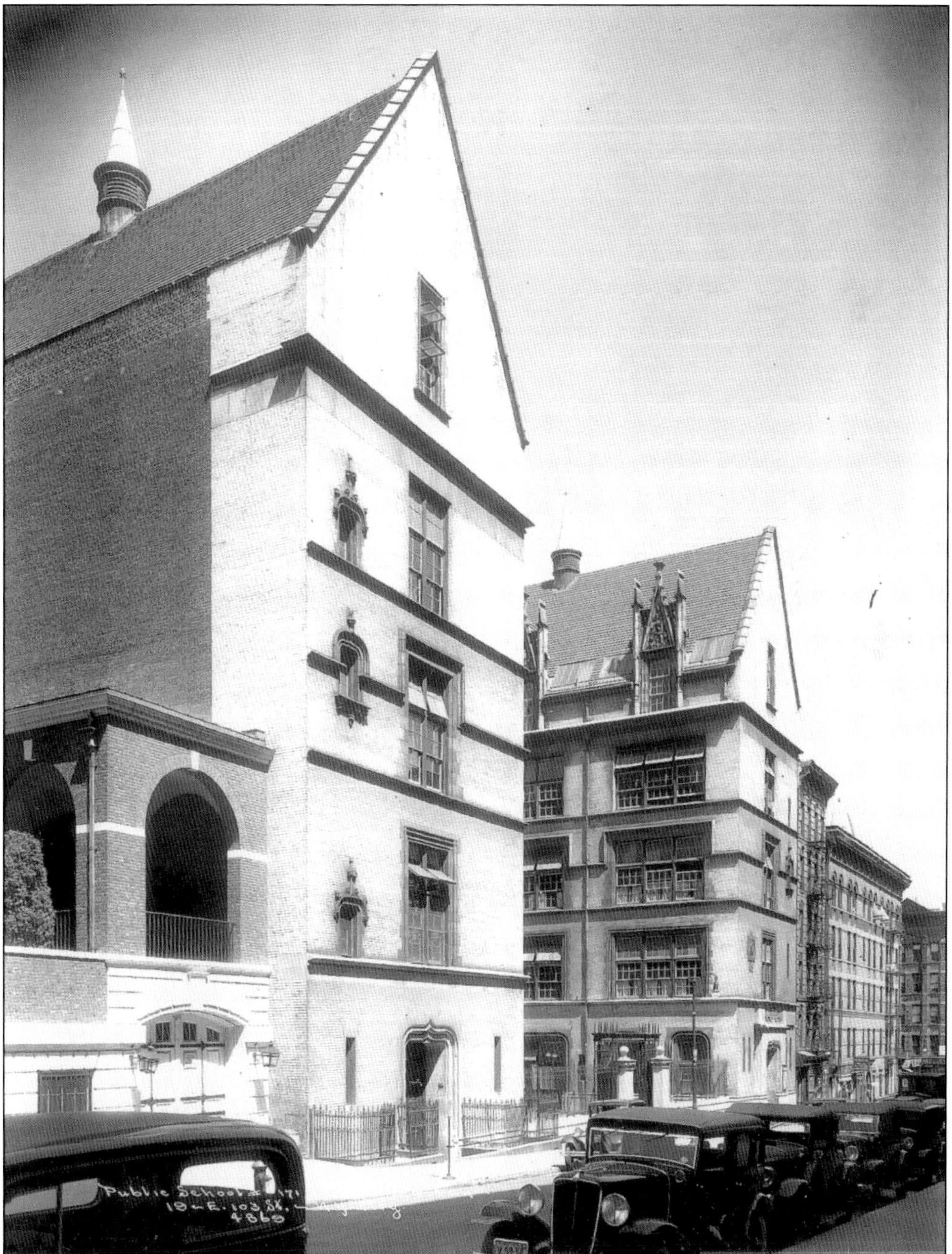

Public School 171, located on 103rd Street between and Fifth and Madison Avenues, is seen in this view.

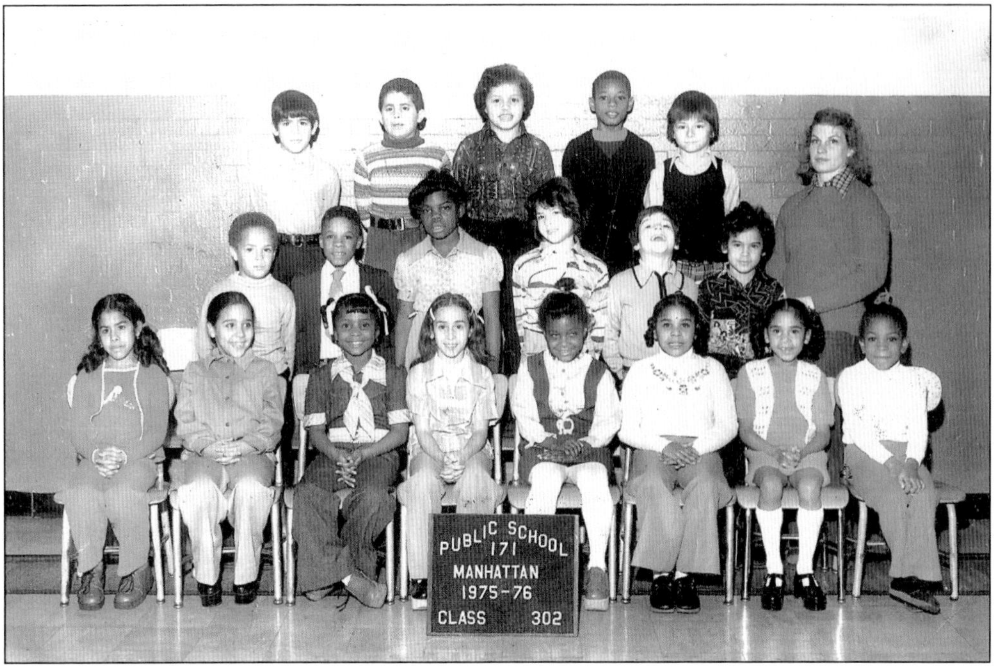


Although the sign says that this is Public School 171's class No. 302 (third grade), the class is a mixture of second and third grades of the 1975–1976 school year. The teacher is Susan Wolf. (Author's collection.)

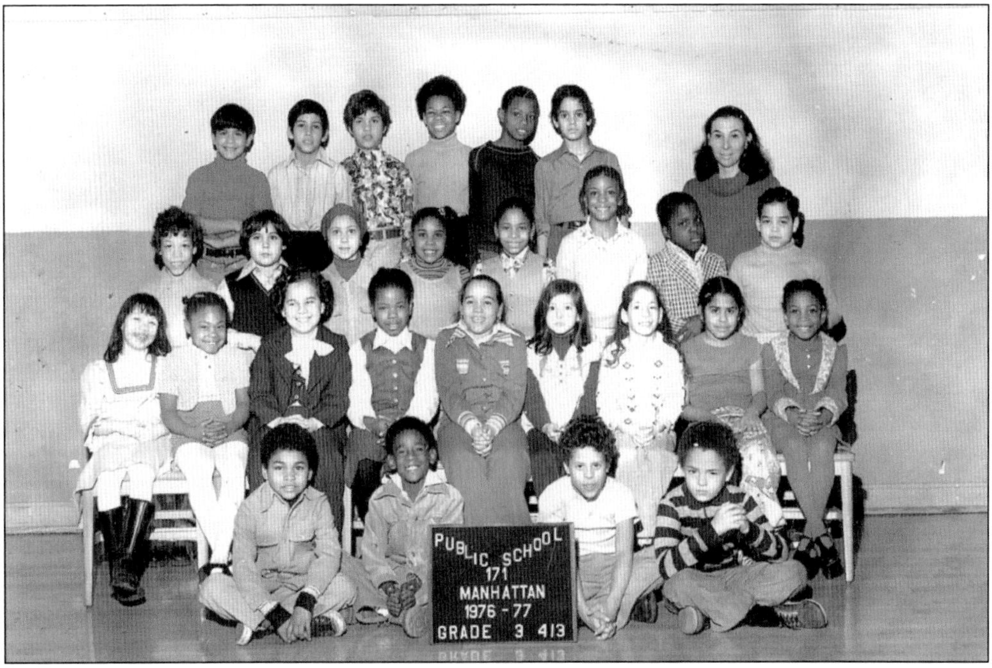


In this Public School 171 photograph, which was taken in a different year than the previous view was, notice that some of the students from the previous photograph are in this one. The teacher is Lynda Ramirez. (Author's collection.)

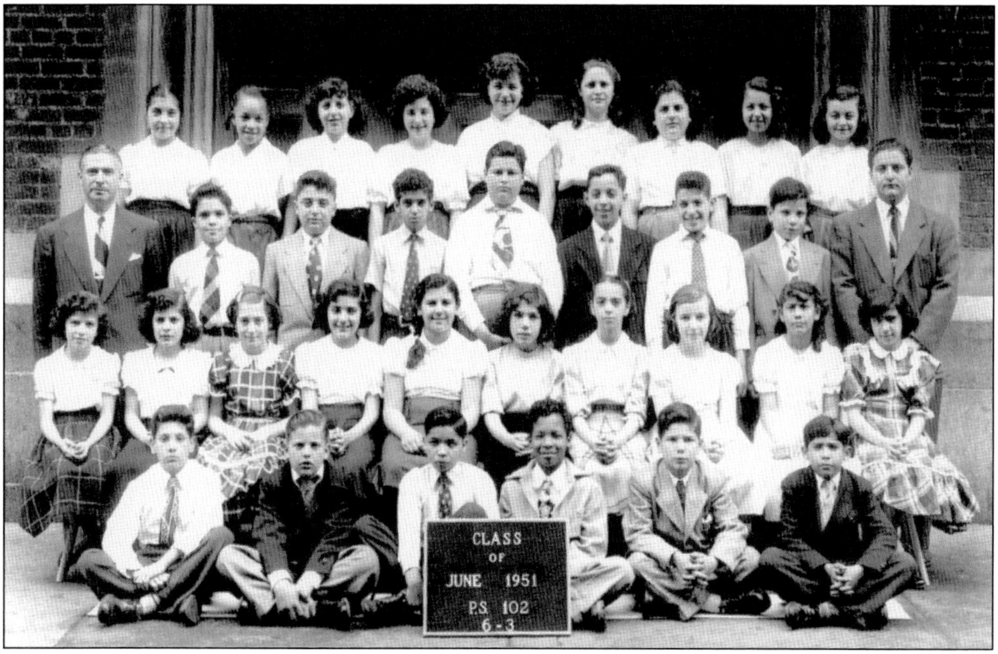


Seen in this June 1951 photograph is the sixth-grade class of Public School 102, located on 113th Street. Fourth from the right in the third row is John Pascale (the son of Rose and Pete Pascale). (Courtesy the Pascale-Evans Photograph Archives.)

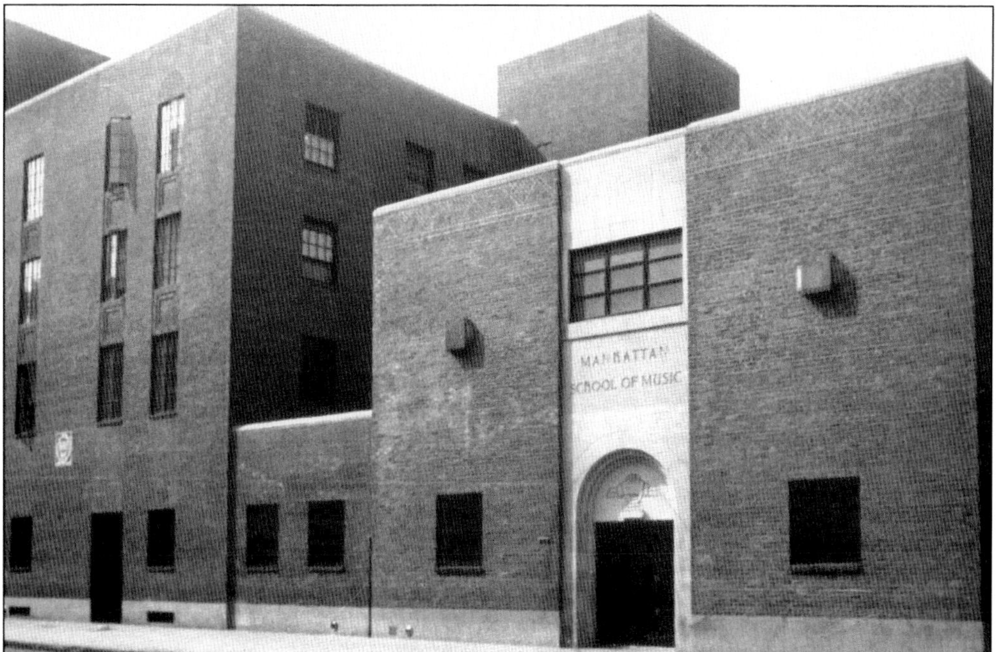


The Manhattan School of Music was founded by Janet B. Schenck in 1918. The school was originally located on 104th street but moved to 105th Street between Second and Third Avenues in 1924. Numerous teachers and artists have lectured at the school, including Pablo Cassals and Harold Bauer. (Courtesy the Manhattan School of Music.)

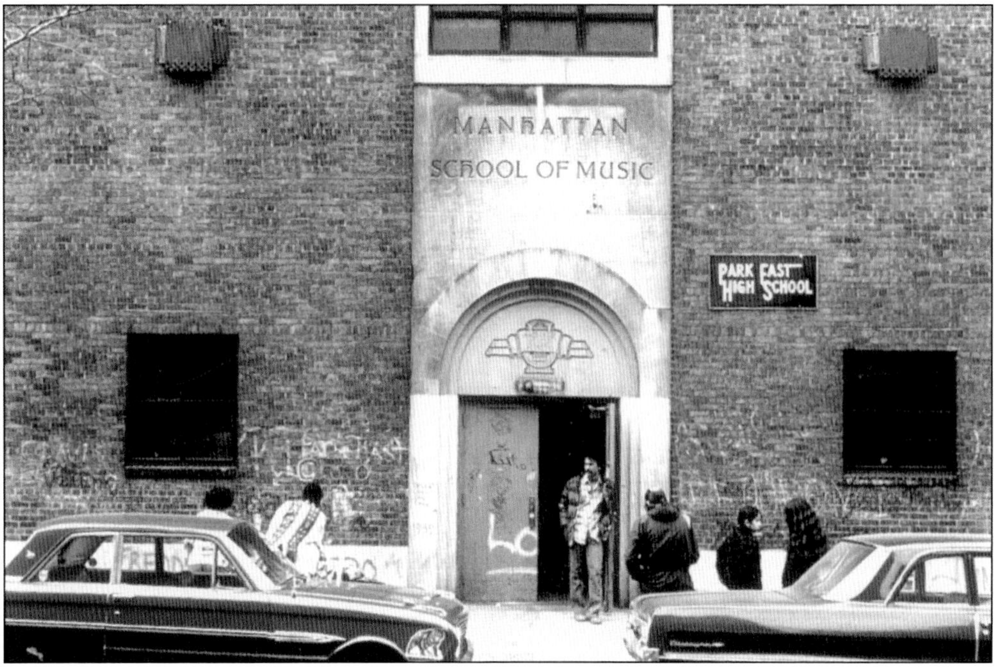


In 1971, Park East High School was founded as an alternative high school on the site of the old Manhattan School of Music. Two years earlier, the music school had moved to the Upper West Side. The engraved carving of the former tenants is a still visible in this 1976 photograph. (Courtesy Jerry and Eleanor Koffler.)

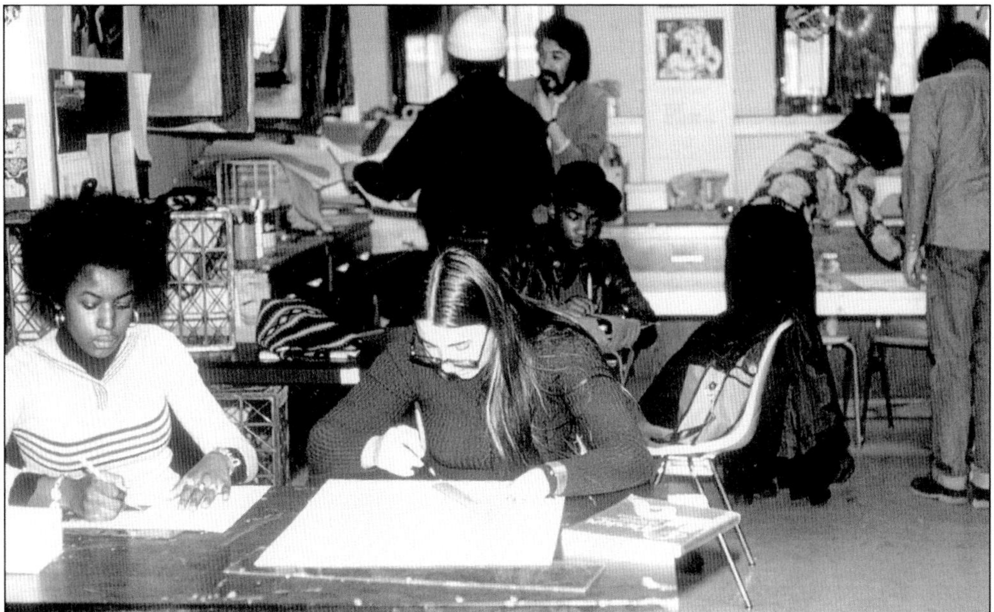

Instead of making beautiful music in this school building, these adolescents are creating beautiful artwork. This photograph was taken in 1976. (Courtesy Jerry and Eleanor Koffler.)

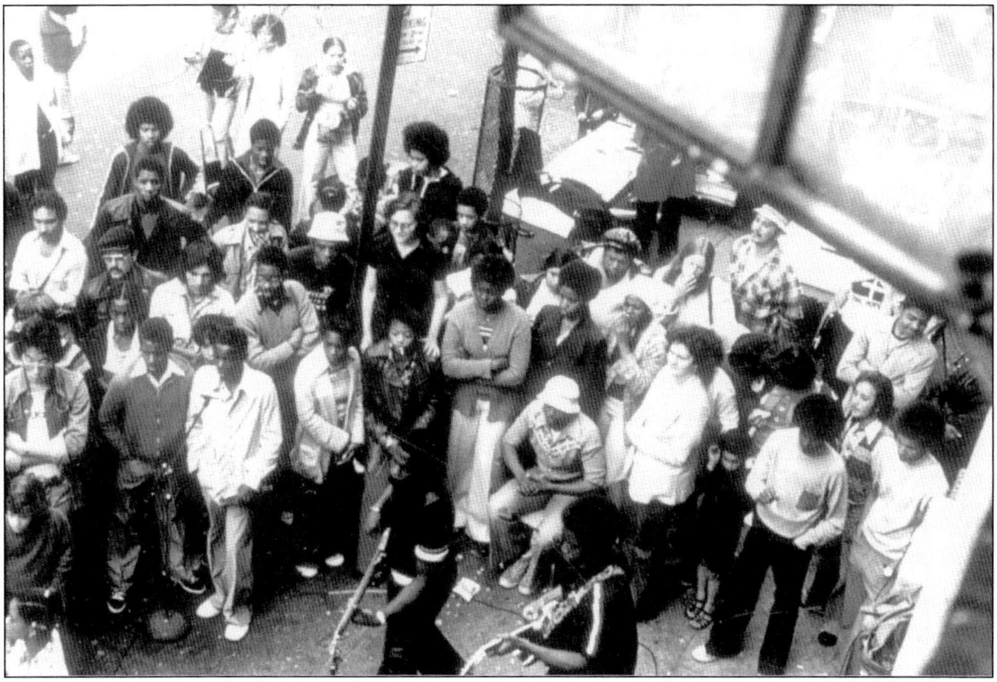

Park East High School students gather outside the school to enjoy the music during the 1977 street festival. (Courtesy Jerry and Eleanor Koffler.)

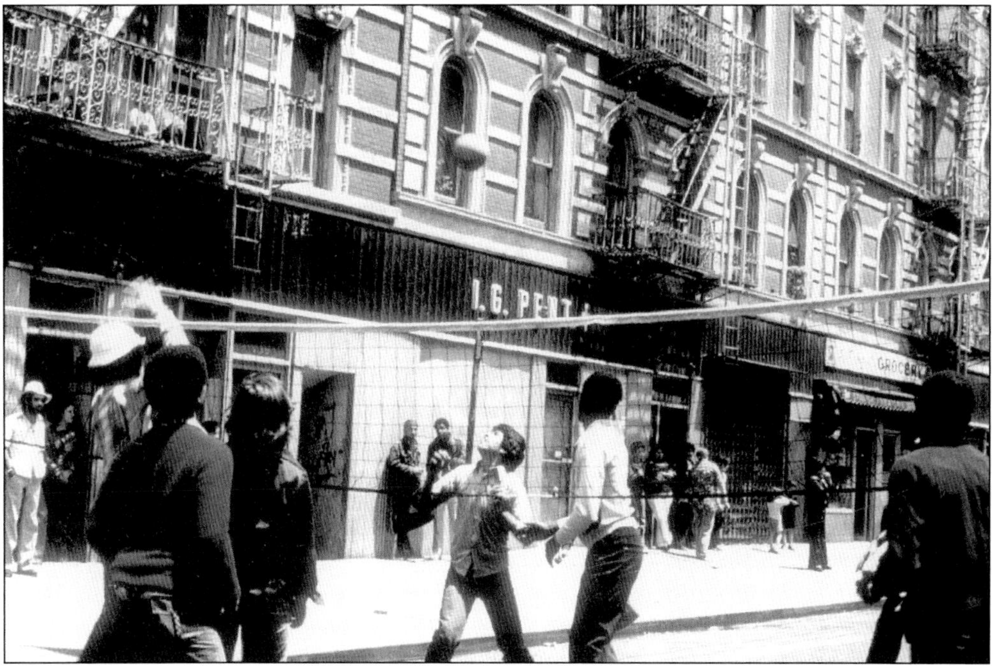

In this 1977 view, Park East students are participating in a volleyball tournament. (Courtesy Jerry and Eleanor Koffler.)

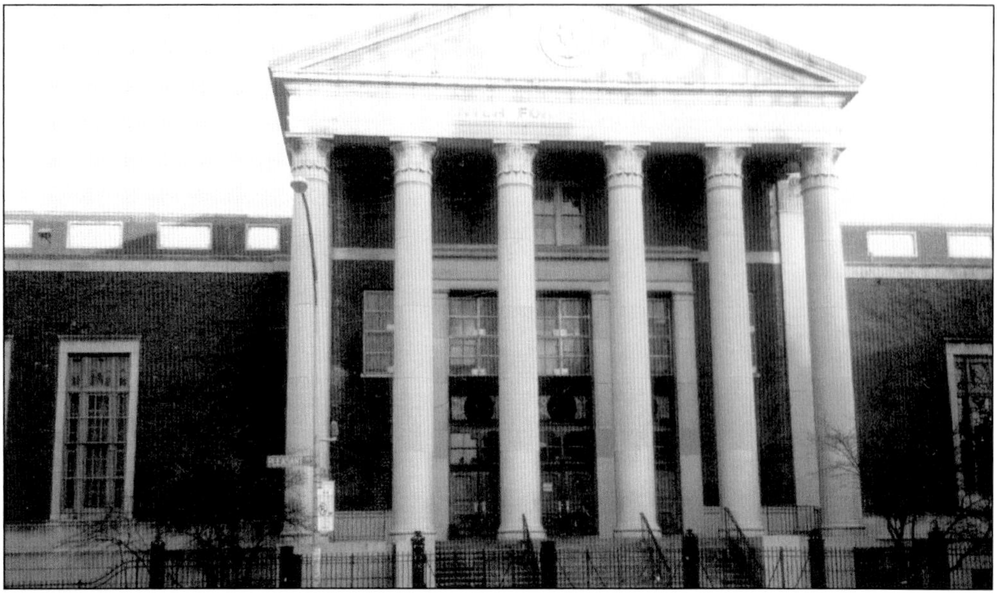

The Manhattan Center for Science and Mathematics (formerly the Benjamin Franklin High School, which was built in 1942) is seen here.

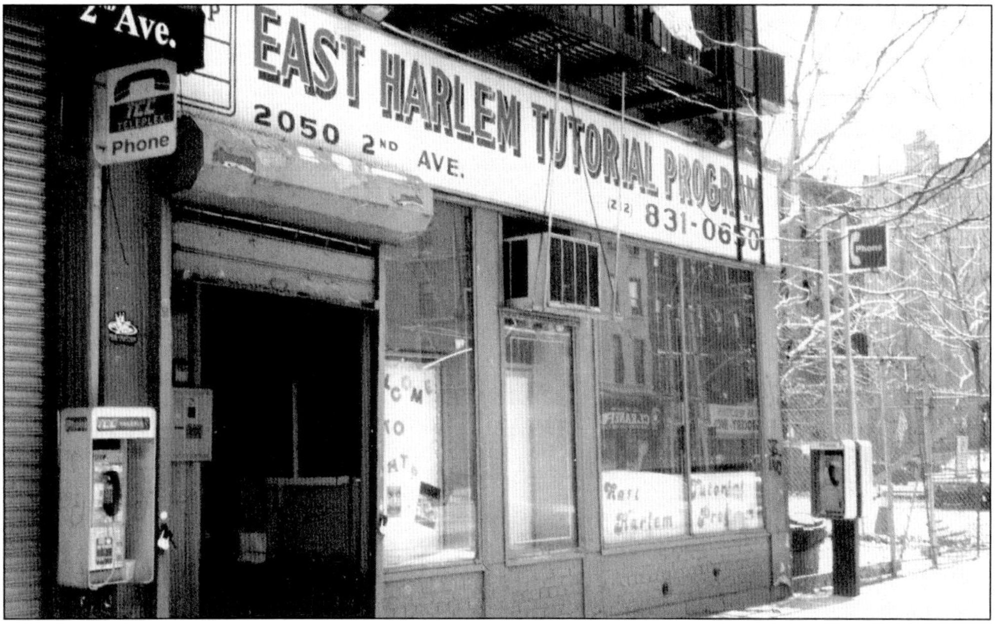


The East Harlem Tutorial Program is located on 105th to 106th Streets and Second Avenue. Helen "Dibby" Webber founded the program in 1958. The center has helped thousands of East Harlemites graduate from high school and continue their education in college. Famous writers and other artists have given their time and energy to promote the well-being of the children in East Harlem. They include, in no specific order, Calvin Trillin, Oscar Hijuelos, Charlayne Hunter-Gault, Maya Angelou, Esmeralda Santiago, George Plimpton, Phylicia Rashad, Piri Thomas, William Styron, Toni Morrison, Wynton Marsalis, Roy Blount Jr., Walter Mosley, Nicholasa Mohr, Ntozake Shange, Anna Quindlen, Ashford and Simpson, and Kurt Vonnegut.

# *Four*

# EAST 100TH STREET REVISITED

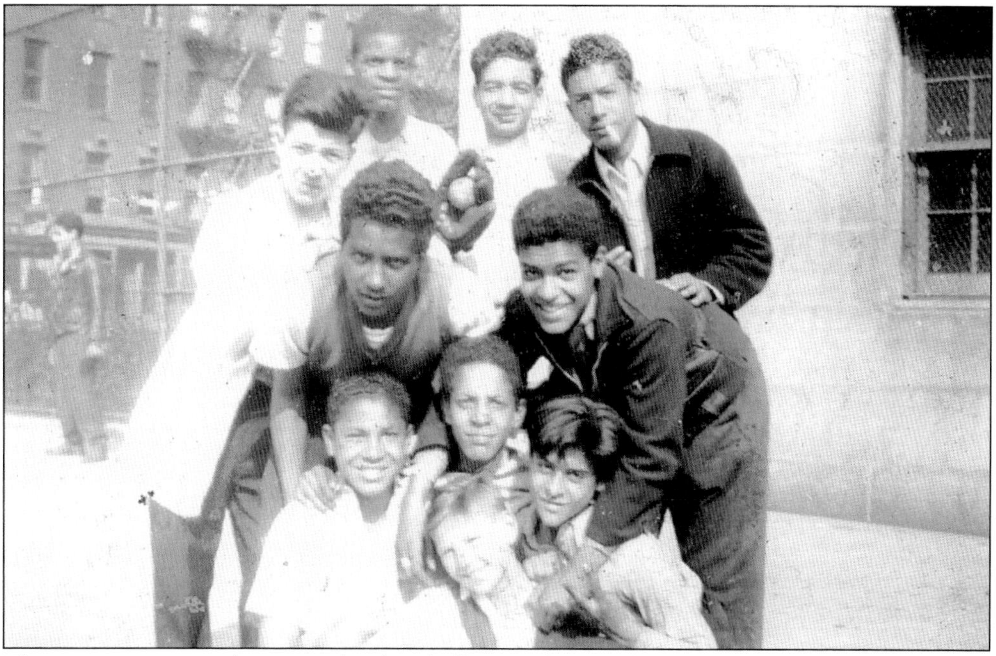

These young men, about to play baseball, pose before the camera on East 100th Street in 1946. The photograph signifies the heterogenous racial make-up of the neighborhood. (Courtesy Raymond Rodriguez.)

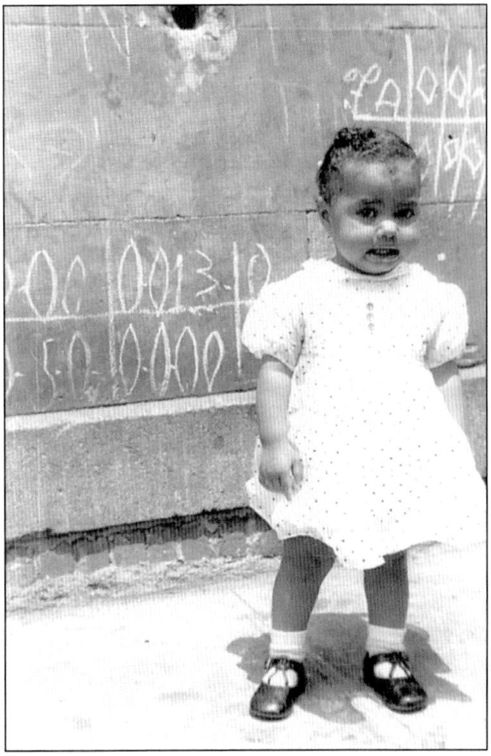

The young Angela Loubriel poses in front of a makeshift scoreboard in 1953. (Courtesy Raymond Rodriguez.)

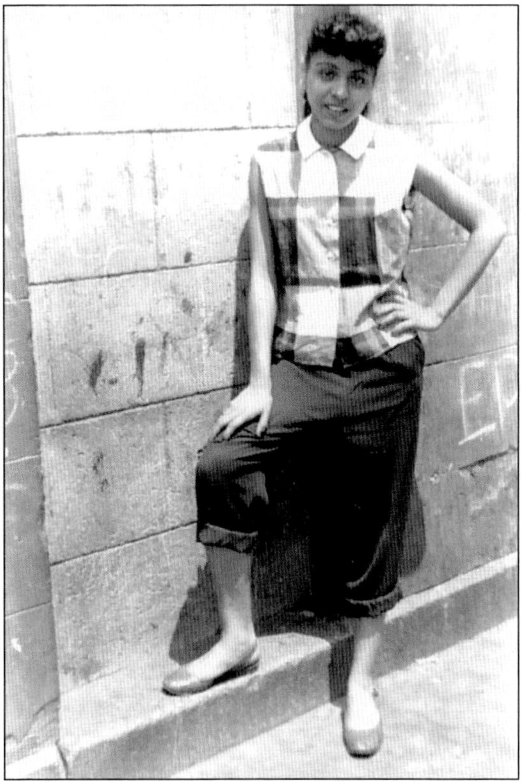

The wall has taken on a new life as the neighborhood stadium, as this 1953 photograph attests. (Courtesy Raymond Rodriguez.)

Three young girls are seen in front of the neighborhood store on 100th Street in 1953. Notice the Pepsi Cola and Orange Mission soda billboards. (Courtesy Raymond Rodriguez.)

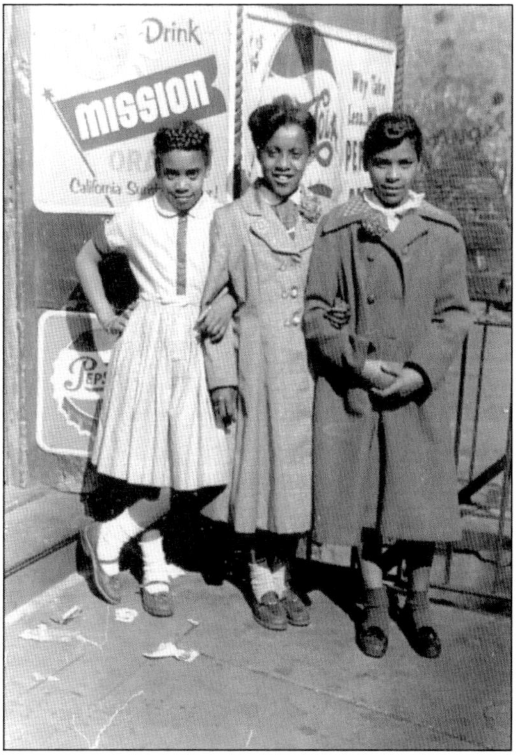


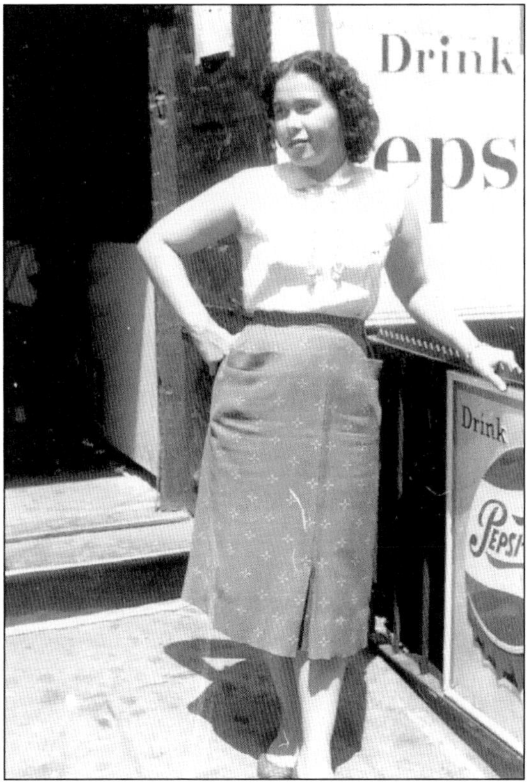


This lovely unidentified woman takes her turn posing in front of the store in 1953. (Courtesy Raymond Rodriguez.)

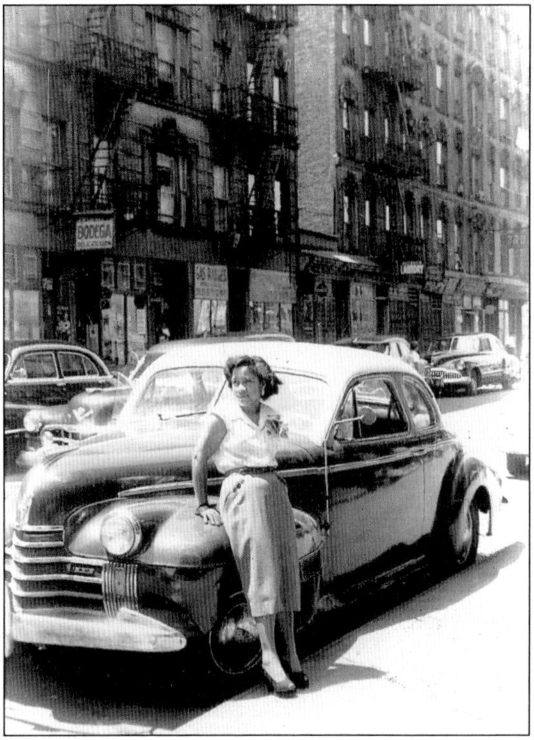


Mercedes Crispin poses with an automobile on 100th Street in 1953. Many businesses and small stores, called bodegas, can be seen in the background. (Courtesy Raymond Rodriguez.)

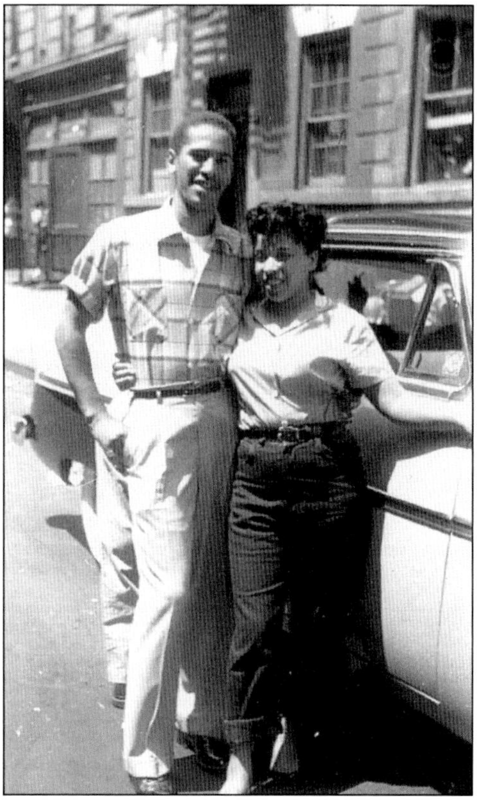

Candido "Butch" Rosado and his friend seem happy on a warm summer day in this 1953 photograph. (Courtesy Ramon Rodriquez.)

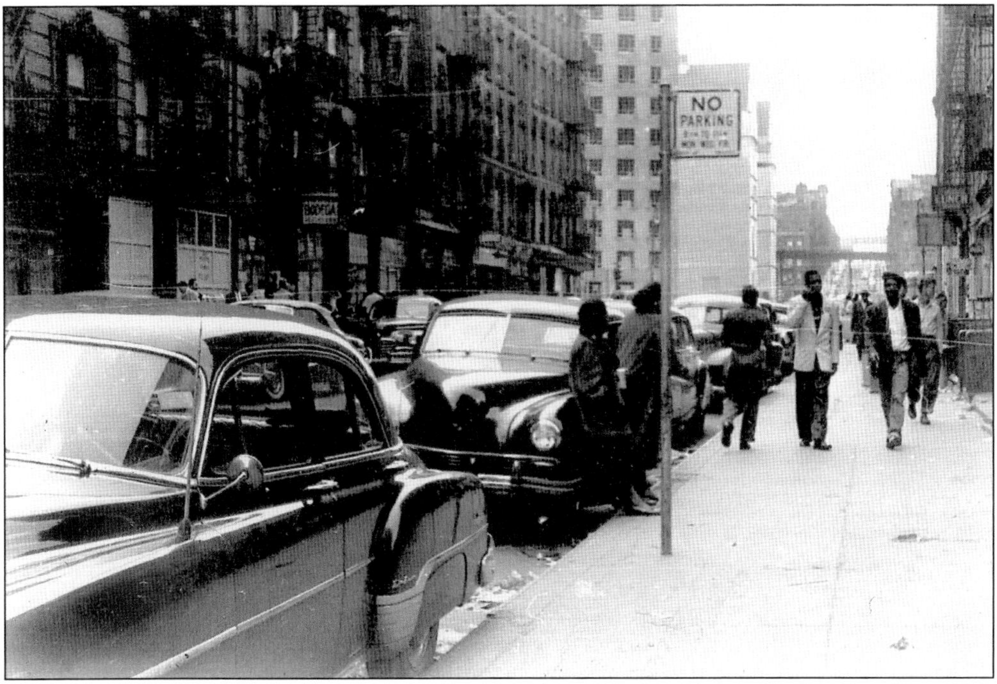


In the autumn of 1953, residents on 100th Street don jackets and coats to keep warm on this cool day. (Courtesy Ramon Rodriquez.)

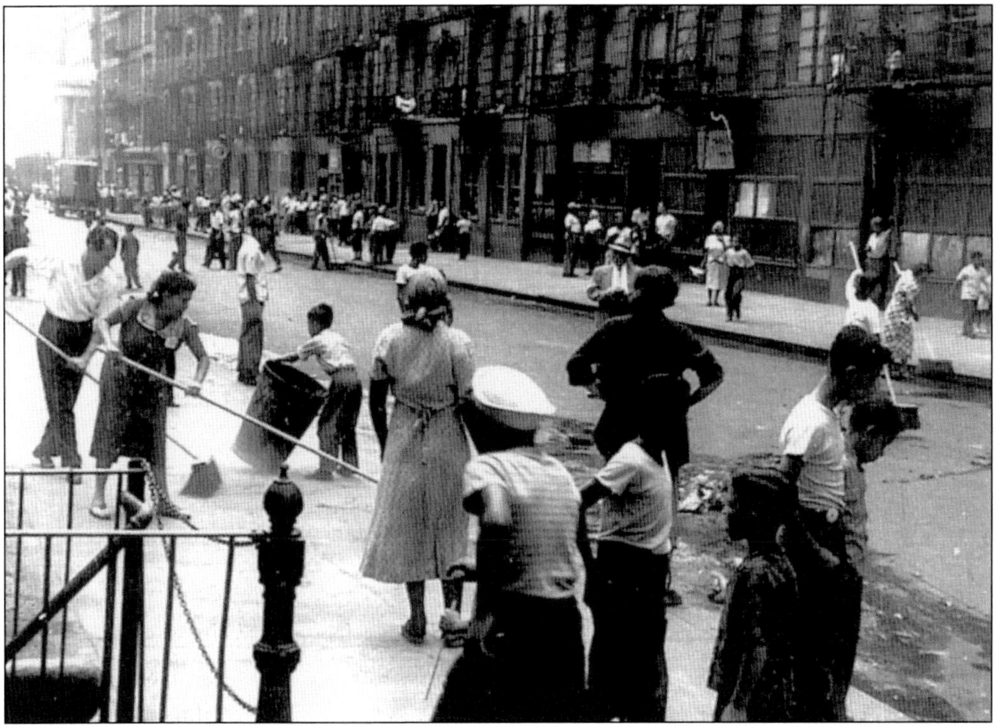

These environmentalists of 100th Street are seen participating in the 100th Street cleanup of 1951. (Courtesy the Reverend Norman C. Eddy.)

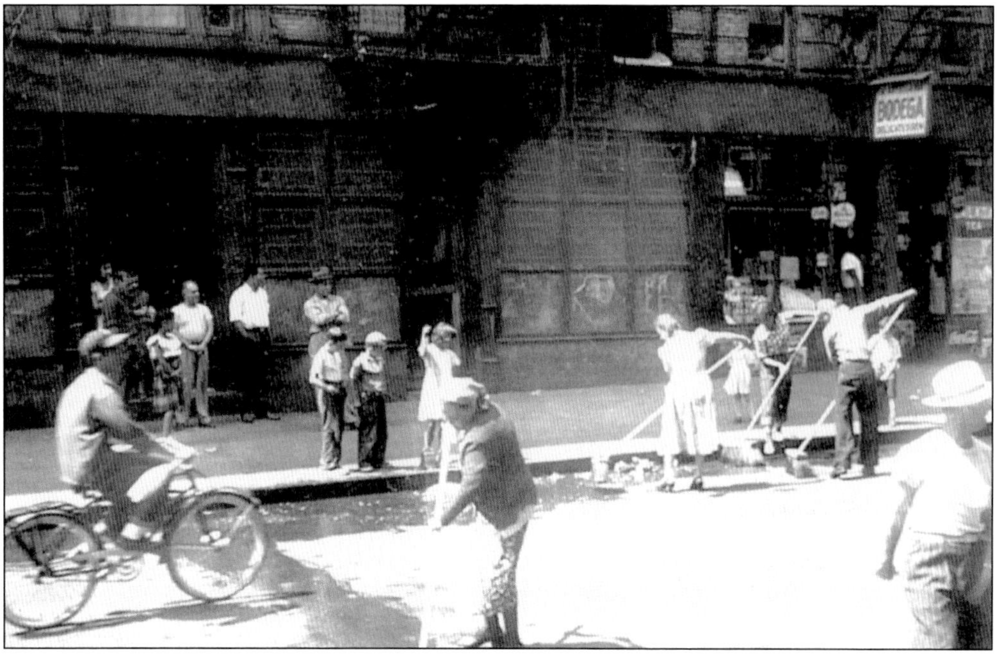

The 100th Street cleanup continues in this 1951 photograph. (Courtesy the Reverend Peg Eddy.)

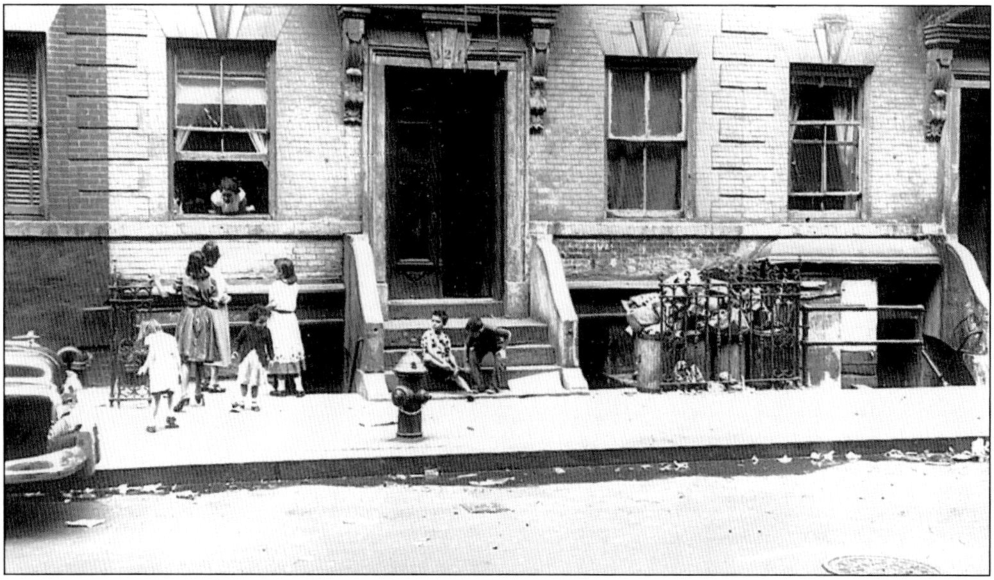

In this 1950s view, the young men are sitting on the stoops as the girls are talking to a friend. The toddlers have their attention elsewhere. (Courtesy the Reverend Norman C. Eddy.)

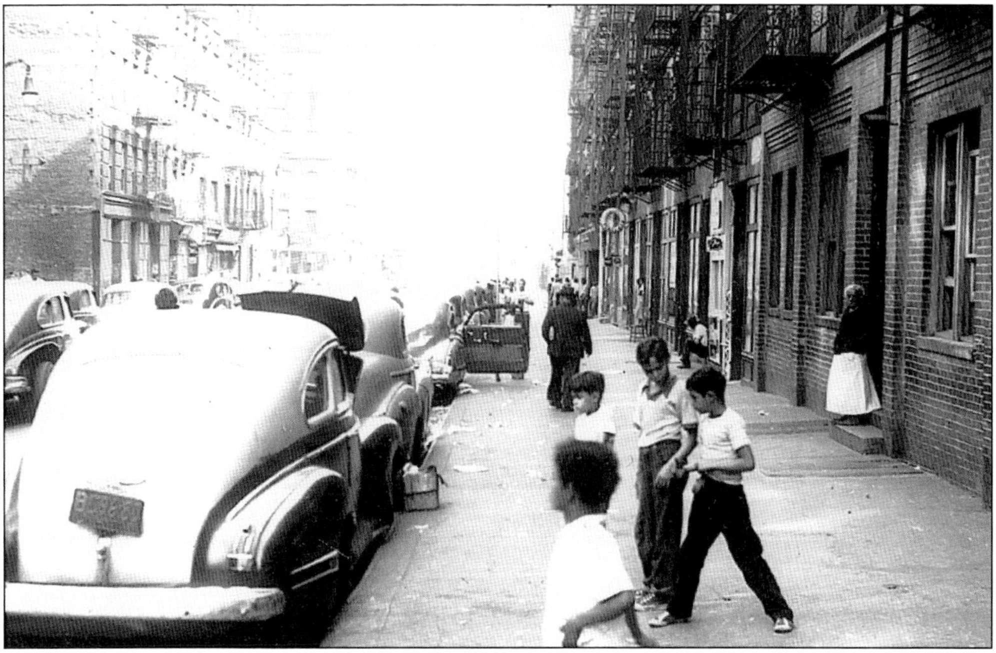

These young men seem drawn to the 1950s vintage cars on 100th Street. (Courtesy the Reverend Norman C. Eddy.)

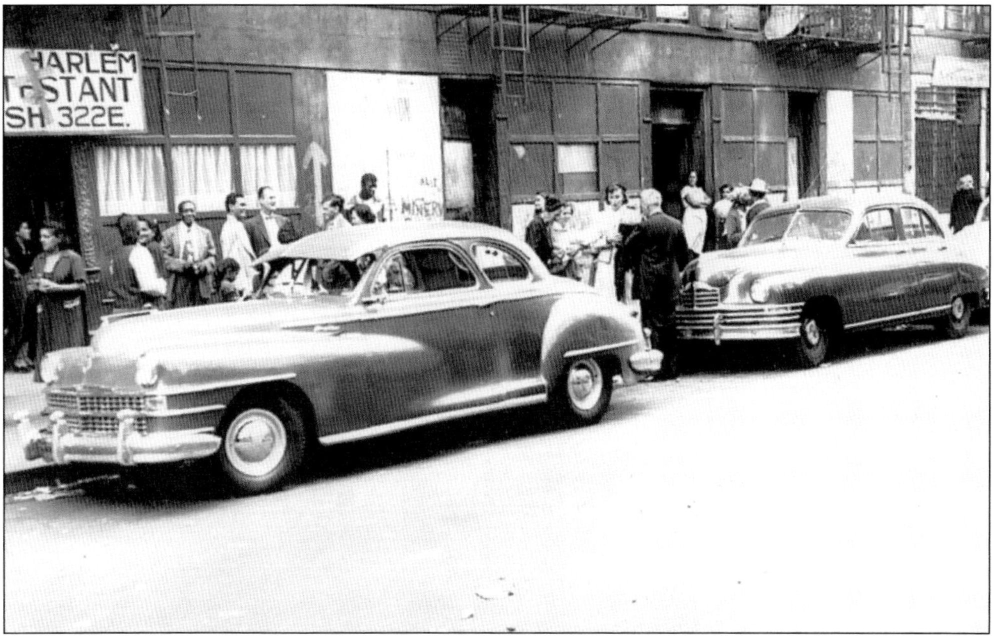


The East Harlem Protestant parish, founded in 1948, established three storefront churches, on 100th, 102nd, 104th Streets. The parish took over ownership of the church on 106th Street to have four houses of worship in East Harlem. Here, parishioners of the 100th Street church gather outside after a service in 1953. (Courtesy the Reverend Norman C. Eddy.)

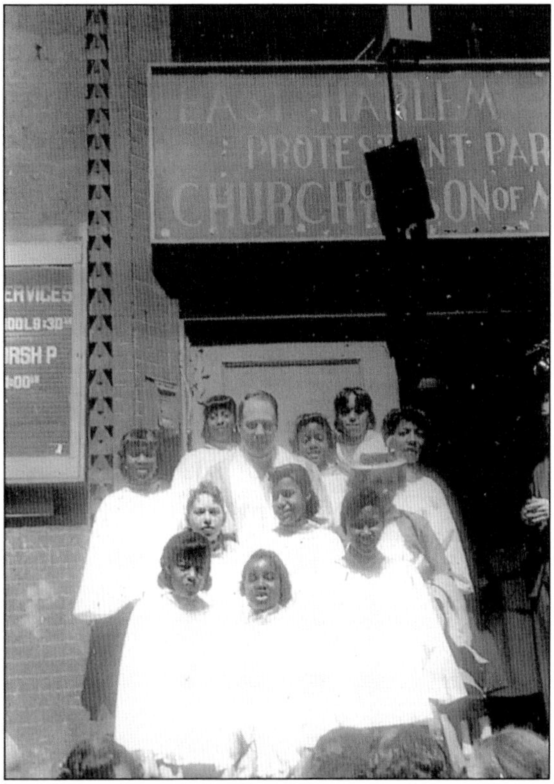

Don and Ann Benedict are surrounded by parishioners in front of the 102nd Street church, called the East Harlem Protestant Parish Church of the Son of Man, in 1954. (Courtesy the Reverend Norman C. Eddy.)

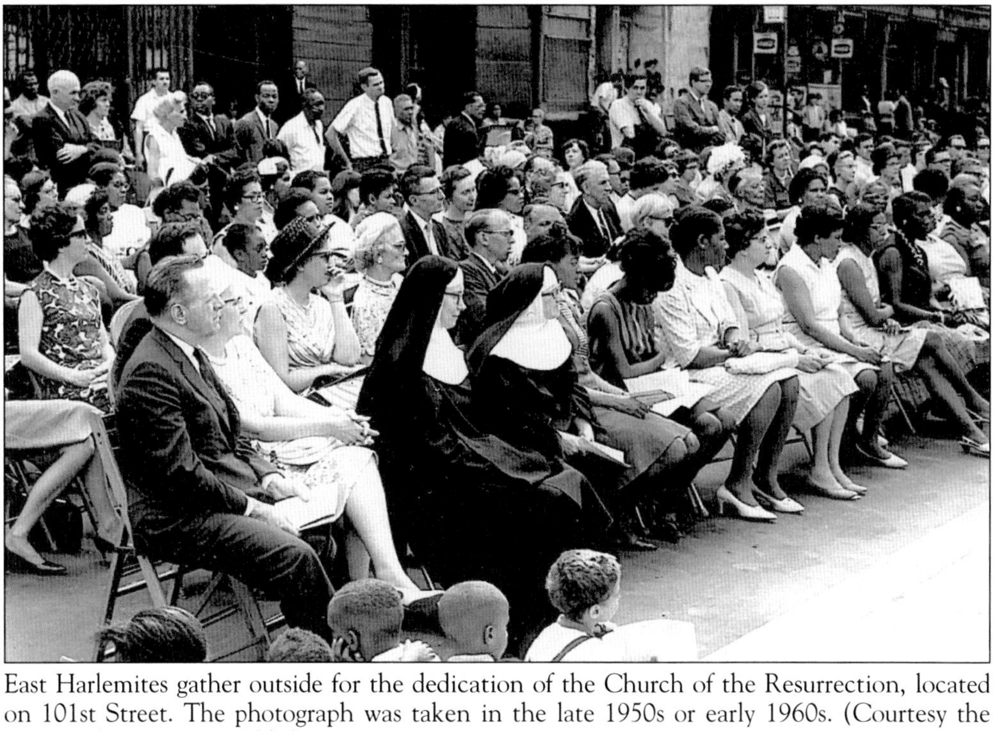

East Harlemites gather outside for the dedication of the Church of the Resurrection, located on 101st Street. The photograph was taken in the late 1950s or early 1960s. (Courtesy the Reverend Norman C. Eddy.)

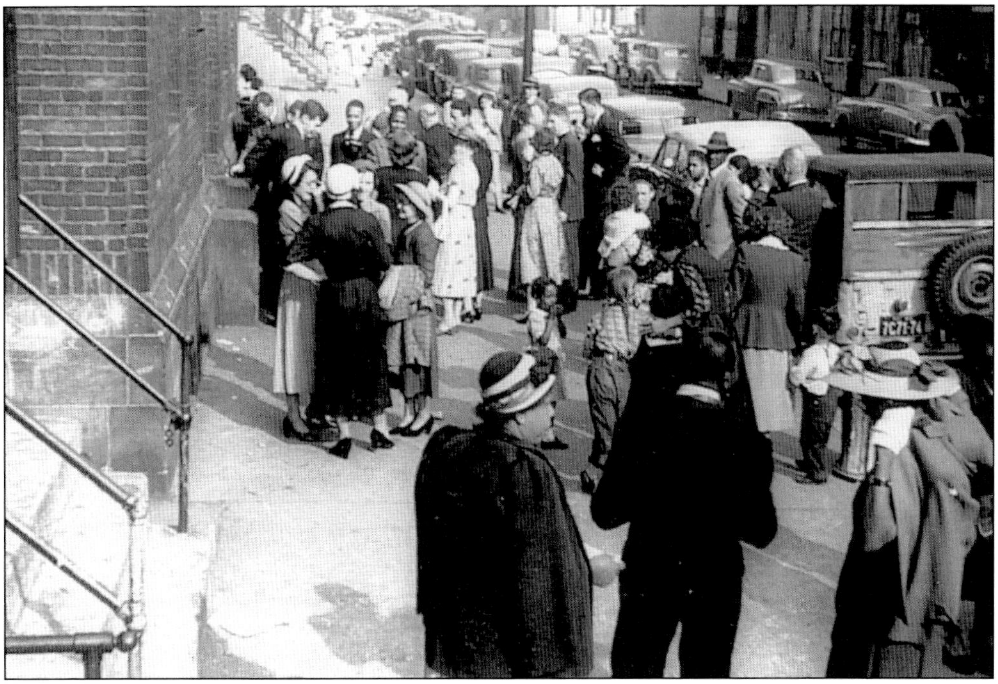

East Harlemites are about to enter the church to attend a wedding in 1950. (Courtesy the Reverend Norman C. Eddy.)

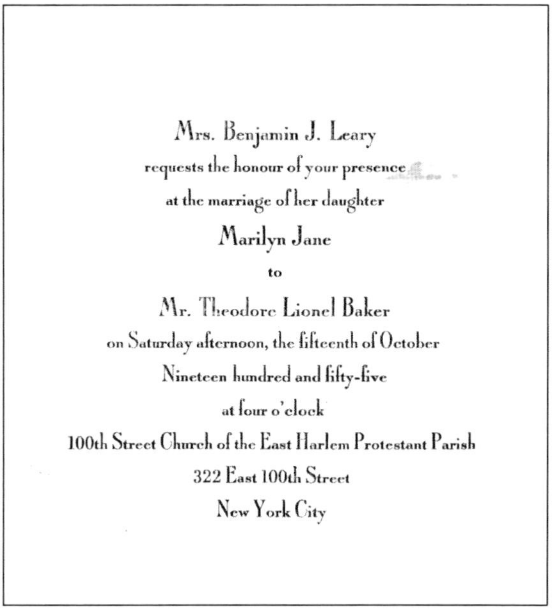

Mrs. Benjamin J. Leary
requests the honour of your presence
at the marriage of her daughter
Marilyn Jane
to
Mr. Theodore Lionel Baker
on Saturday afternoon, the fifteenth of October
Nineteen hundred and fifty-five
at four o'clock
100th Street Church of the East Harlem Protestant Parish
322 East 100th Street
New York City

Seen here is a wedding invitation from Mrs. Benjamin J. Leary, whose daughter Marilyn Jane married Theodore Lionel Baker. (Courtesy Raymond Rodriguez.)

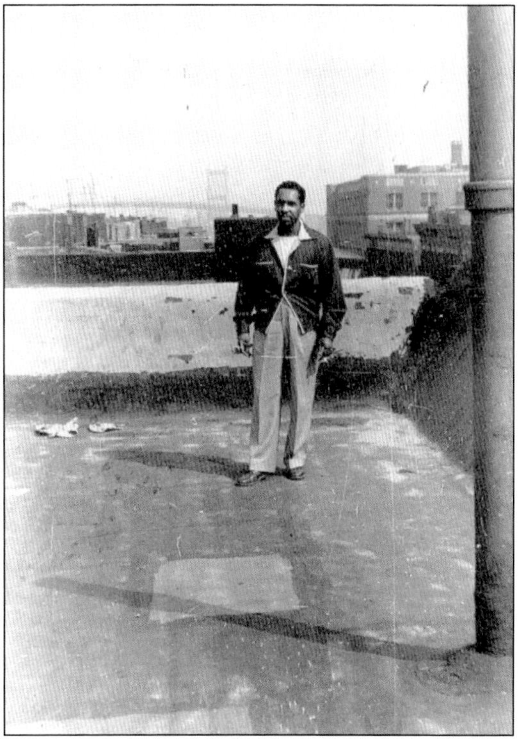

Victor Sanchez is seen with a cigarette in hand on the roof of 321 East 100th Street in this 1953 photograph. Public School 99 can be seen to the right, and the Triborough Bridge is in the background. (Courtesy Raymond Rodriguez.)

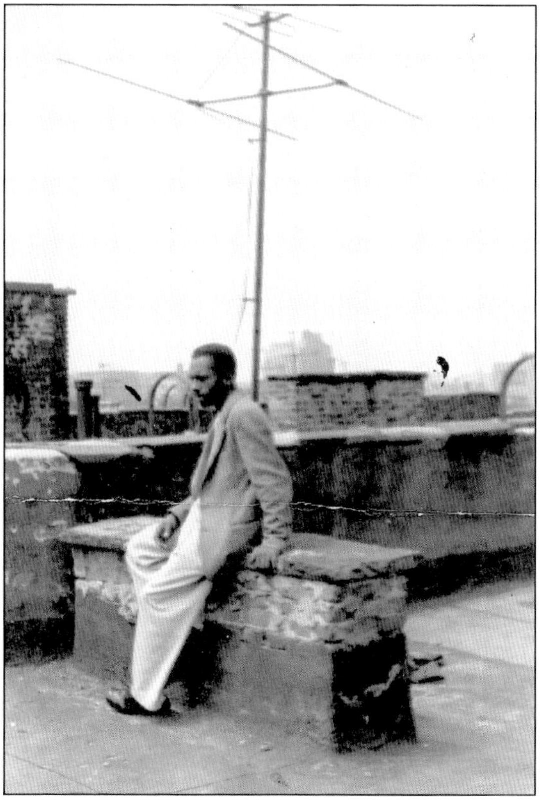

Raymond Rodriguez is reclining on the roof of 321 East 100th Street in this 1953 photograph. Notice the old-style antennas designed to give reception to the radios and first-generation television sets. (Courtesy Raymond Rodriguez.)

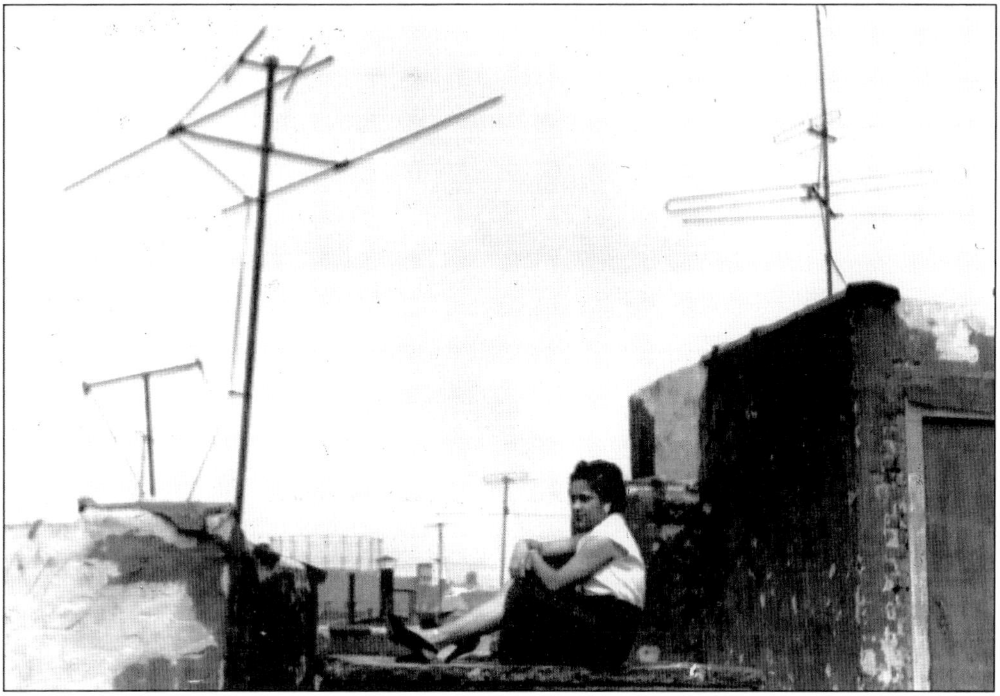

Mercedes Crispin, where have you been? Crispin is seen in this 1953 photograph on the roof of 321 East 100th Street. Again, note the old-style antennas that adorned the roofs of many tenement buildings on this block. A water tower is in the distance. (Courtesy Raymond Rodriguez.)

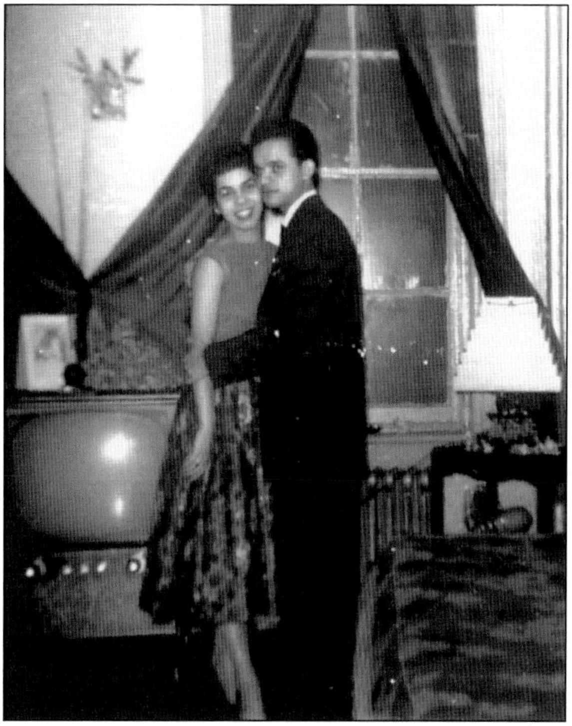

Seen here is a 1950s television in the apartment of Roberto and Andy Ortiz on 103rd Street in 1957. (Courtesy Robert Ortiz.)

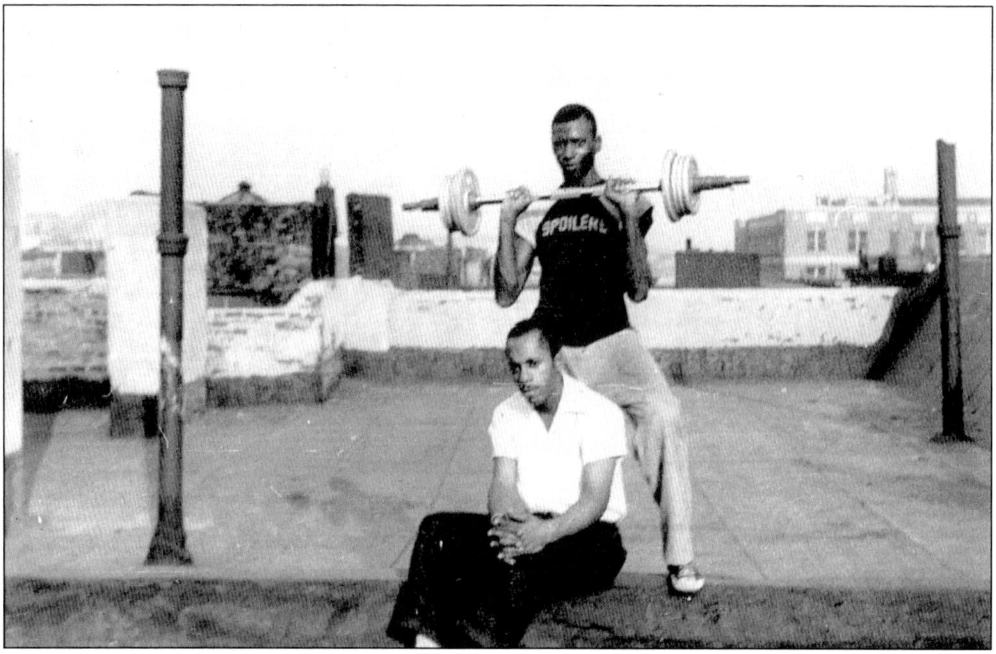

While Raymond Rodriguez sits on the roof of 321 East 100th Street in this 1954 photograph, his friend is pumping iron. Well, it is really sand. (Courtesy Raymond Rodriguez.)

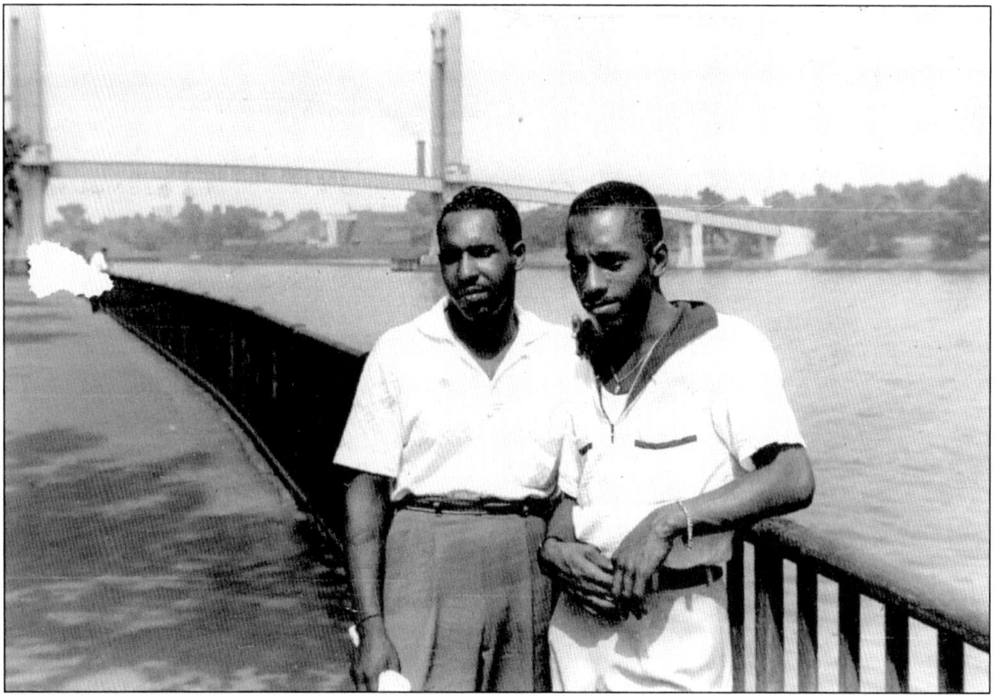

Victor Sanchez (left) and Raymond Rodriguez pose in front of the East River. In the background is the bridge that leads to Wards Island. The year is 1953. (Courtesy Raymond Rodriguez.)

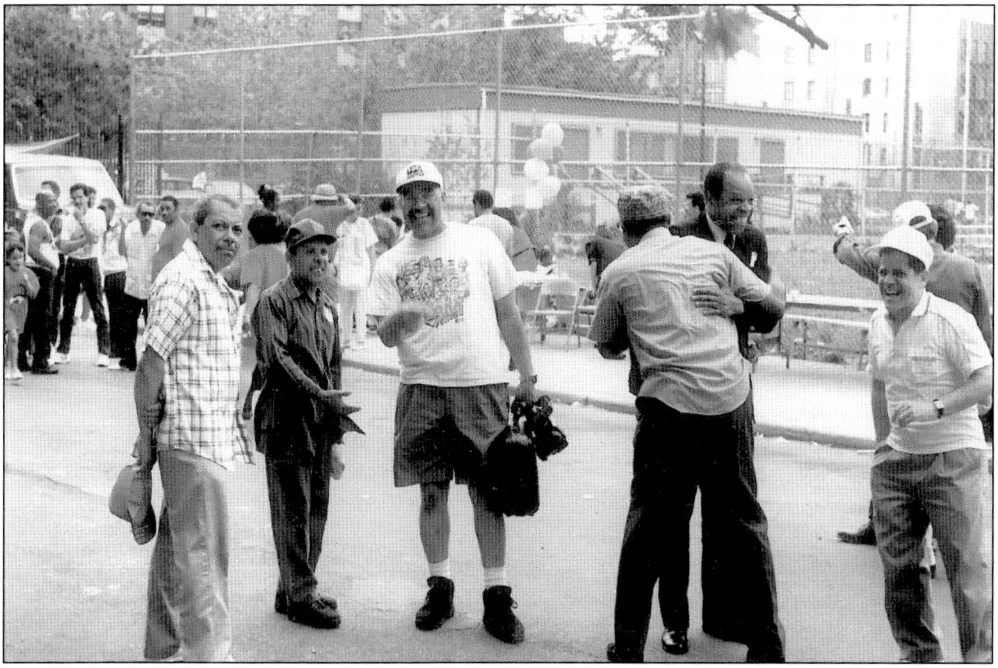

In 1970, the New York City government felt that the apartments along 100th Street between First and Second Avenues were unsafe for habitation and the buildings were razed. In 1994, residents of 100th Street reunited to relive the past. (Courtesy Raymond Rodriguez.)

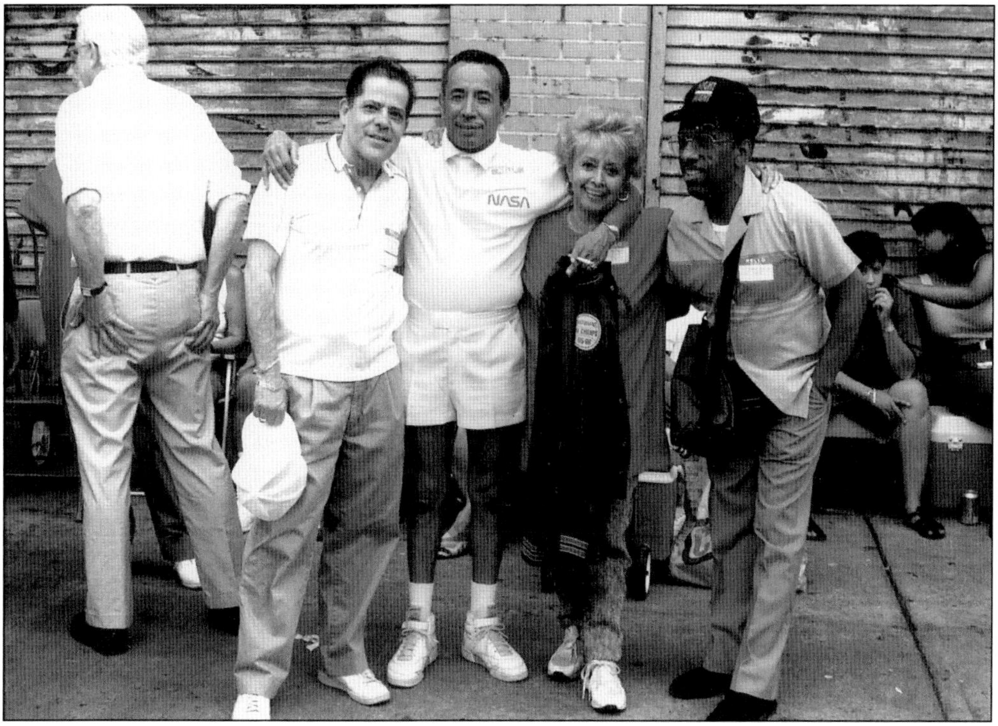


Bob Montesi (in shorts) and Raymond Rodriguez (in a cap), along with two former residents of 100th Street, gather on 101st Street in 1994. (Courtesy Raymond Rodriguez.)

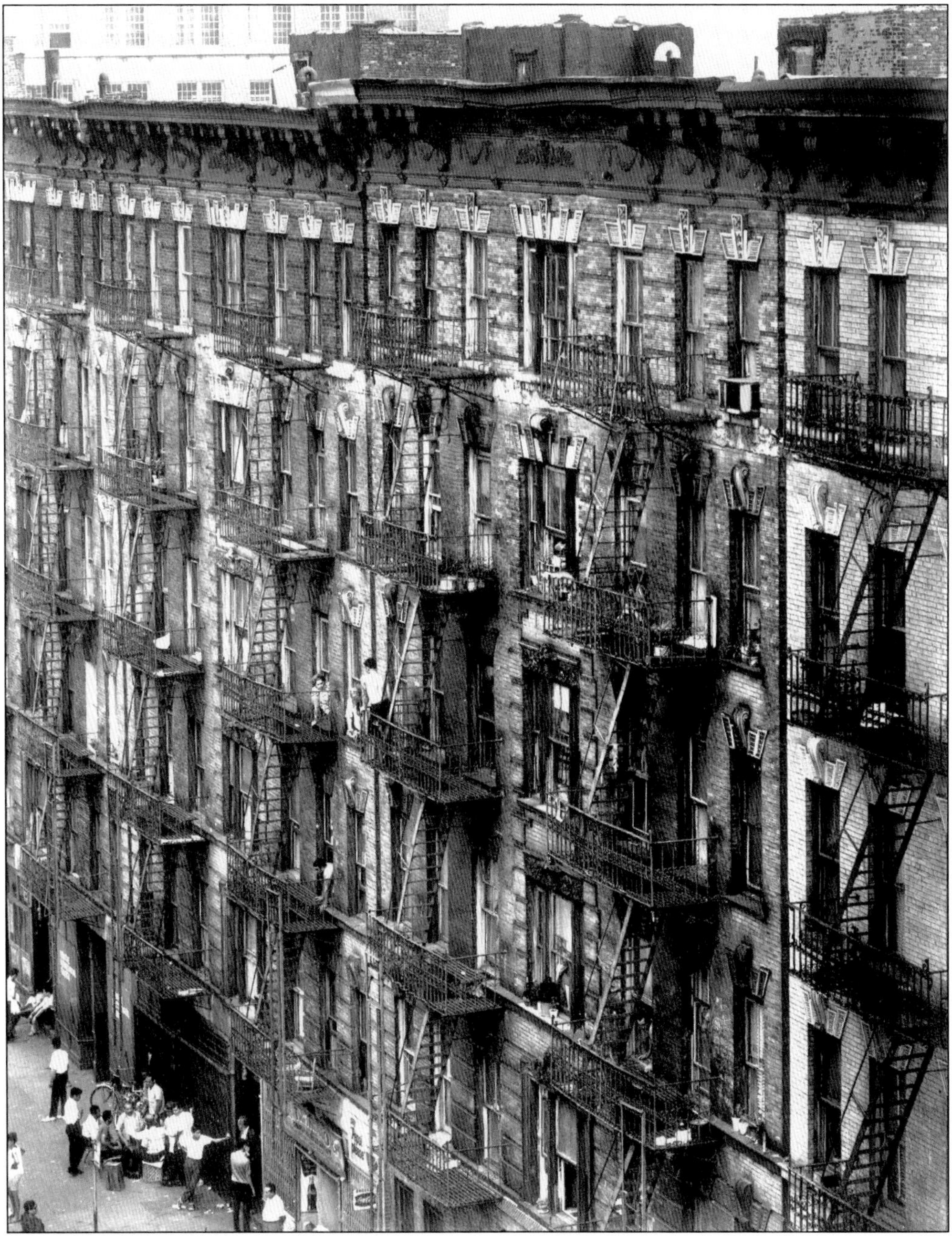

Bruce Davidson took this photograph of 100th Street. Davidson's portrait captures the mood of the neighborhood on this summer day in 1968. Residents can be seen milling around outside or hanging out on the fire escape talking with another neighbor who has opened her window. The contiguous tenement buildings are reminiscent of an earlier East Harlem of six-story tenements, which allowed everyone in the neighborhood to know and look after each other.

# *Five*

# Changing Scenes

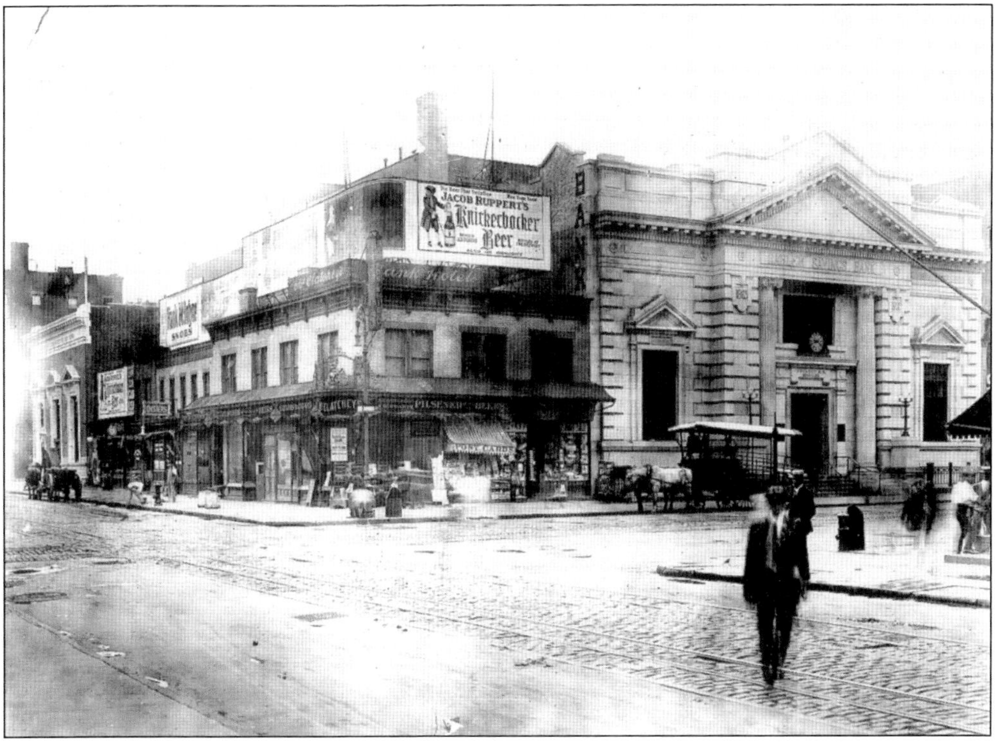


This photograph of 125th Street and Lexington Avenue portrays early-20th-century East Harlem. Men in straw hats are strolling through the neighborhood. A horse-drawn carriage is right in front of the Harlem Savings Bank, which was founded in 1863 and housed in this edifice, completed in 1907. A sign over the newsstand reads, "Jacob Rupert's Knickerbocker Beer." Rupert's brewery was located two blocks south, on 123rd Street. The year is 1911, eight years before Prohibition outlawed the sale of alcohol and before the completion of the Lexington Avenue subway. (Courtesy the New York Public Library.)

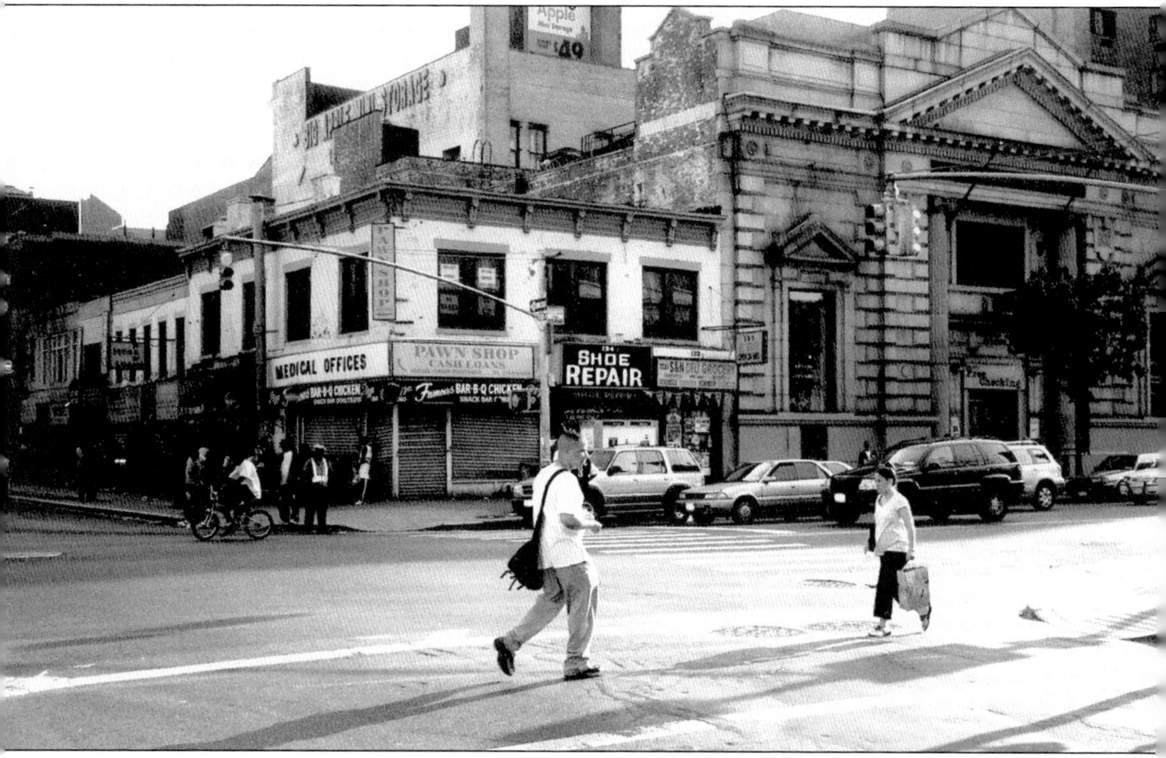


Today, most of the buildings seen in the previous photograph are still standing. Apple Savings Bank is the present tenant holding the neighborhood's deposits. The 125th Street and Lexington Avenue subway has replaced the horse-drawn carriage. Big Apple Mini Storage occupies the location previously owned by Rupert's brewery. (Author's collection.)

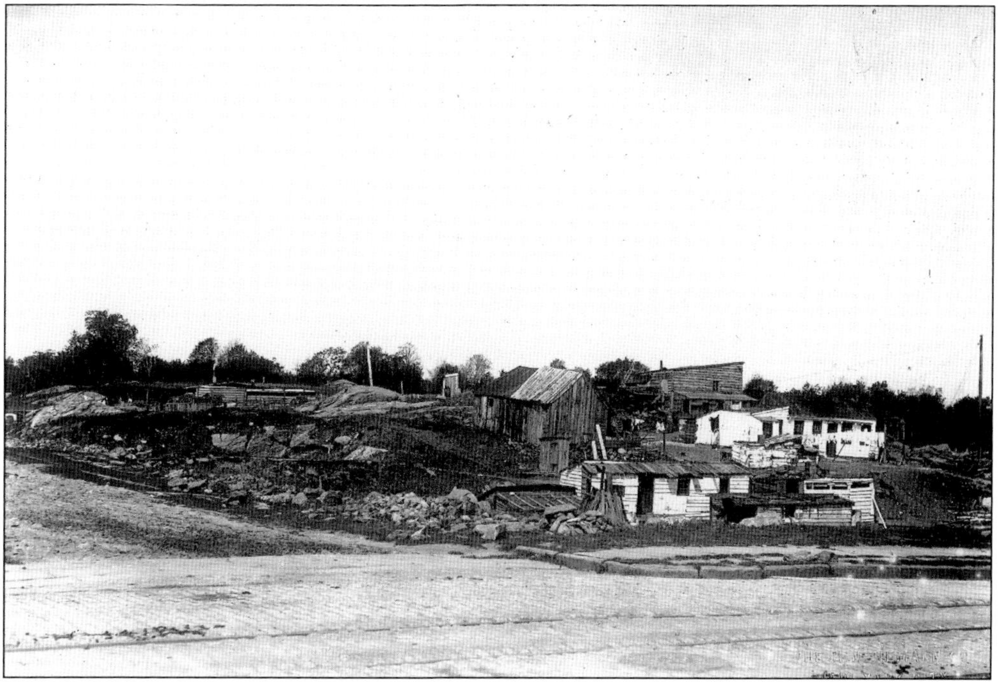

During this period, shacks and shantytowns made from discarded factory debris and jetsam were located along Madison Avenue, such as this one on 100th Street. This photograph was taken in 1894. (Courtesy the New York Public Library.)

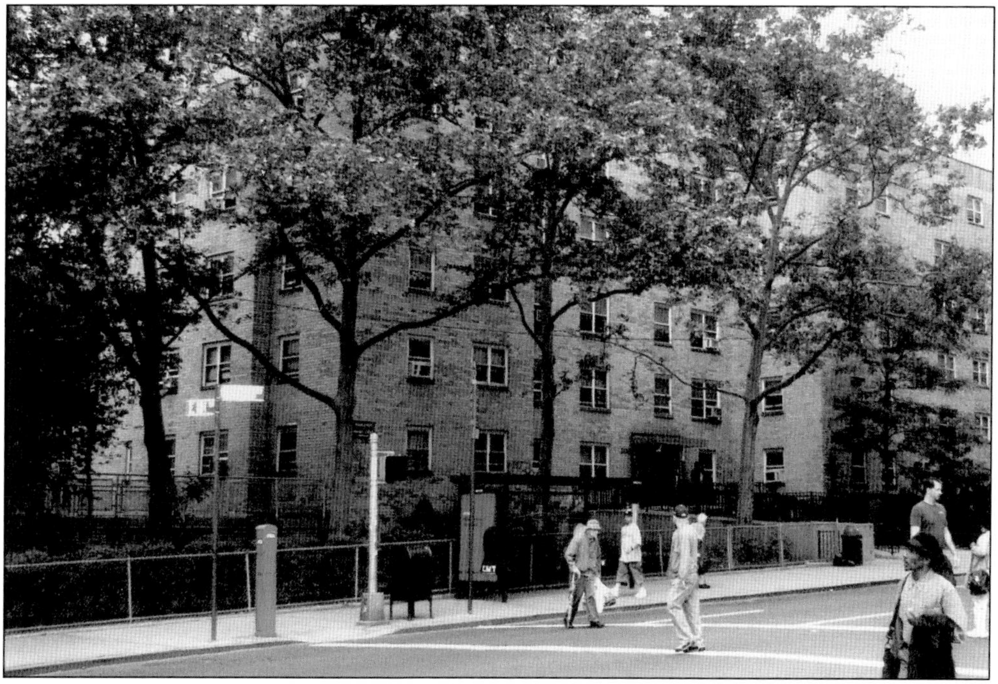

Today, the George Washington Carver Houses, which began construction in 1955 and were completed in 1958, occupy the space once filled with shacks and shantytowns on this site. (Author's collection.)

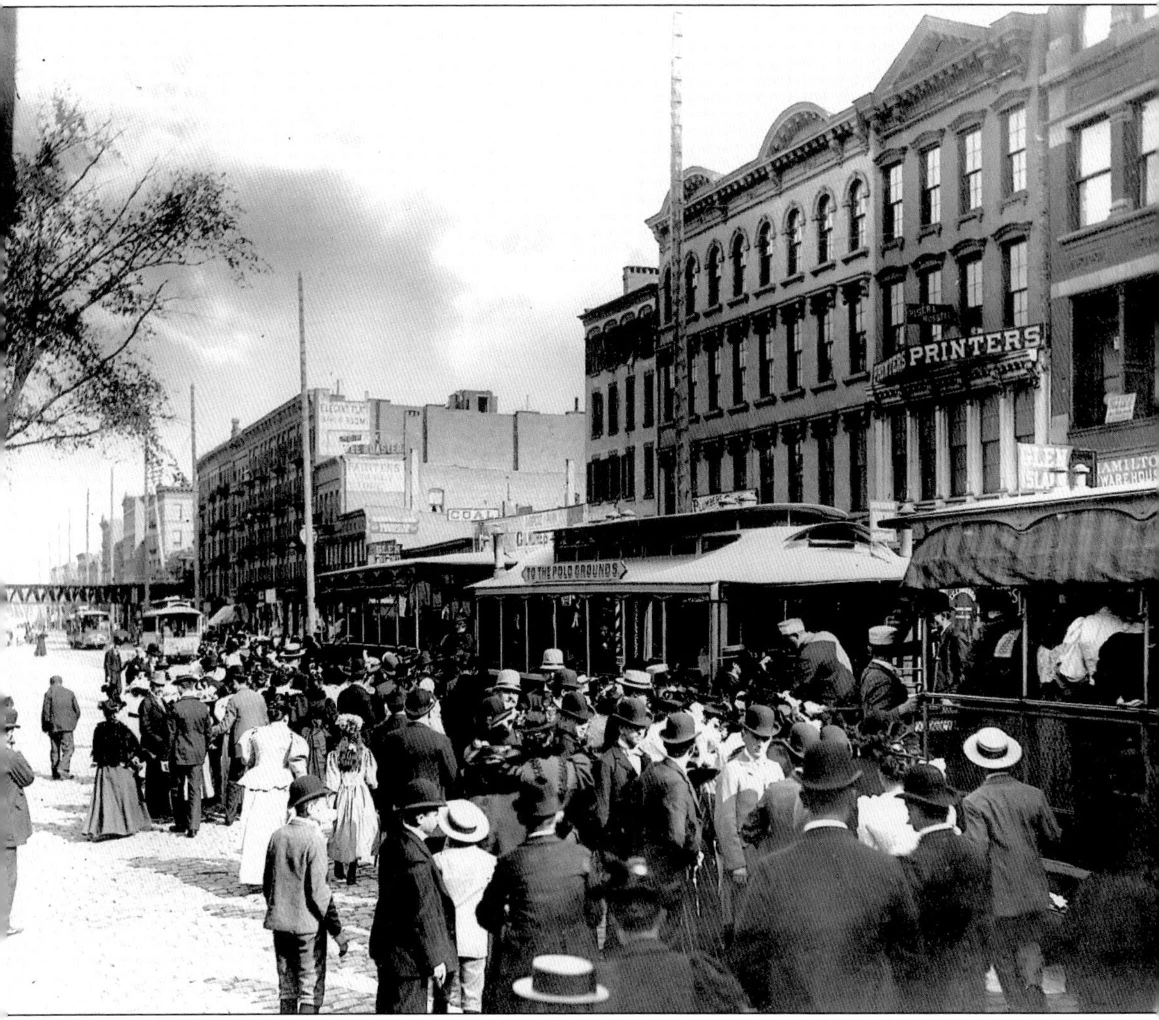


Seen in this 1895 photograph is the trolley car, at 125th Street and Third Avenue, headed for the Polo Grounds, once located on 110th Street between Fifth and Sixth Avenues. Polo matches were played by at the grounds by wealthy New Yorkers. Also, the New York Giants baseball team played on this same site until 1890, when they were evicted by the city government. (Courtesy the Museum of the City of New York, Byron and J. Clarence Davies collection.)

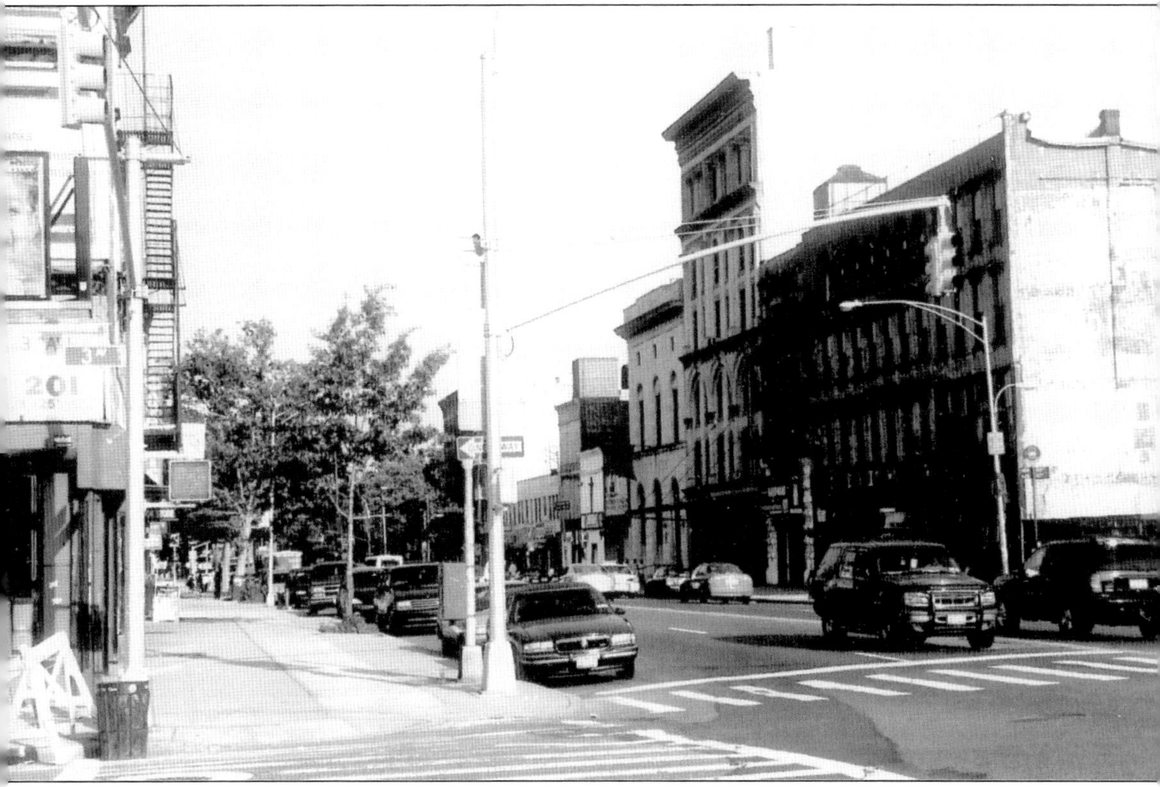

Today, a carpet and linoleum store is on the corner of 125th Street and Third Avenue. The sign reads, "Cada Niño Merece un Padre," meaning "each child deserves a father." (Author's collection.)

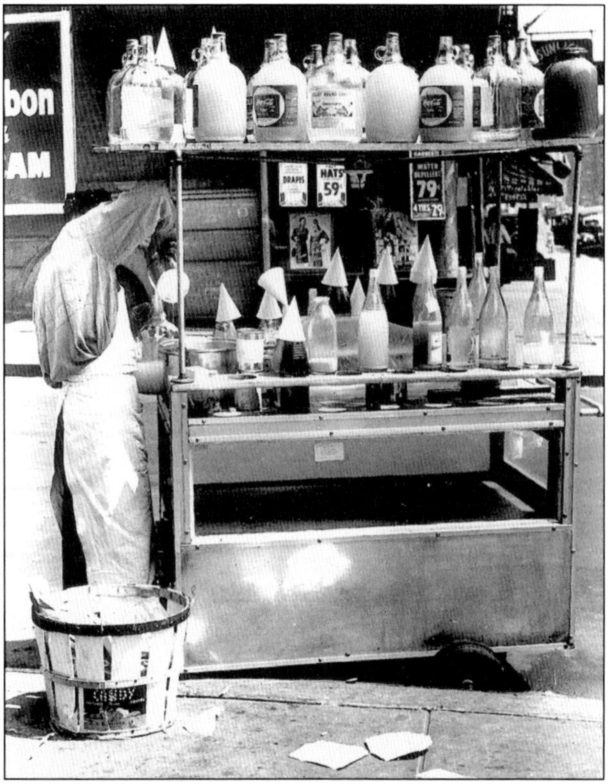

John Albok had an affinity for East Harlem, as evident in this 1940 photograph taken of the ice-cone man on East 110th Street. (Courtesy the Museum of the City of New York, Ilona Albok Vitarius.)

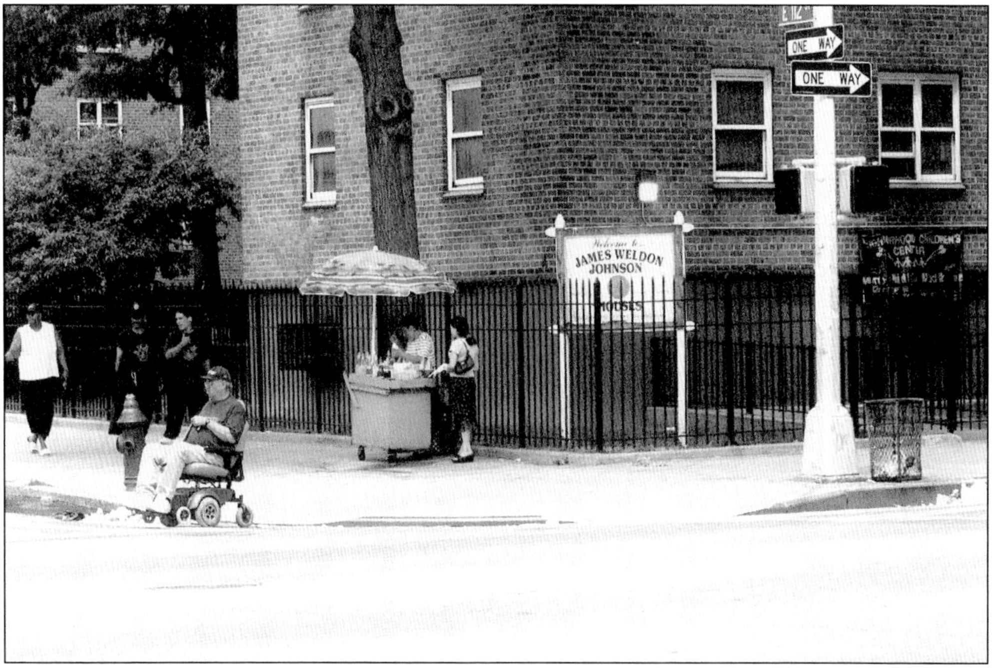


Today, East Harlemites can still cool off with an ice cone, but the tasty treat is called piragua. Here, a piragua saleswoman is fixing a piragua for a customer on 112th Street and Third Avenue. (Author's collection.)

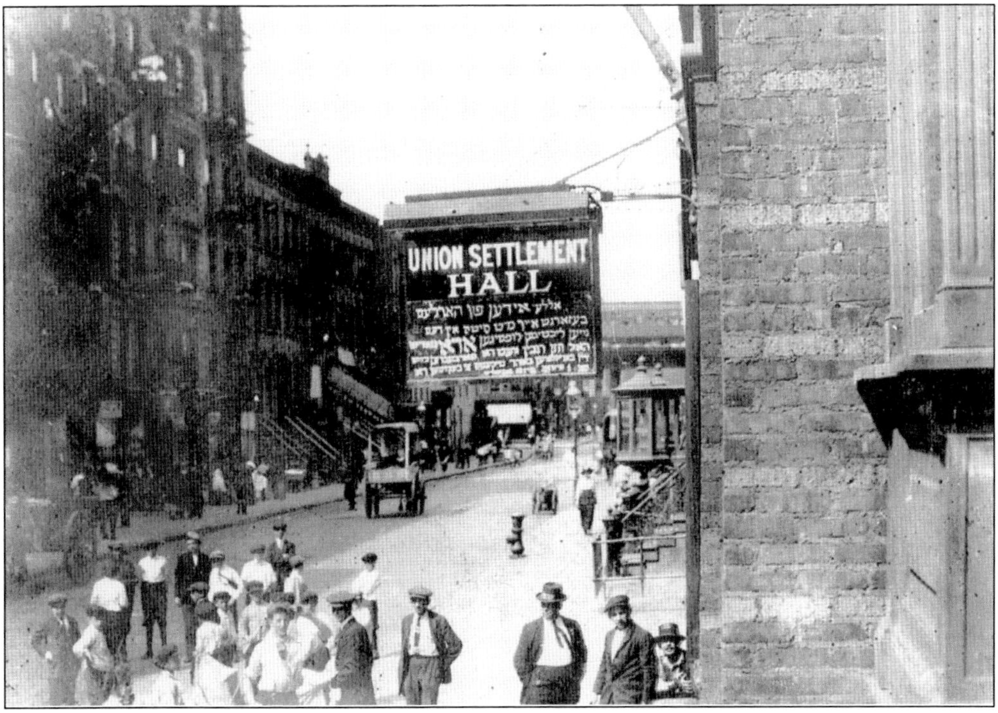


Union Settlement, located on 104th Street between Second and Third Avenues, was founded in 1895 by the alumni club of Union Theological Seminary to help immigrant Jews from Poland. The sign is written in Yiddish. This photograph was taken in 1900. (Courtesy the Union Settlement Association.)

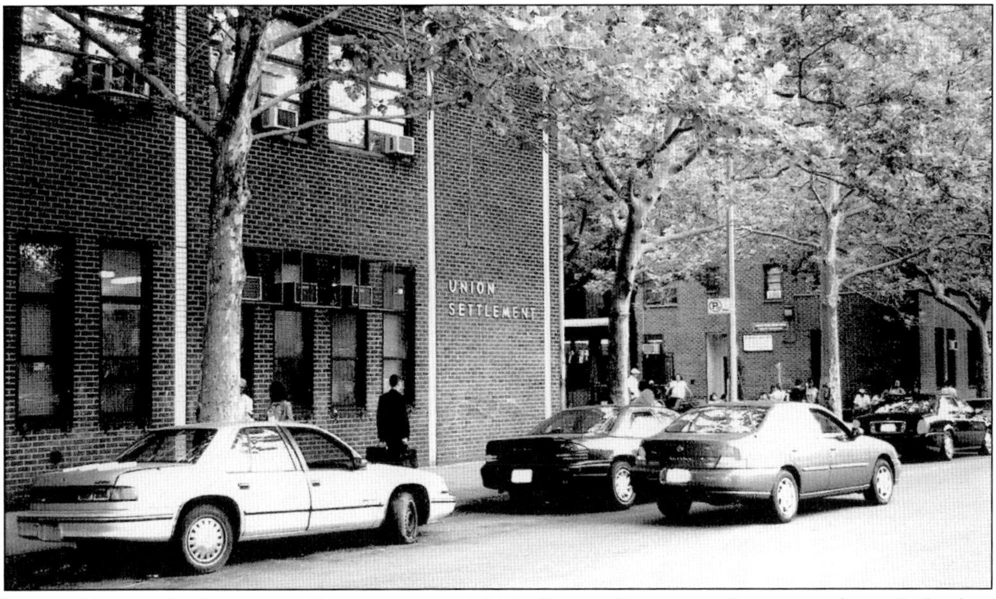


Today, Union Settlement still operates on 104th Street. Programs they provide include, but are not limited to, a senior citizen center, a head start program, a day-care program, college readiness programs, an adult education department, a job training program, the East Harlem HIV care network, and a credit union. (Author's collection.)

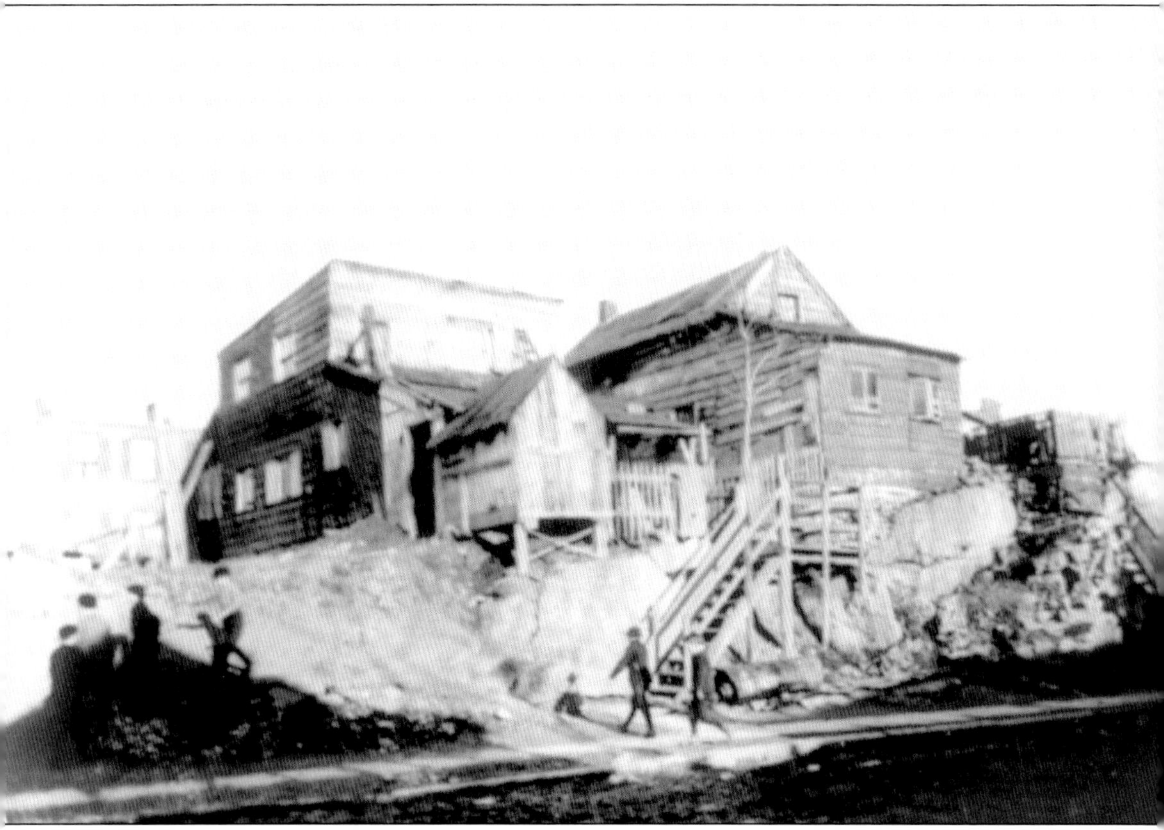

A little farther north, young men play in front of the shantytowns located on 118th Street and Madison Avenue. (Courtesy the Museum of the City of New York Print Archives.)

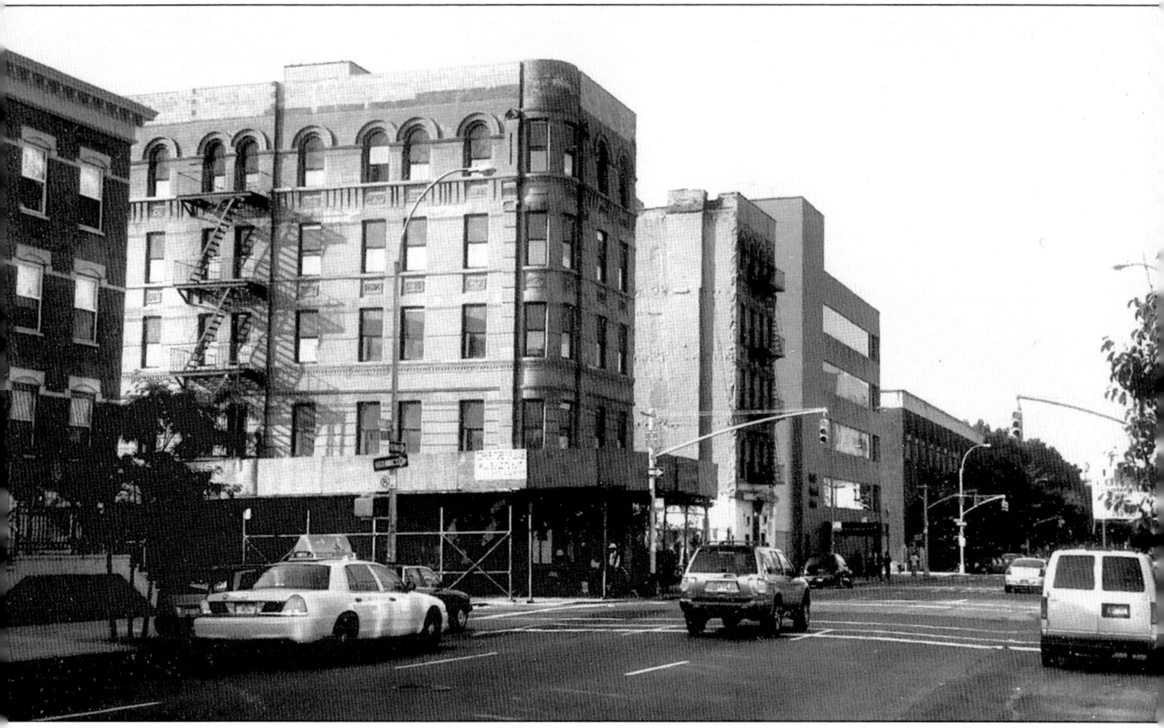

Today, recently renovated apartments have arisen on 118th Street and Madison Avenue. (Author's collection.)

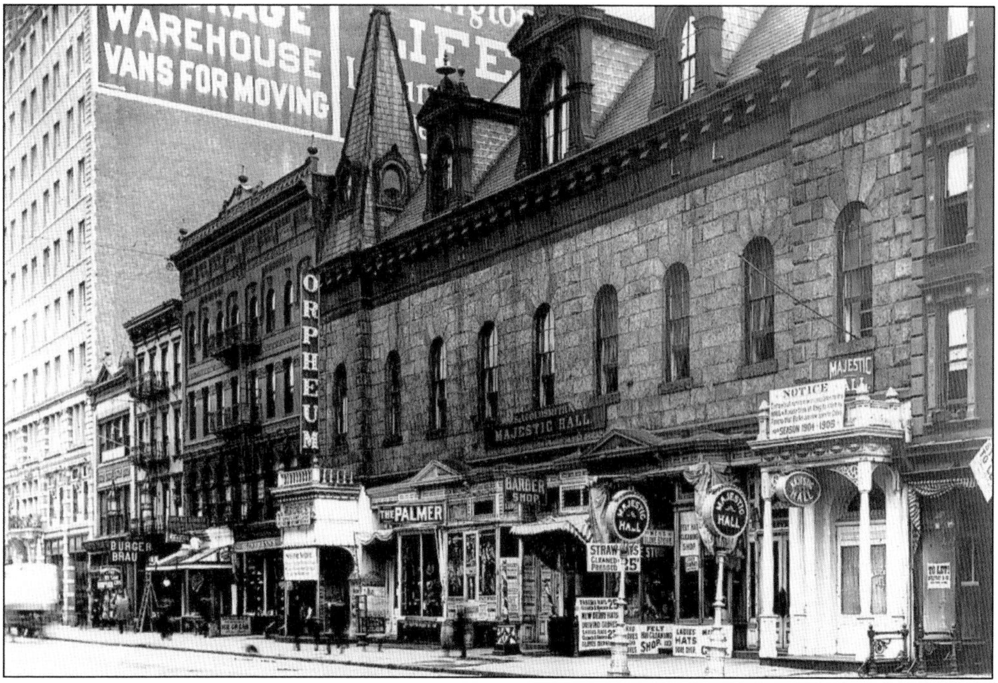


On 125th Street and Park Avenue (formerly Fourth Avenue) is a commercial strip where many businesses operate. Along the Majestic Hall, customers could purchase ice cream, have their clothes tailored, have their hair cut, and have their gloves and hats cleaned and repaired. This location remained open for the 1904–1905 season. (Courtesy the New York Public Library.)

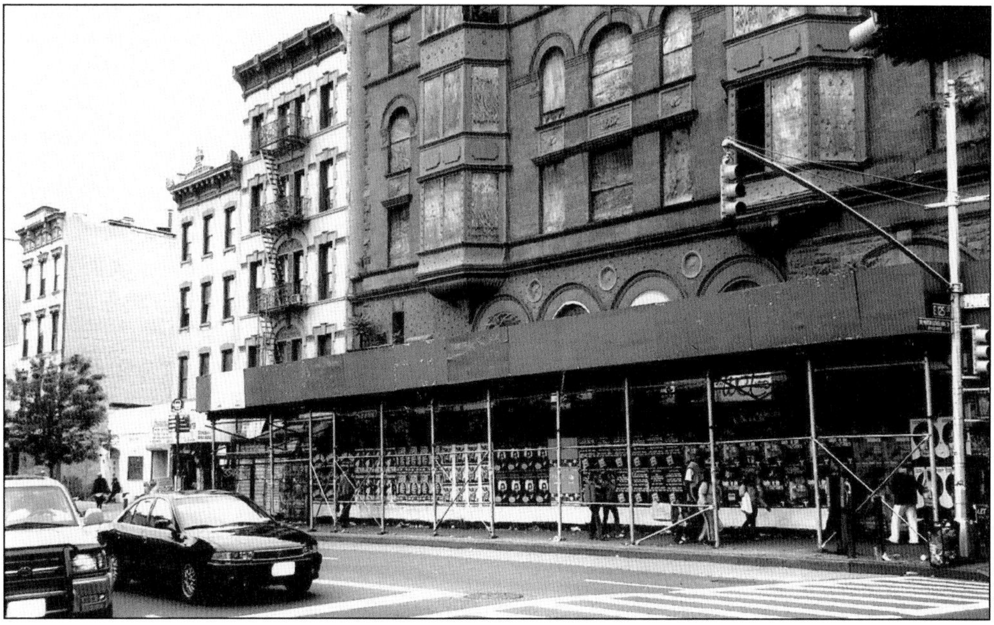

Today, unfortunately, the Majestic Hall is not open, nor are any of the other businesses mentioned above. These buildings are set for renovation, and hopefully people and businesses will be alive again on this block. (Author's collection.)

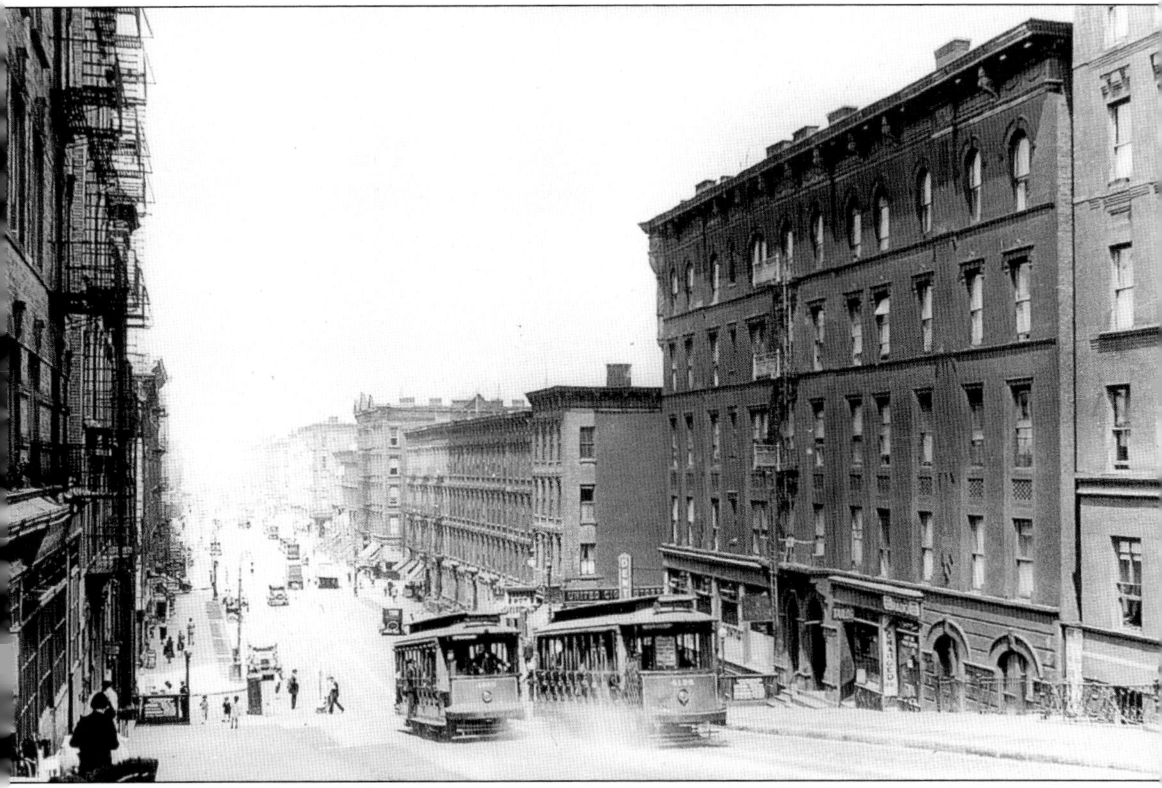

In this 1934 photograph, trolley cars, another common sight in East Harlem during this period, are seen traveling through many streets. These two trolleys are ascending the Hill, located on 102nd Street and Lexington Avenue. In the distance to the left is the 103rd Street and Lexington Avenue subway station. Many automobiles drove alongside the trolley cars in both directions. (Courtesy the New York Public Library.)

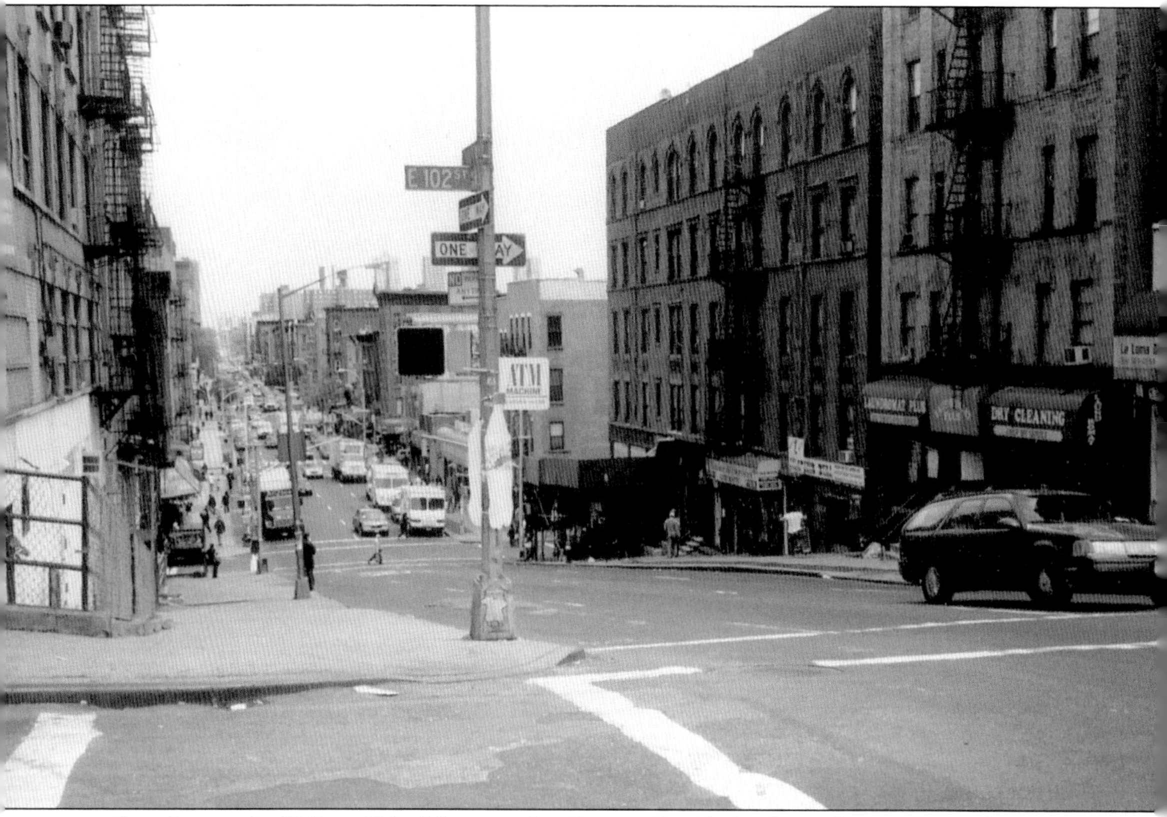


Seen here is the Hill on 102nd Street today. During the 1940s, the trolley cars ceased operation, and the cobblestone streets were paved over. Automobiles keep the tradition of traveling up the Hill alive; however, the traffic flows in one direction. The buildings in the previous photograph are still standing and rented by tenants. (Author's collection.)

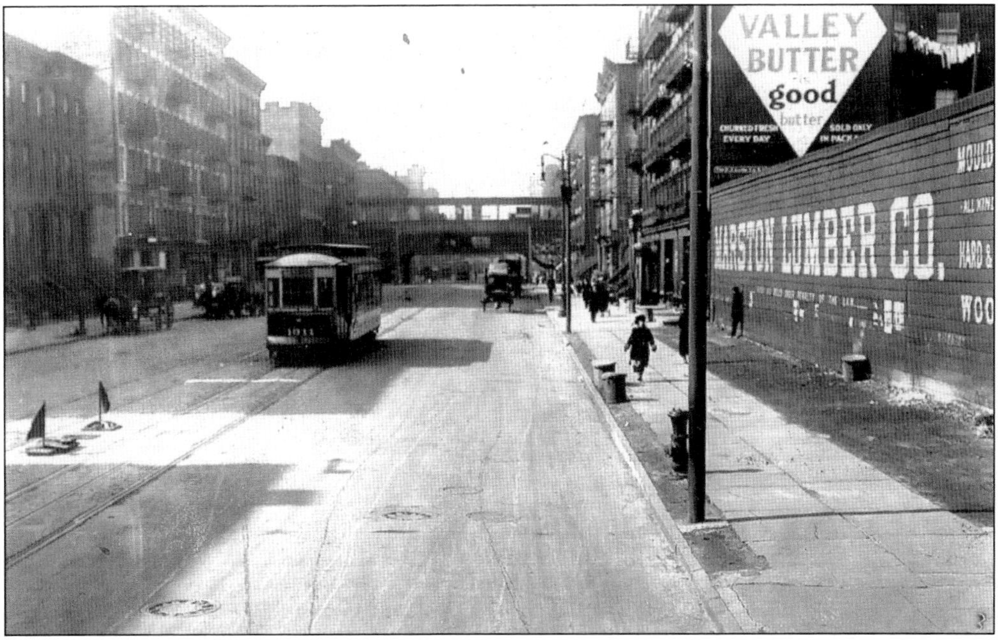


Seen in this 1898 photograph is another trolley traveling up 125th Street between First and Second Avenues. The Second Avenue elevated train is in the distance. On the right is the Marston Lumber Company. In the upper right corner is an advertisement for the Blue Valley Butter Company. As with the automobile, the horse-drawn carriages traveled in both directions. The year is 1898. (Courtesy the New York Public Library.)

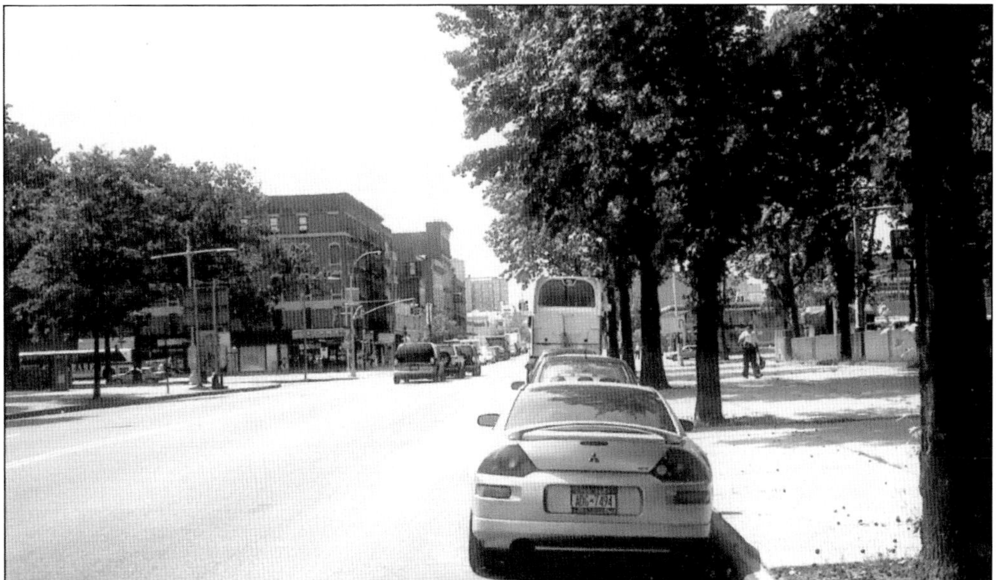

Today, the area is completely void of any reminder that this street was once a busy intersection for commuters. In the early 1930s, this neighborhood was remodeled for the construction of the Triborough Bridge. (Author's collection.)

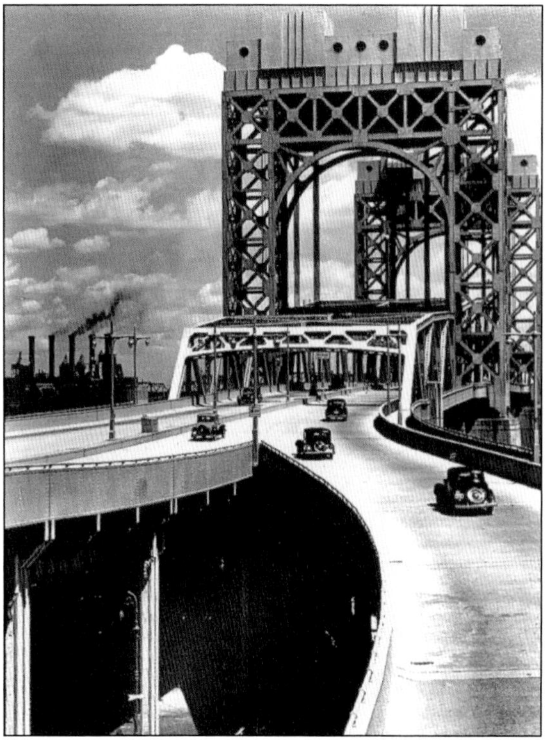

In this 1937 photograph are many cars entering the 125th Street approach to the Triborough Bridge, built in 1936. The car was at first a luxury and later became a necessity to escape the congested city. Roads and bridges were created to accommodate such a vehicle. However, the construction was to the consternation of the many residents who resided in developed areas and were relocated. (Photograph by Bernice Abbott; courtesy the Museum of the City of New York.)

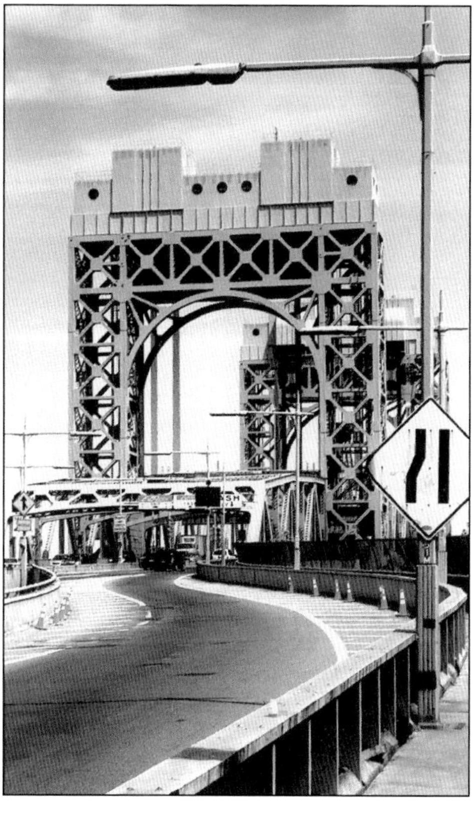

Today, 67 years after its construction, the Triborough Bridge is still in use. The only difference in the bridge is the new lights that were installed to illuminate it at nightfall. (Author's collection.)

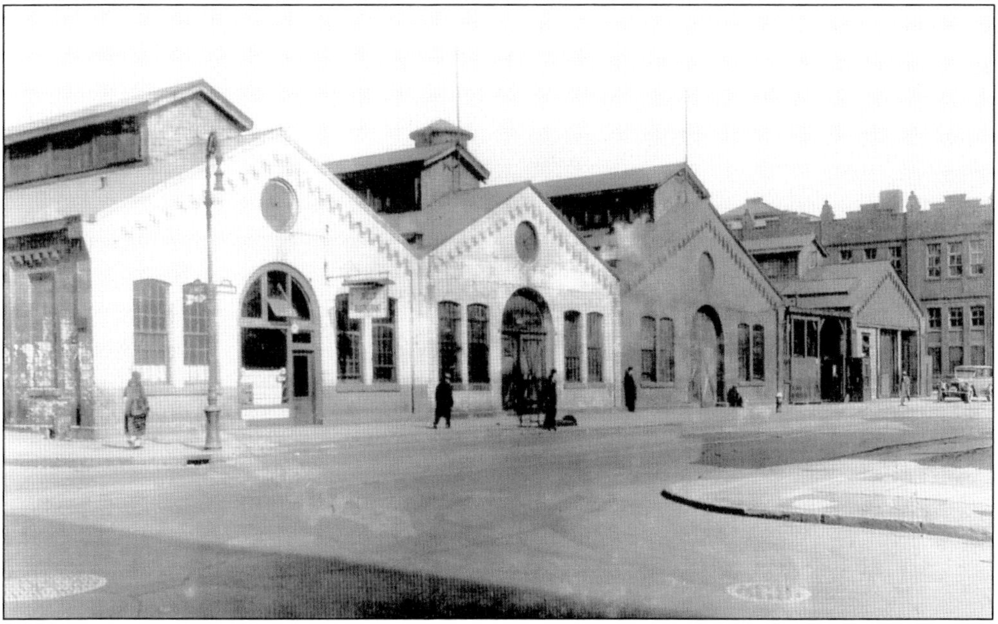

Seen in this 1931 photograph are the Interborough Rapid Transit (IRT) subway repair shop and the Green Line carbarn, located on 98th and 99th Streets and Lexington Avenue. A trolley car depot, which later became a bus depot, is adjacent to these houses.

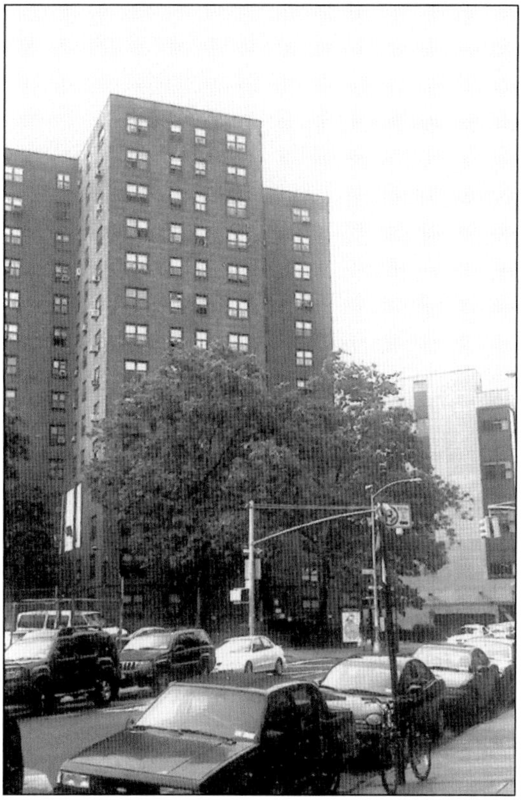

Today, the Lexington Houses, a 15-story housing development built in the early 1950s, occupies this location. On the right is a newly renovated 100th Street bus depot. (Author's collection.)

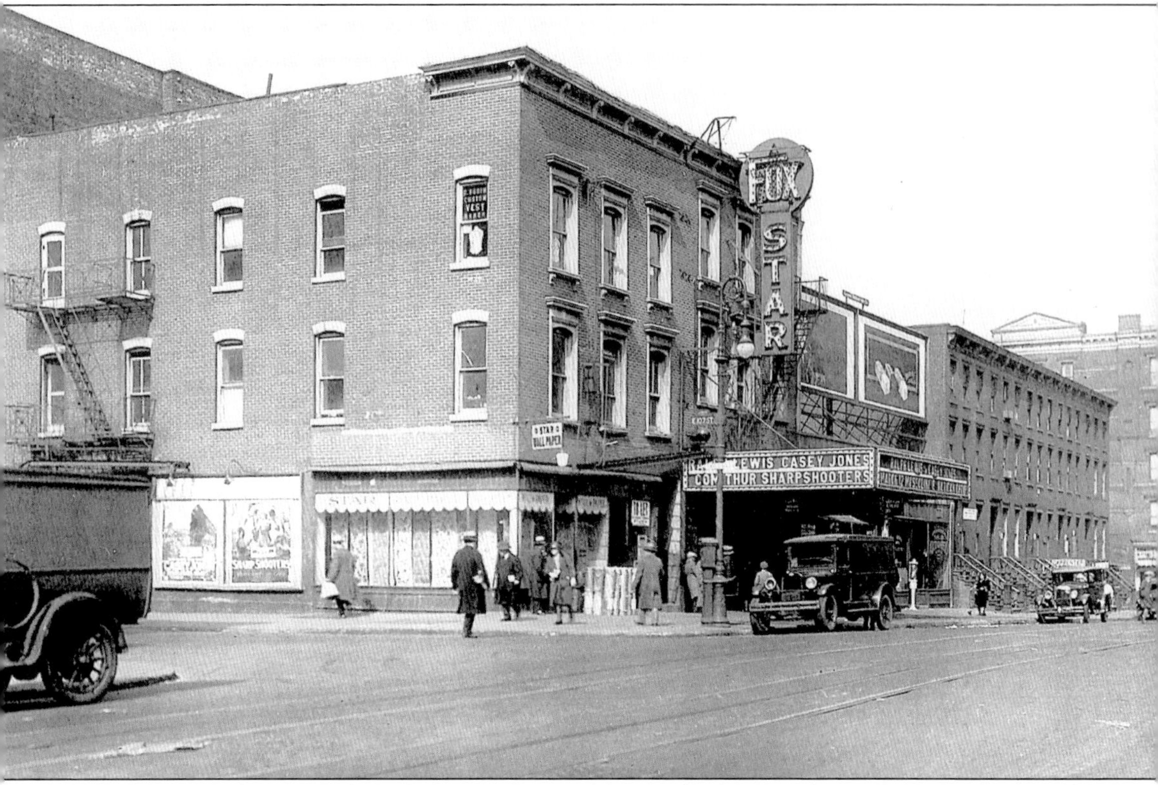


Throughout East Harlem there were many movie theaters, such as the Fox Star Studio, located on 107th Street and Lexington Avenue. To the left of the studio is a wallpaper store. To the right are tenement apartments where many small businesses operated on the ground floor, including a carpentry store. This photograph was taken in 1928. (Courtesy the New York Public Library.)

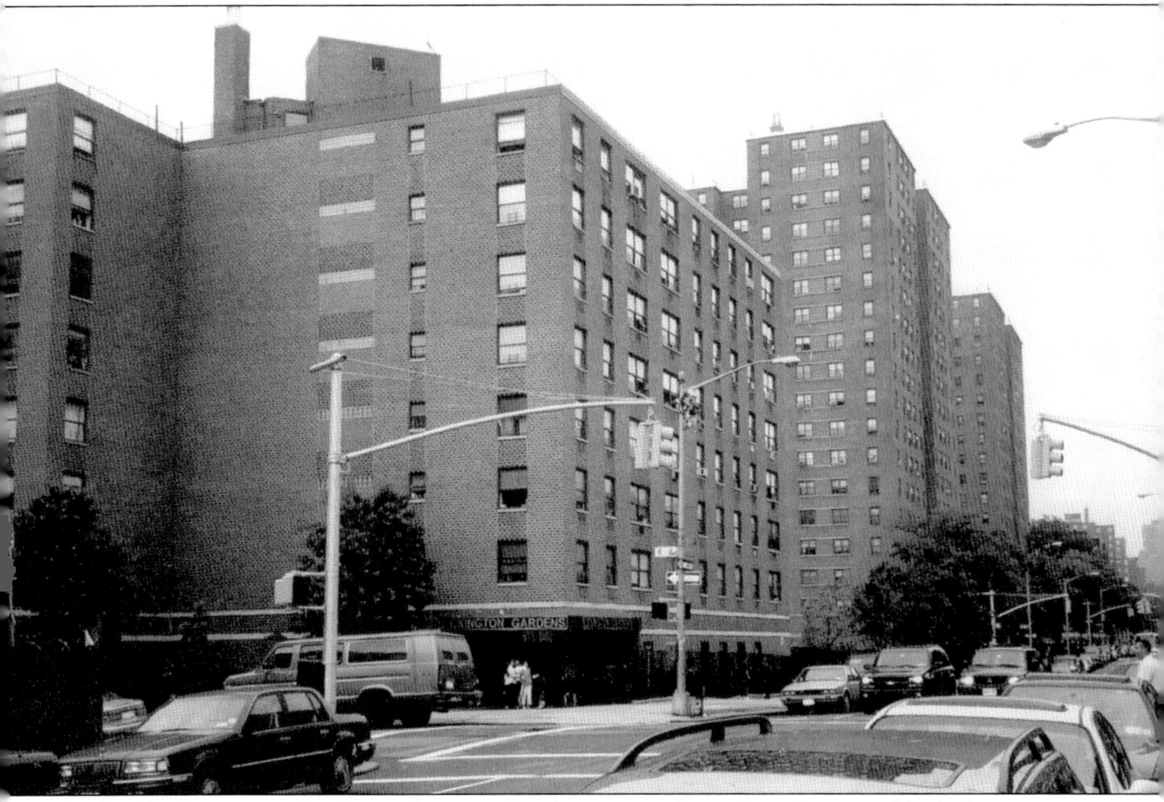

Today, the Lexington Gardens, a housing development, is located on the same block that once teemed with moviegoers. (Author's collection.)

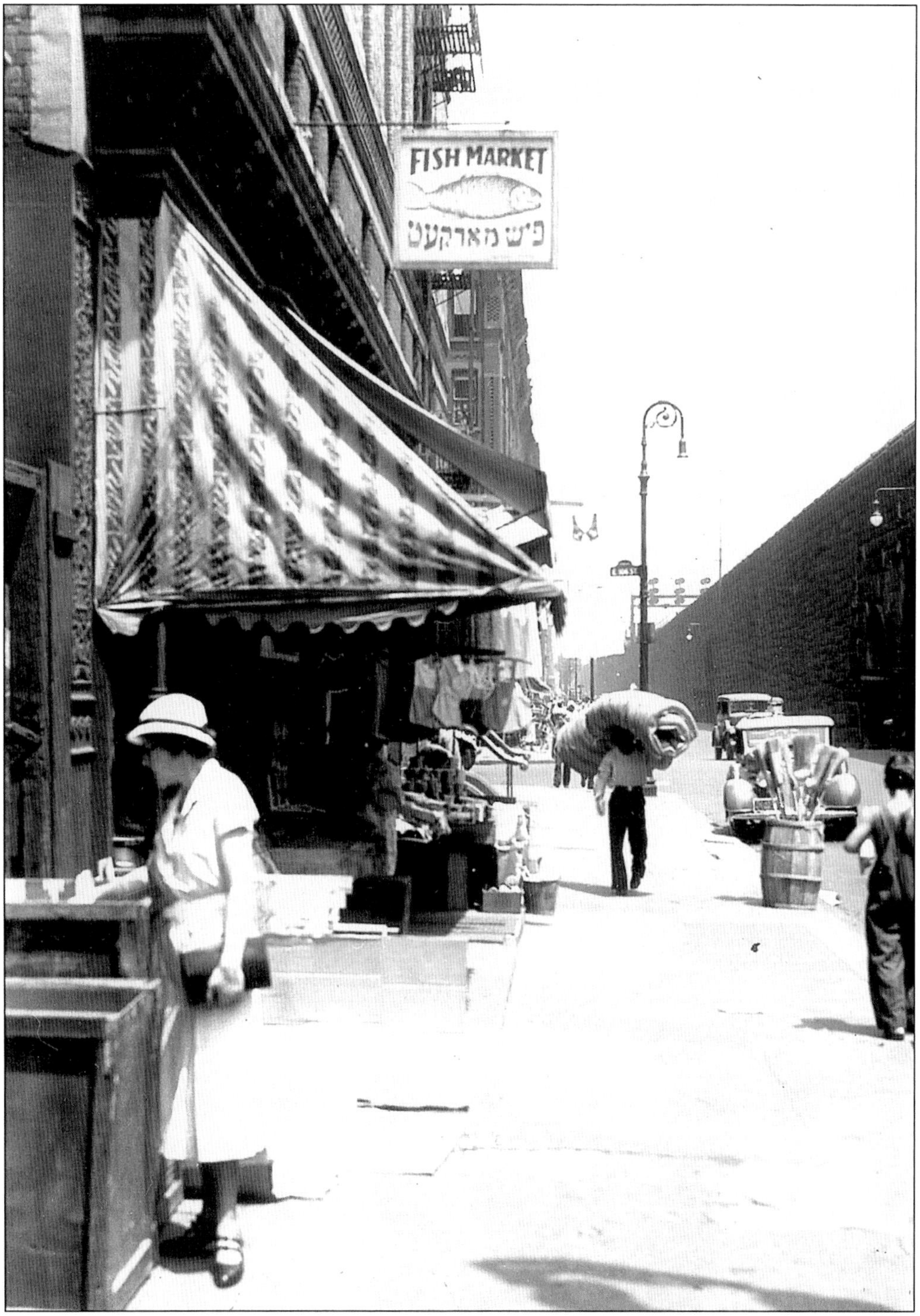


Near 106th Street and Park Avenue, next to the New York Central Railroad, were many businesses on one block. East Harlemites could buy their groceries and other goods without traveling far, as seen in this 1938 photograph. The fish market sign is written twice, in English and in Hebrew. On the right is a clothing store. (Courtesy the New York Public Library.)

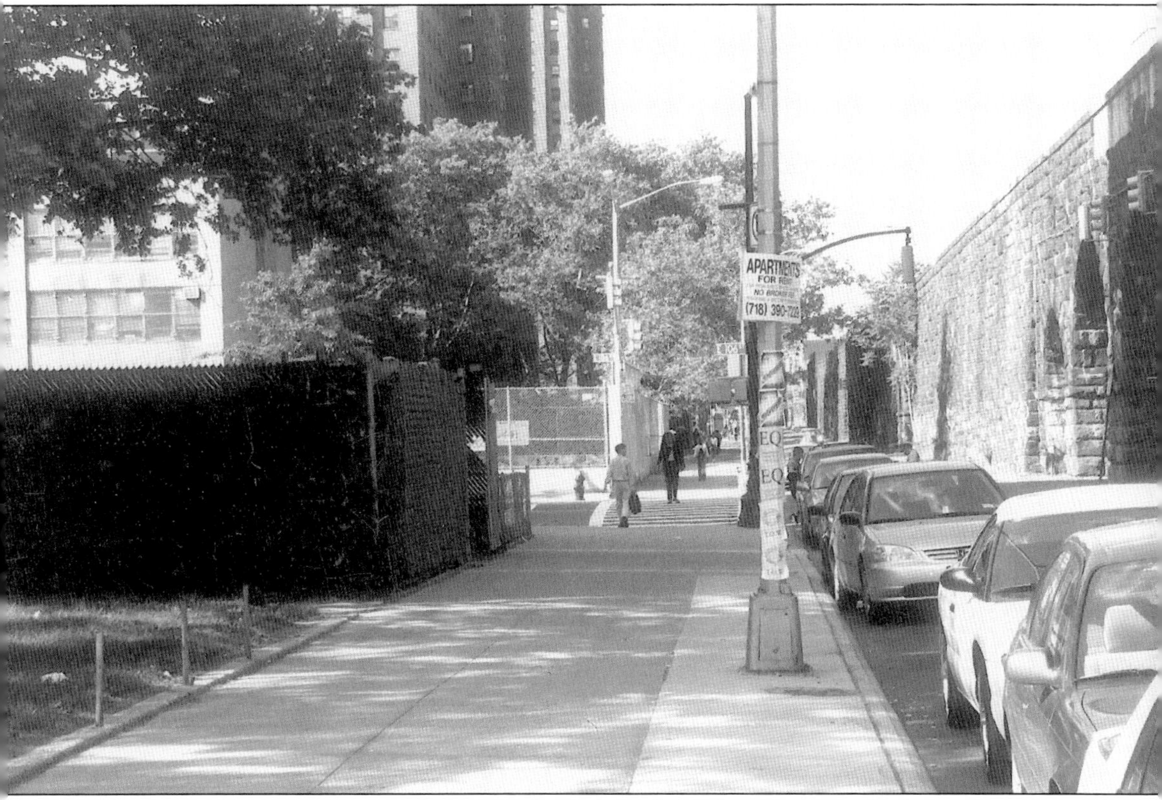


Today, the tenements and other businesses that adorned this block were demolished to make way for the George Washington Carver Houses, which stretch from 99th to 106th Streets along Park Avenue. The only thing that remains from the previous photograph is the New York Central Railroad, which became the Metro North Railroad.

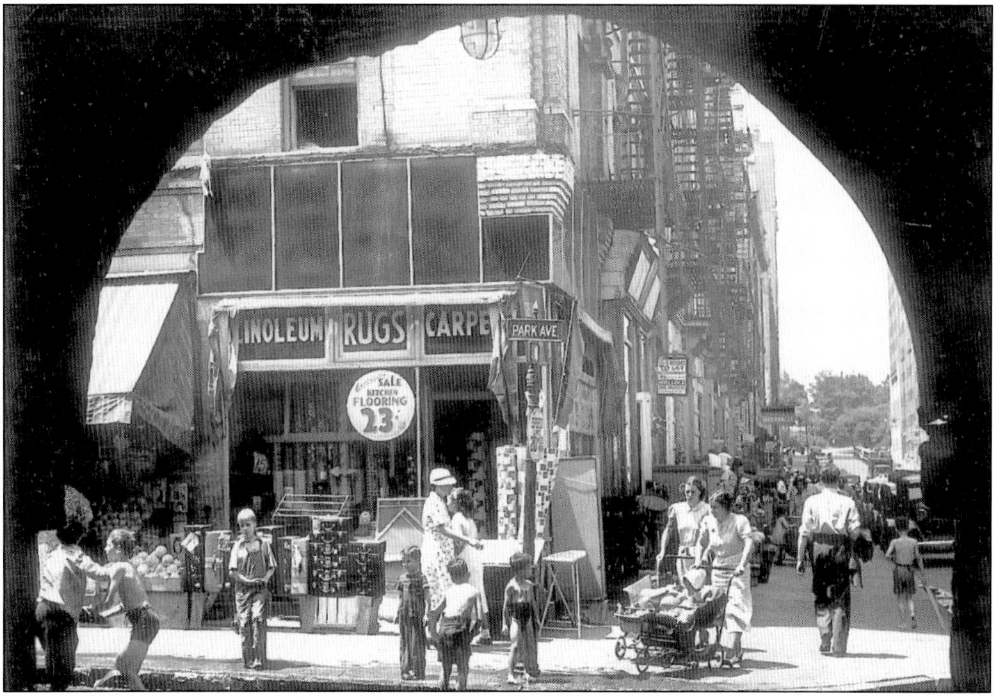


Seen is a view under the walkway of the New York Central Railroad on 106th Street and Park Avenue. The lack of cars allowed children to play in the street free from injury. Also seen are two young women with baby carriages strolling through this busy block. There is a grocery store on the left, and in the center is a linoleum, rugs, and carpet store. Luggage accessories could also be purchased here. There are apartments for rent, and the People's Tabernacle Church also appears in this view from the 1930s.

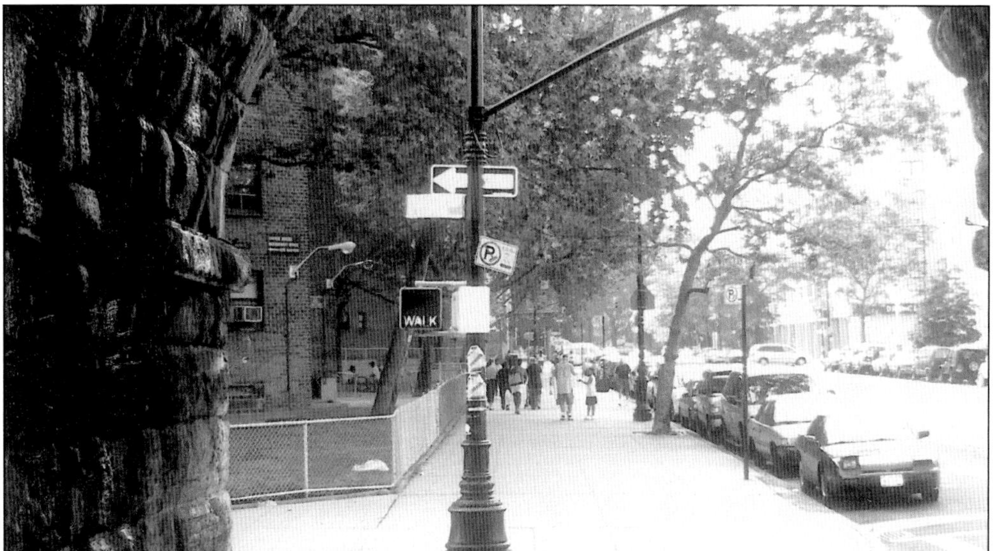


Today, people still partake a view of East Harlem, but the stores are gone, and the residents of George Washington Carver Houses are the main beneficiaries of this location. (Author's collection.)

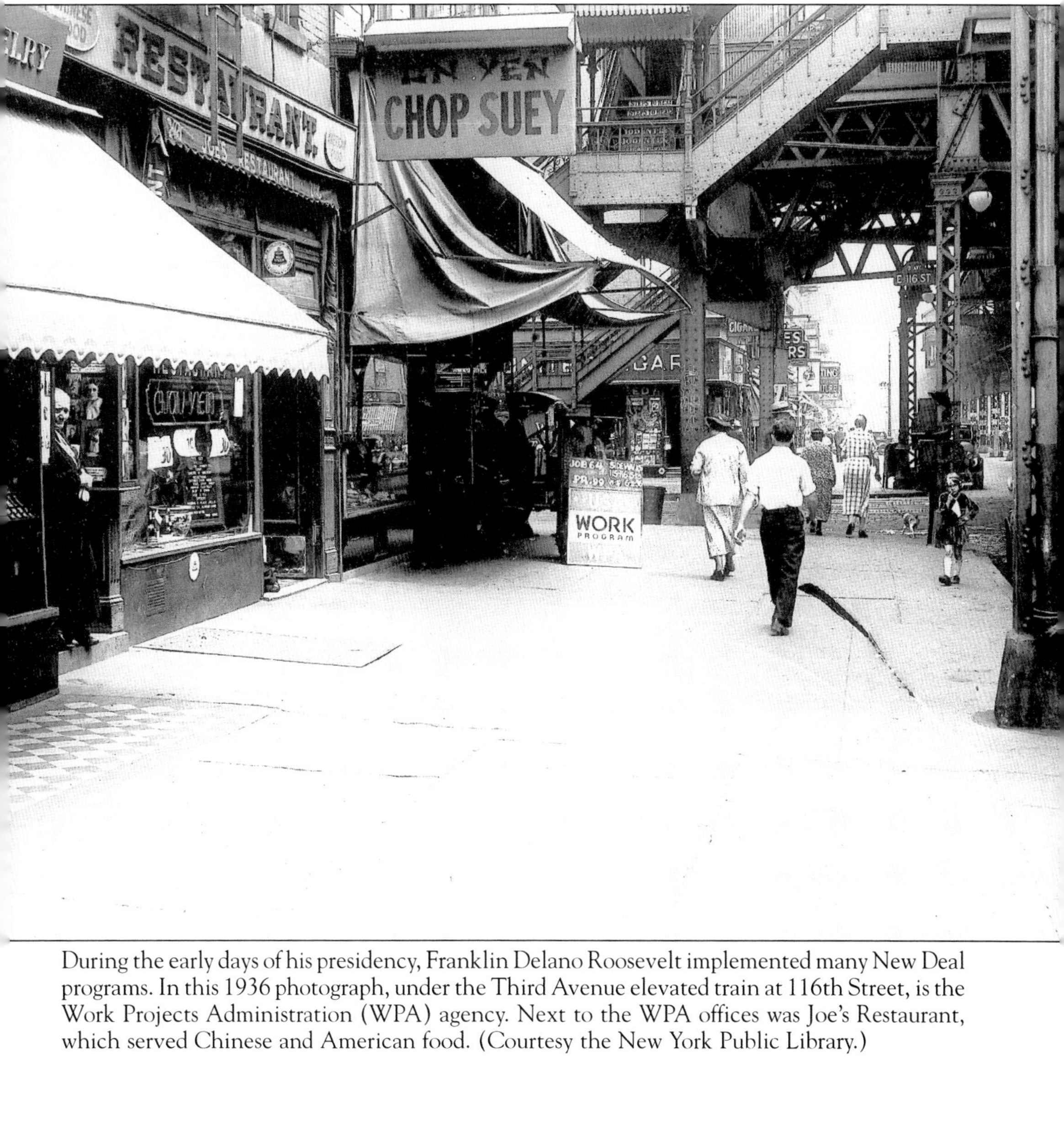


During the early days of his presidency, Franklin Delano Roosevelt implemented many New Deal programs. In this 1936 photograph, under the Third Avenue elevated train at 116th Street, is the Work Projects Administration (WPA) agency. Next to the WPA offices was Joe's Restaurant, which served Chinese and American food. (Courtesy the New York Public Library.)

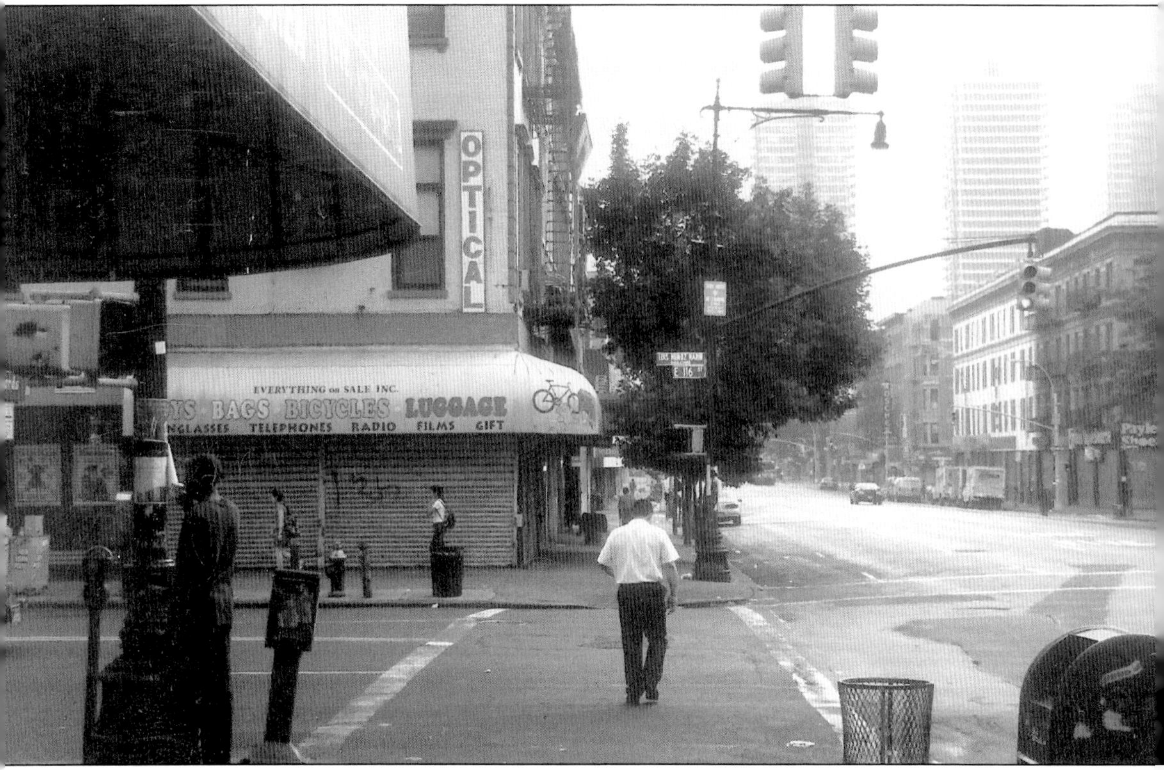


Seen here are today's Third Avenue and 116th Street. The Third Avenue elevated line ceased operation in 1955. Although the el is gone, many stores are still a staple of the neighborhood, making 116th Street a viable component of the businesses in East Harlem. From Fifth to First Avenues, 116th Street was renamed Luis Muñoz Marin Boulevard in honor of the first elected Puerto Rican governor (1948). (Author's collection.)

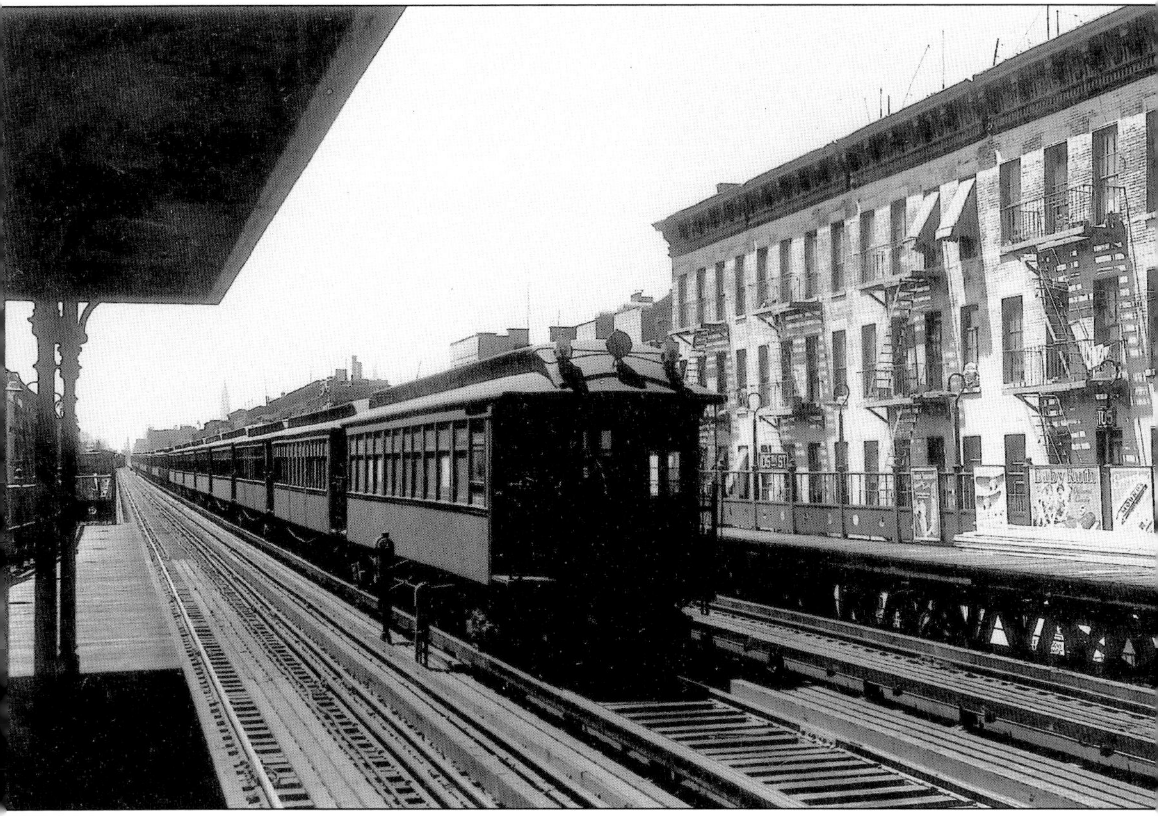


A few years after the Civil War, New Yorkers commuted on a cable-drawn line. This transportation method grew into the elevated railroad system. By 1880, elevated subways were located on Second, Third, Sixth, and Ninth Avenues. A Second Avenue elevated express subway is seen passing 105th Street in this 1934 view. In the distance is a local elevated subway on 111th street. (Courtesy the New York Public Library.)

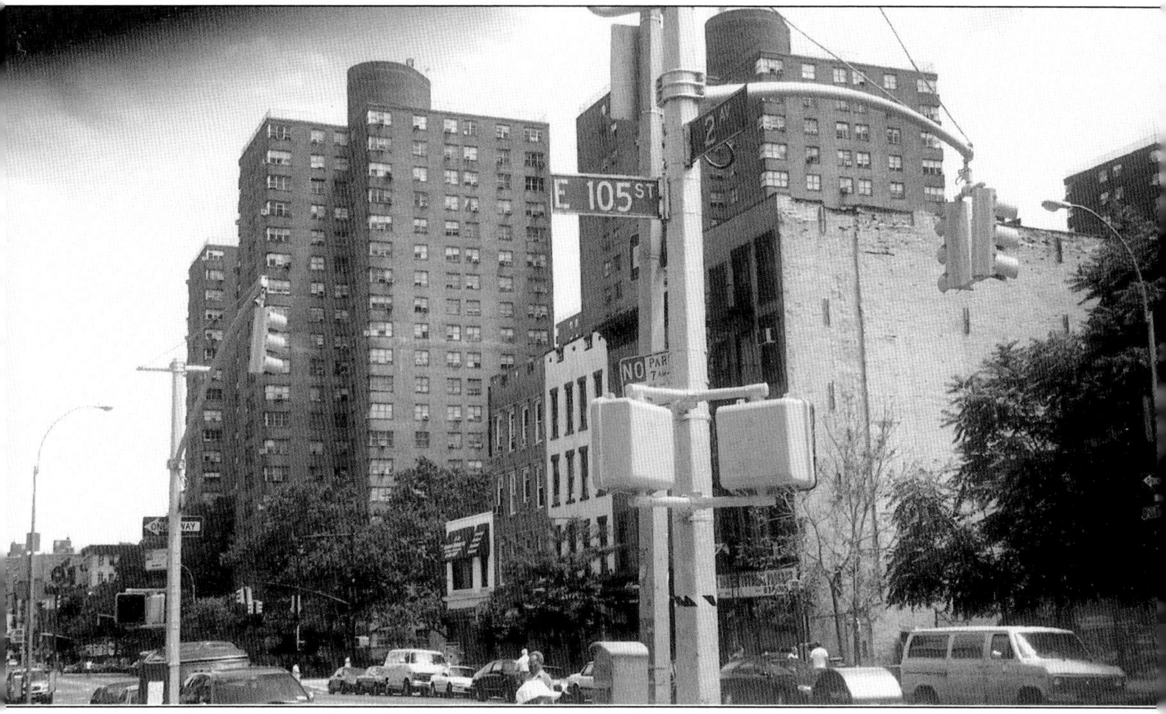


Second Avenue and 105th Street are seen in this modern-day view. The second elevated subway was demolished in 1940. In 2002, East Harlemites and all New Yorkers reveled in the resumption of the construction for the underground Second Avenue subway, which was discontinued in 1975 due to the fiscal crises that nearly bankrupted New York City.

*Six*

# Famous People and Places

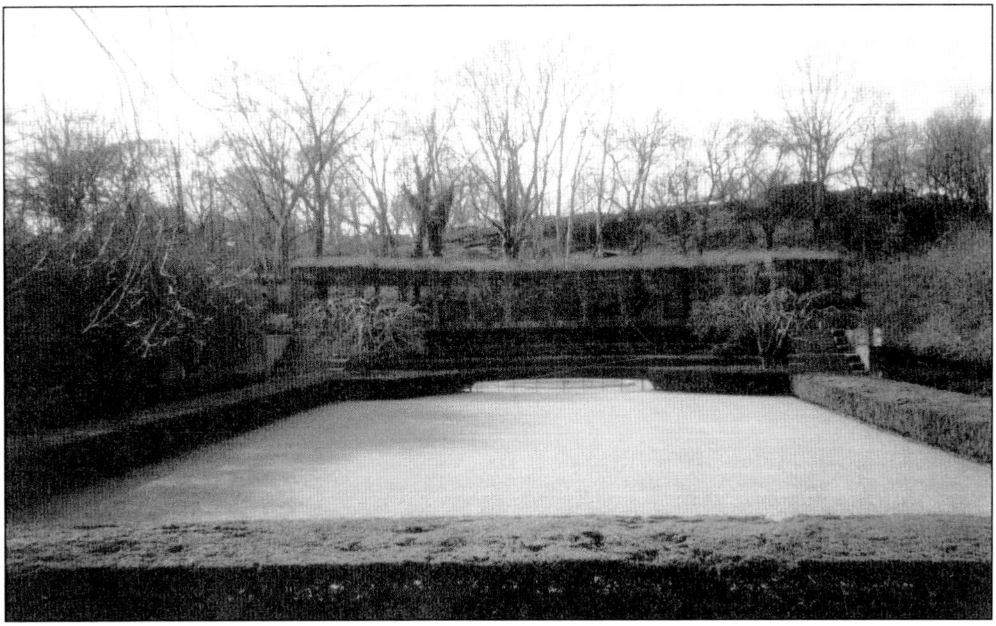

The Conservatory Garden is located on 105th Street and Fifth Avenue. It is a favorite destination for newlyweds to take their first photographs.

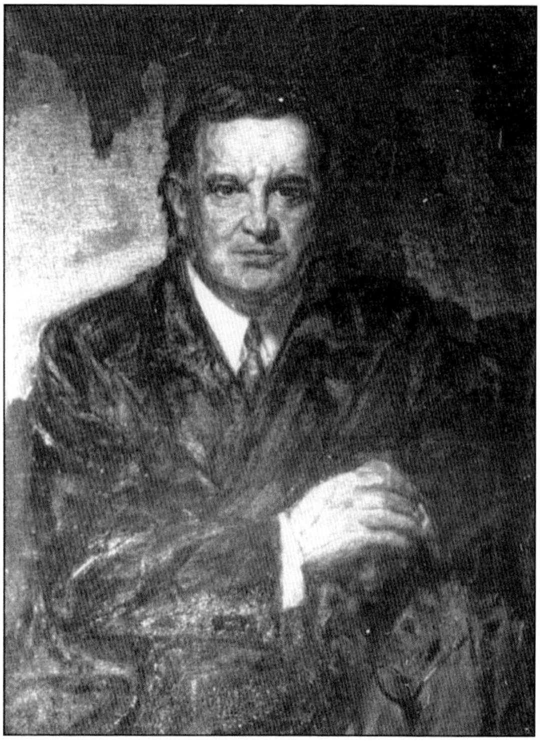

Fiorello H. La Guardia was also known as "the Little Flower." La Guardia represented two neighborhoods in Congress: the Lower East Side and East Harlem. Even after he became mayor of New York City, La Guardia continued to live in East Harlem on East 107th Street. (Courtesy the Fiorello H. La Guardia Community Center.)

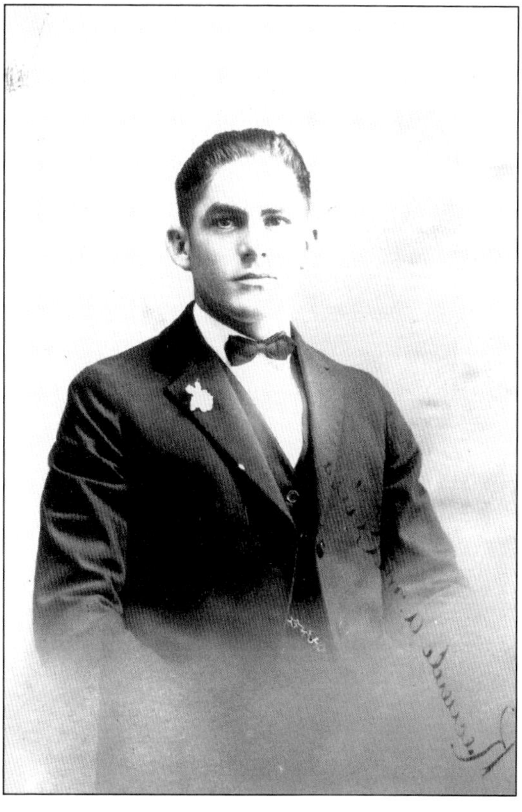

This portrait of Oscar Garcia Rivera was taken in 1926. An exceptional leader, Garcia Rivera was born in Mayaguez, Puerto Rico, in 1900. Garcia Rivera arrived in New York City first in 1917, and returned to the city in 1926. After he graduated from St. John's University School of Law in 1930, Garcia Rivera opened up law firms throughout New York City, including one in East Harlem. He even offered pro-bono work for East Harlemites who were too poor to retain his services. In 1937, Garcia Rivera was elected to the state assembly, becoming the first Puerto Rican elected to public office in the United States. (Courtesy the Center for Puerto Rican Studies, Hunter College, City University of New York.)

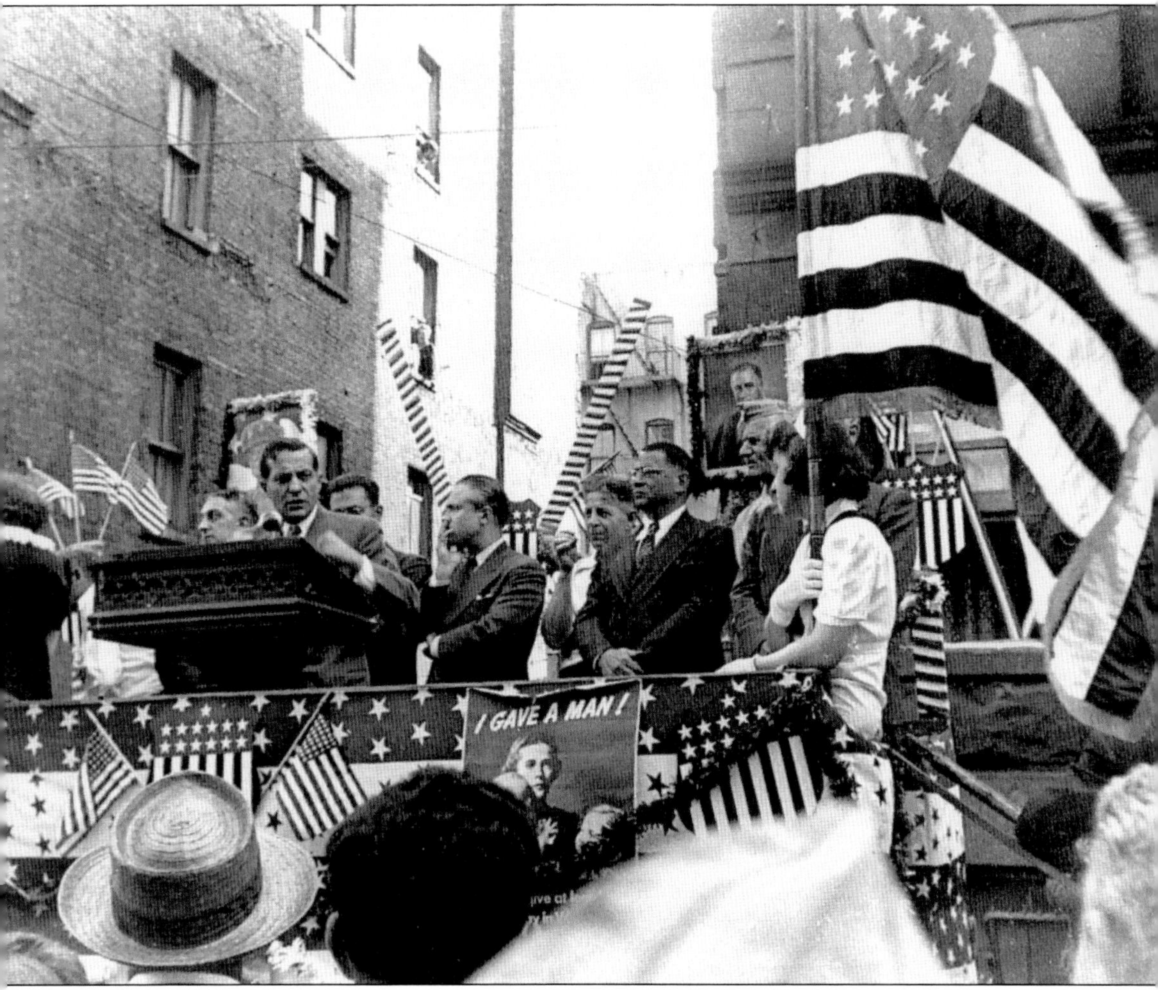


Vito Marcantonio was a La Guardia protégé and an eventual successor in Congress. Although he was attacked for his progressive viewpoints, no one can deny his indefatigable service to his East Harlem constituents. Affectingly called "Marc" by his friends, he is seen here making an address at a 105th Street victory celebration. (Photograph by John Albok; courtesy the Museum of the City of New York, Ilona Albok Vitarius.)

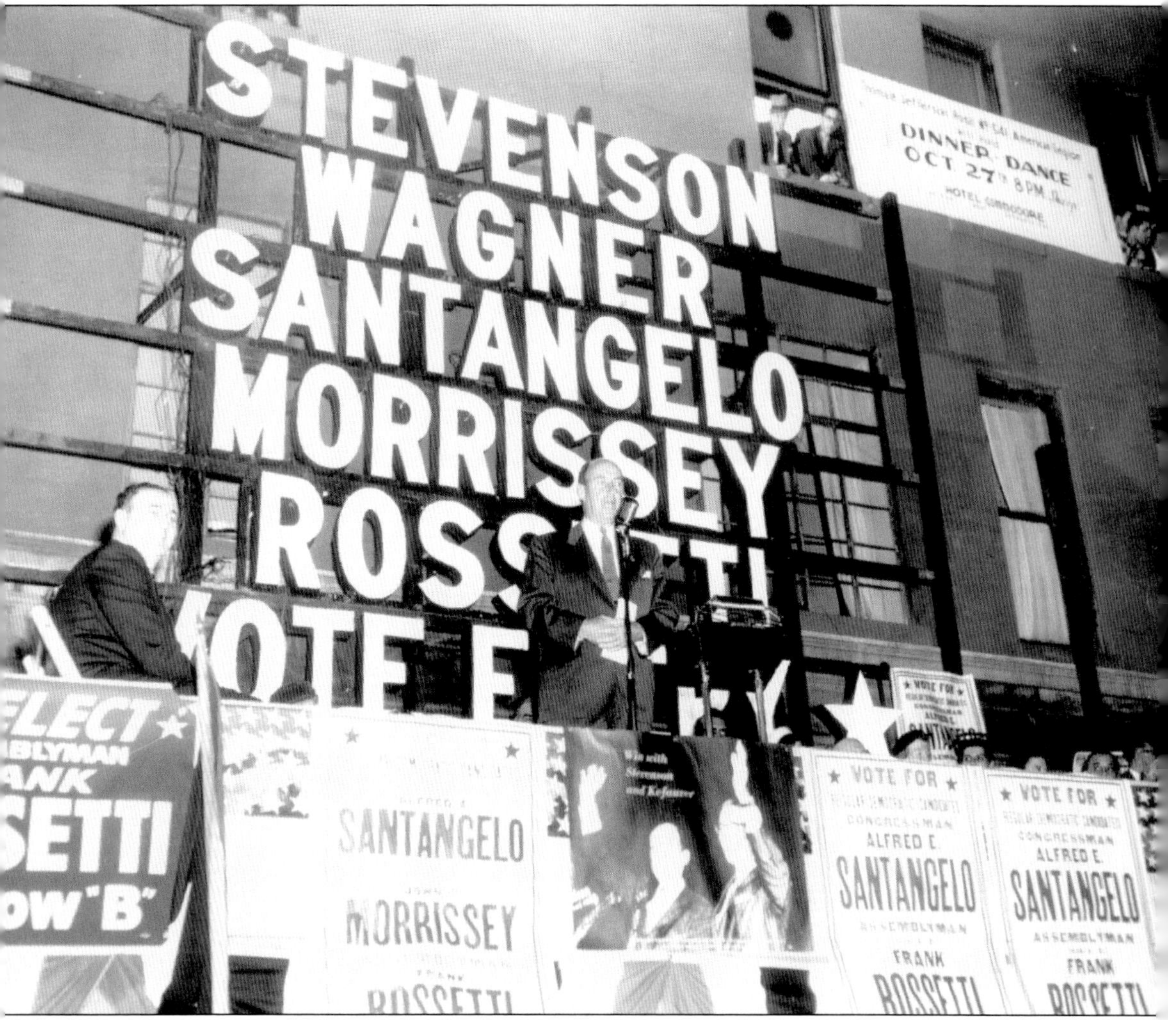


Democratic candidate Adlai Stevenson is seen here speaking at the Lucky Corner on 116th Street and Lexington Avenue in his second bid for the presidency, in 1956. The Lucky Corner, popularized by Fiorello La Guardia, has become a rite of passage for many East Harlem politicians to announce their candidacy for political office. Stevenson went on to lose the presidential election to incumbent Dwight D. Eisenhower. Seated to Stevenson's left is state senator Alfred Santangelo, who was elected to Congress that year. (Courtesy the Center for Puerto Rican Studies, Hunter College, City University of New York, Justo A. Marti collection.)

A Lucky Corner rally flyer, mentioning many of East Harlem's prominent politicians during the late 1930s, is seen here. (Courtesy the Center for Puerto Rican Studies, Hunter College, City University of New York, Oscar Garcia Rivera papers.)

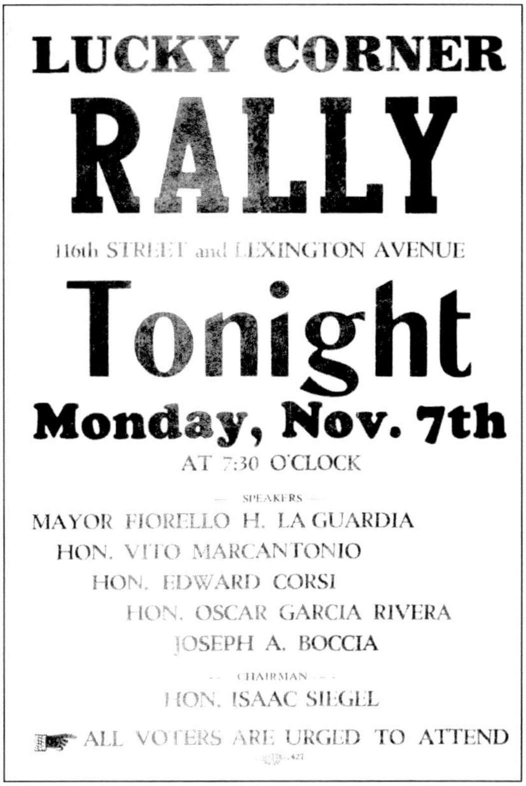


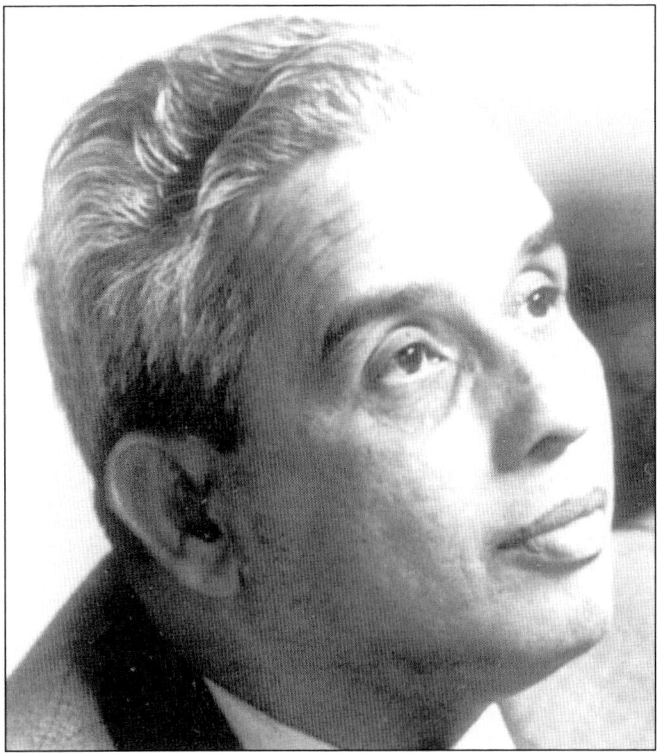

Carlos Rios, a lay minister from the East Harlem Protestant parish and later a New York assemblyman from East Harlem, is seen here *c.* 1960. (Courtesy the Reverend Norman C. Eddy.)

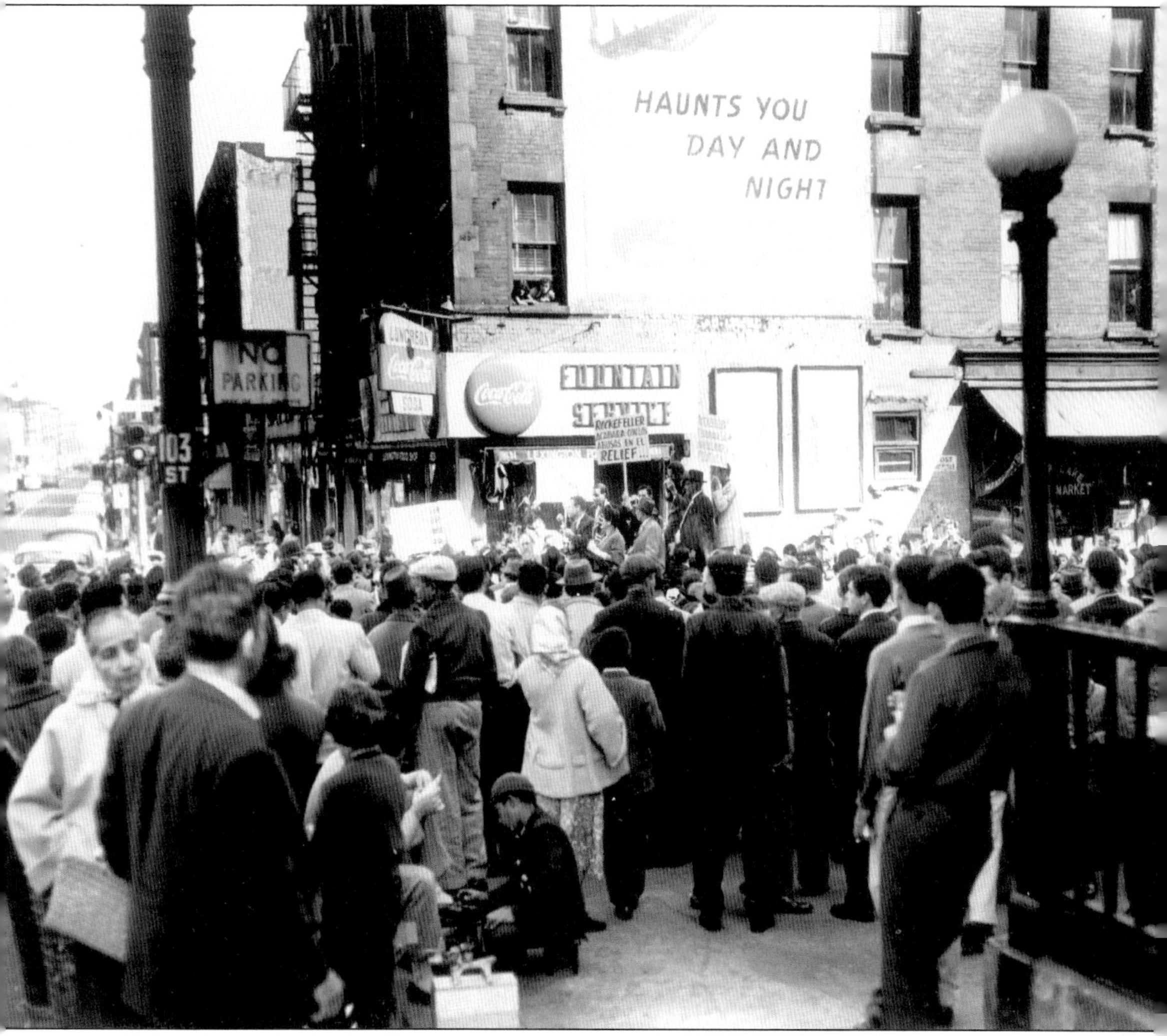


Although not the Lucky Corner, the location is advantageous to Nelson Rockefeller, who is in the center of the photograph in his first campaign for governor, in 1958. Here, Rockefeller addresses a crowd on 103rd Street and Lexington Avenue. Rockefeller went on defeat the incumbent governor, Averill Harriman. (Courtesy the Center for Puerto Rican Studies, Hunter College City University of New York, Justo A. Marti collection.)

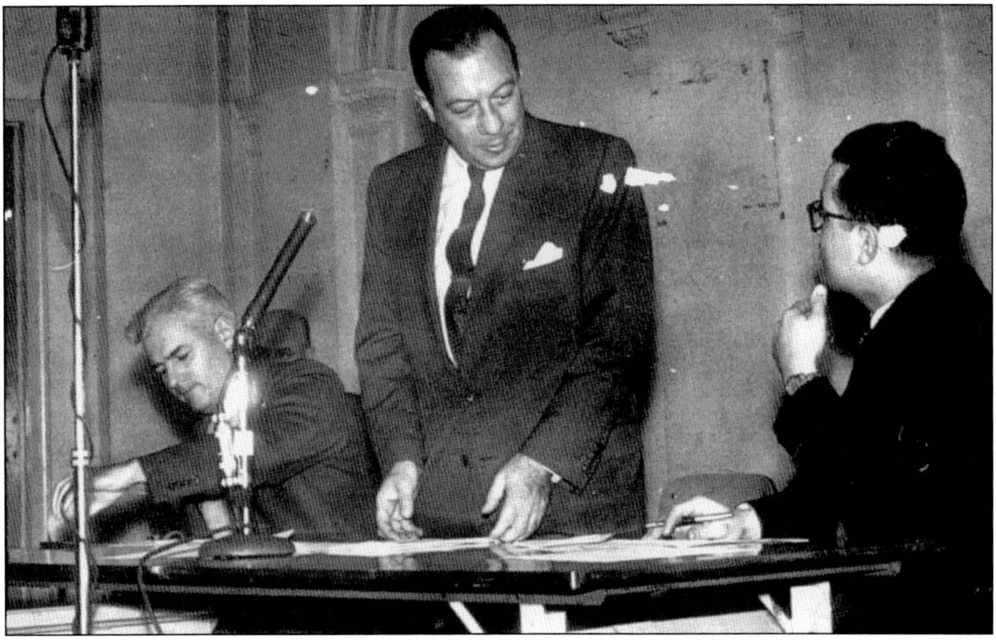

The Reverend Norman C. Eddy is seated on the left at a 1956 community political meeting in East Harlem. Standing in the center of the photograph is the former New York City mayor, Robert Wagner. Jose Fortoul is seated to the right of the mayor. (Courtesy the Reverend Norman C. Eddy.)

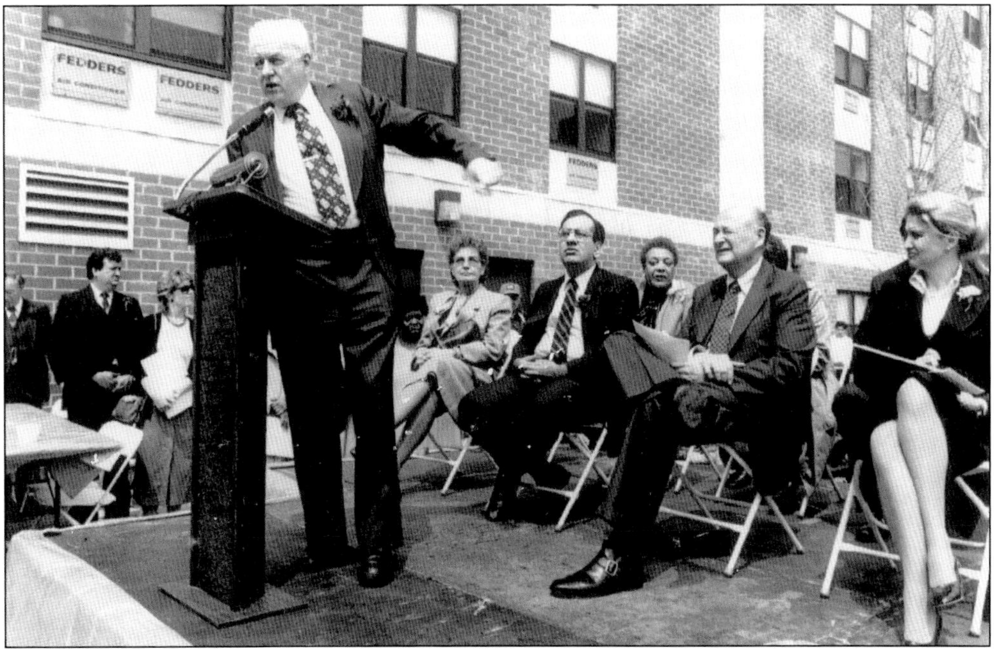


Here, the Reverend Norman C. Eddy speaks at the dedication of a new housing development in East Harlem. Seated is Sen. Olga A. Mendez. Also seen are former state assemblyman Angelo Del Toro, former city councilwoman Carolyn M. Maloney, and former mayor Edward I. Koch. (Courtesy the Reverend Norman C. Eddy.)

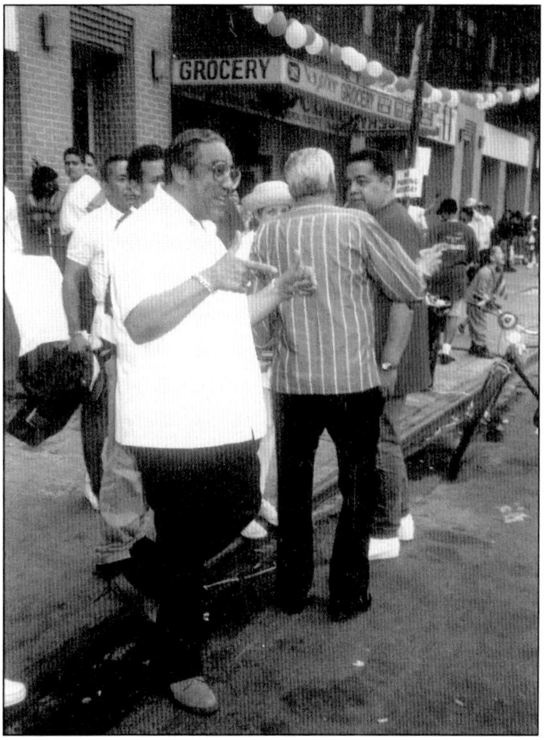


Congressman Charles Bernard Rangel has represented East Harlem in Congress since 1971. Now in his 17th term, Rangel is the highest-ranking Democrat on the powerful Committee on Ways and Means. Rangel has also distinguished himself as a decorated Korean War veteran, assistant district attorney, and state assemblyman. Here, Rangel is enjoying festivities held on 100th Street in 1994. (Courtesy Raymond Rodriguez.)

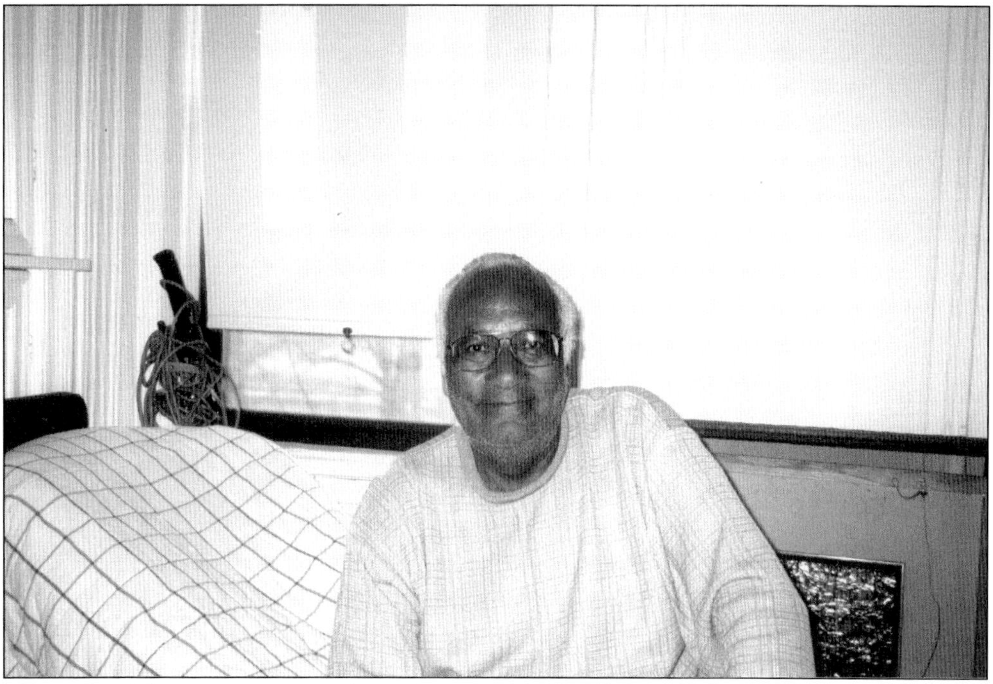

Writer Piri Thomas is seen in the apartment of Claude Brown (author of *Manchild in the Promised Land*). Thomas grew up on 104th Street between Madison and Park Avenues. Thomas's autobiography, *Down These Mean Streets*, has become a classic in American literature. (Author's collection.)

Actor Burt Lancaster was born on 106th Street and Second Avenue. His athleticism earned him a scholarship to New York University. Lancaster dropped out of college and became an acrobat with skills learned at Union Settlement. After World War II, Lancaster became an actor. His credits include *The Rose Tattoo*, *Sweet Smell of Success*, *From Here to Eternity*, *Elmer Gantry* (for which he won the Academy Award), and *Field of Dreams*. This photograph was taken in the 1940s. (Courtesy Ellen Simon.)

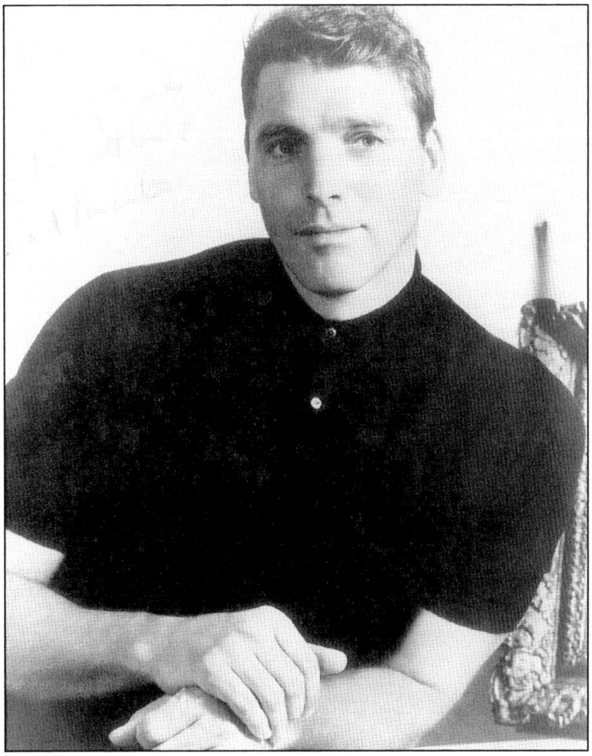

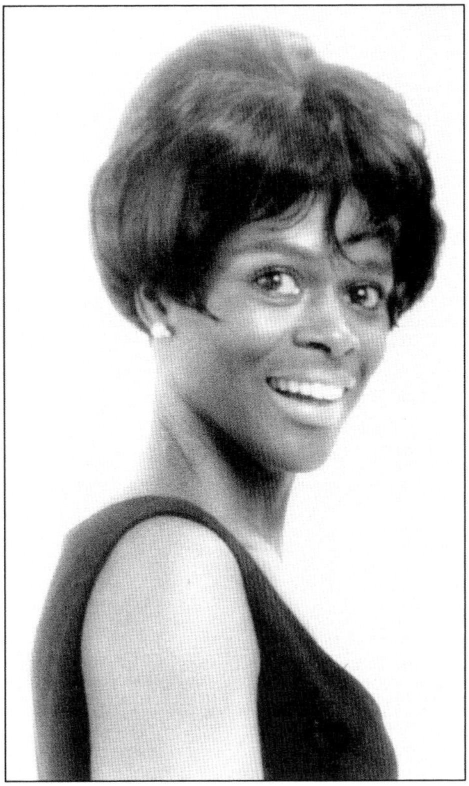

This lovely portrait of actress Cicely Tyson was taken during the 1960s. Tyson's parents immigrated to the United States from the Island of Nevis in the Caribbean. Tyson grew up on 101st Street near Lexington Avenue. She was an Academy Award nominee for her role in *Sounder*. Tyson's other credits include *The Autobiography of Jane Pittman* (for which she won an Emmy Award), *Roots*, and *Hoodlum*. (Courtesy the Schomburg Center for Research in Black Culture, the New York Public Library.)

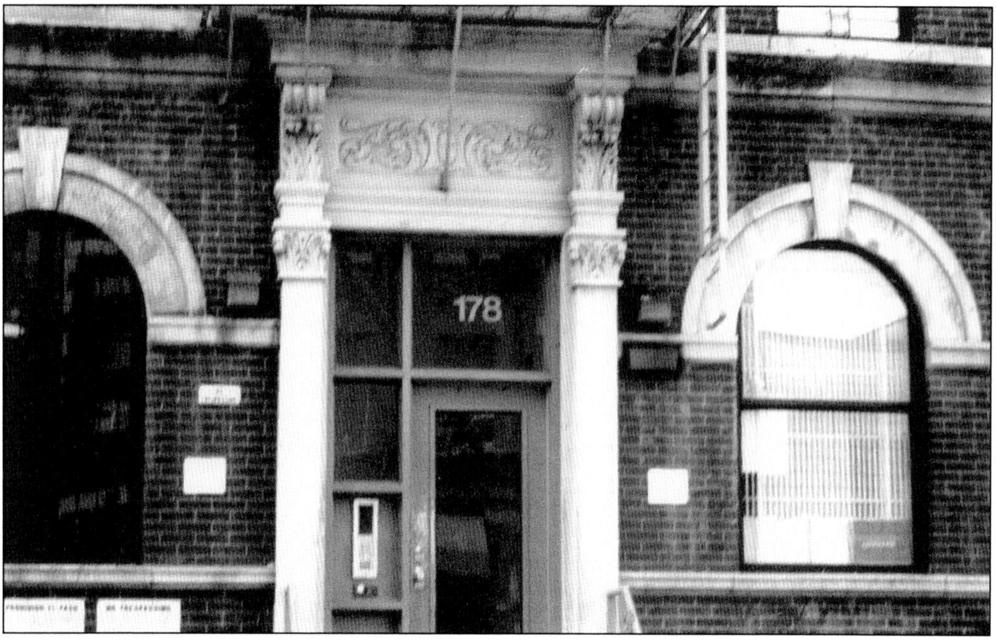


In 1994, the building where Cicely Tyson was reared became the Cicely Tyson House with the assistance of Fr. Robert V. Lott of St. Francis De Sales. This location and three other buildings were refurbished for 58 low-income families. (Author's collection.)

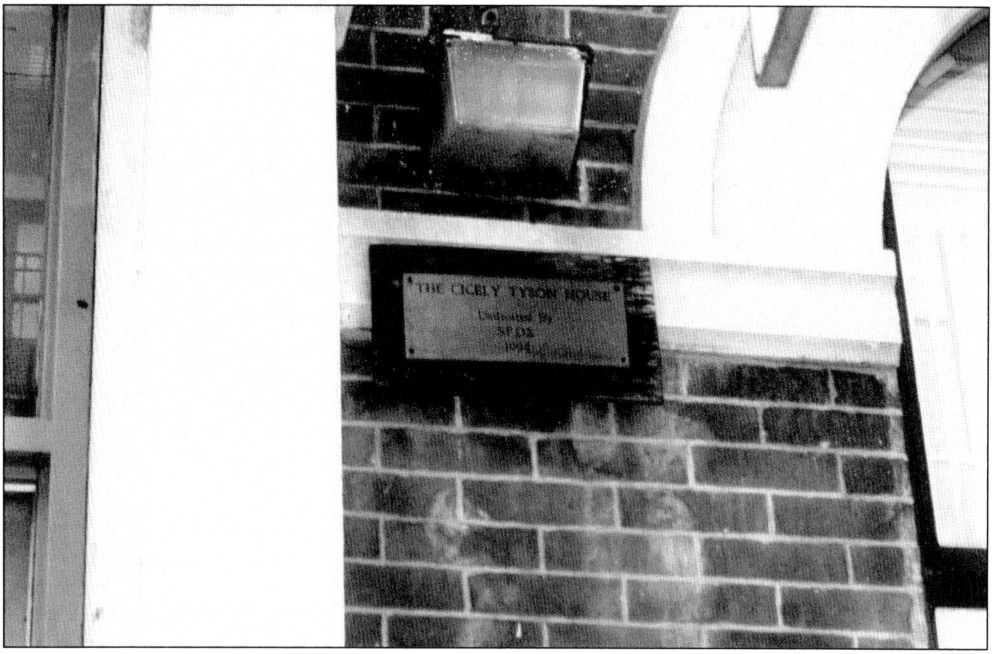


Pictured here is the plaque at the Cicely Tyson House. (Author's collection.)

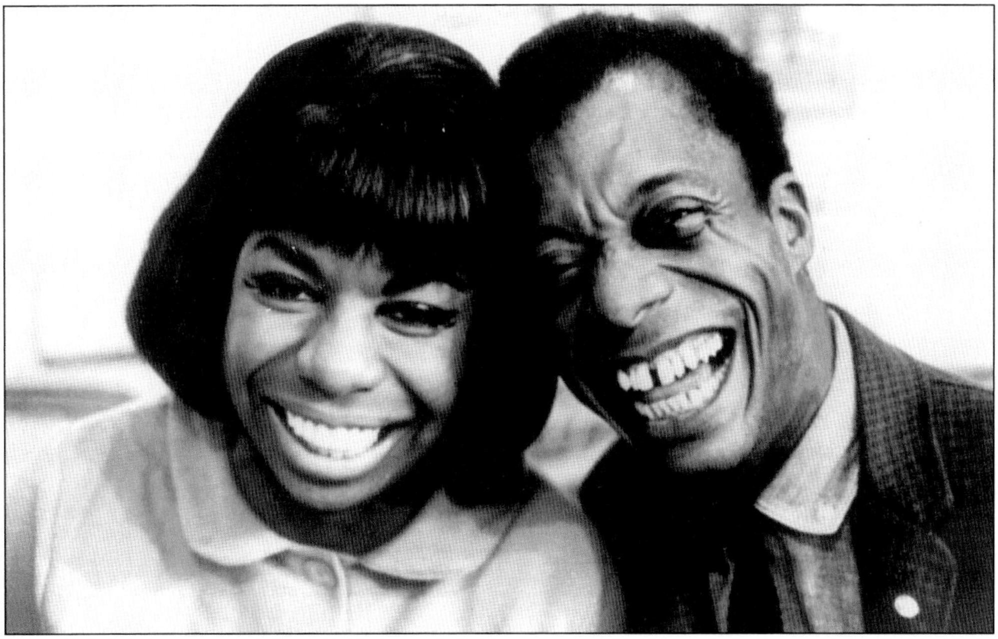

James Baldwin is pictured here with Nina Simone in the 1960s. Both artists would leave the United States for France. Baldwin grew up on 132nd and 133rd Streets and Park Avenue and attended Public School 24, located on 128th Street and Madison Avenue. His semiautobiographical novel *Go Tell It on the Mountain*, published in 1953, established Baldwin as a major American writer. Baldwin's works include *Another Country* and the *Fire Next Time*. Later, Baldwin became a leading spokesman for the civil rights movement. (Courtesy the Schomburg Center for Research in Black Culture, the New York Public Library.)

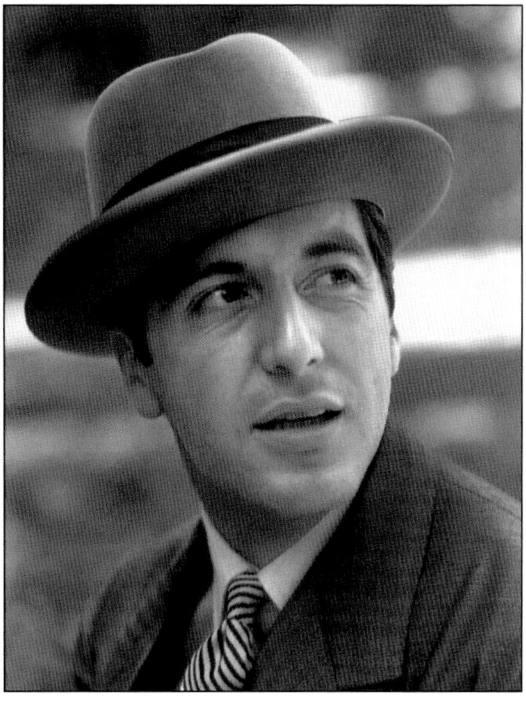

Although he grew up in the South Bronx, Al Pacino was born in East Harlem. Pacino has the distinction of being nominated for the Academy Award four years in a row for his roles in *The Godfather*, *Serpico*, *The Godfather: Part II*, and *Dog Day Afternoon*. He later won the Academy Award for best actor for *Scent of a Woman*. (Courtesy Corbis.)

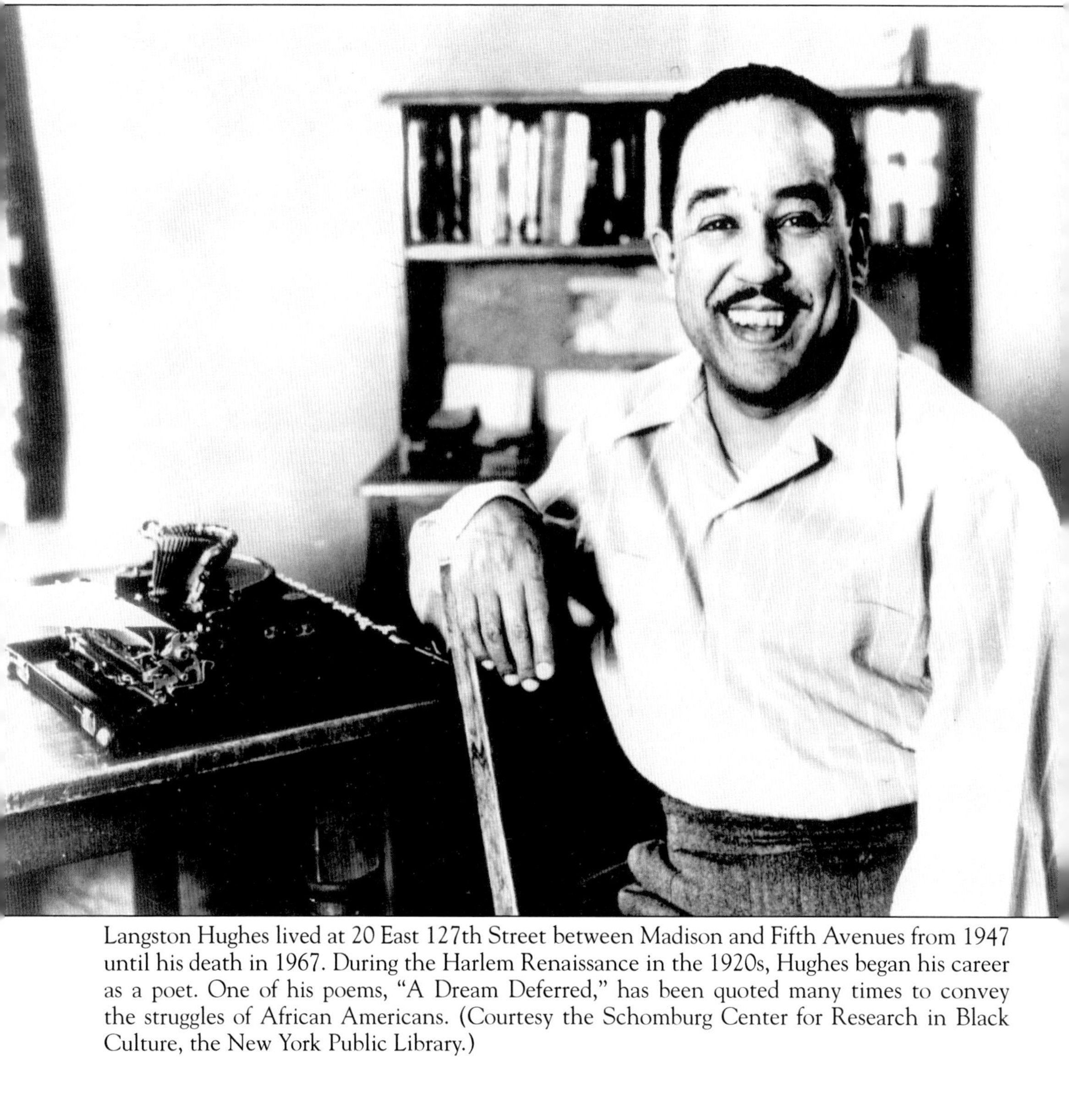

Langston Hughes lived at 20 East 127th Street between Madison and Fifth Avenues from 1947 until his death in 1967. During the Harlem Renaissance in the 1920s, Hughes began his career as a poet. One of his poems, "A Dream Deferred," has been quoted many times to convey the struggles of African Americans. (Courtesy the Schomburg Center for Research in Black Culture, the New York Public Library.)

This brownstone, where Hughes lived, was built in 1869 at 20 East 127th Street between Fifth and Madison Avenues. (Author's collection.)

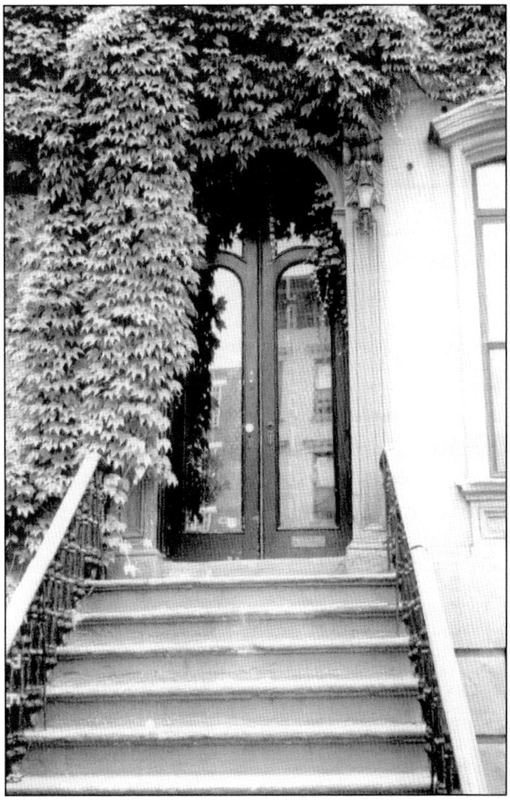

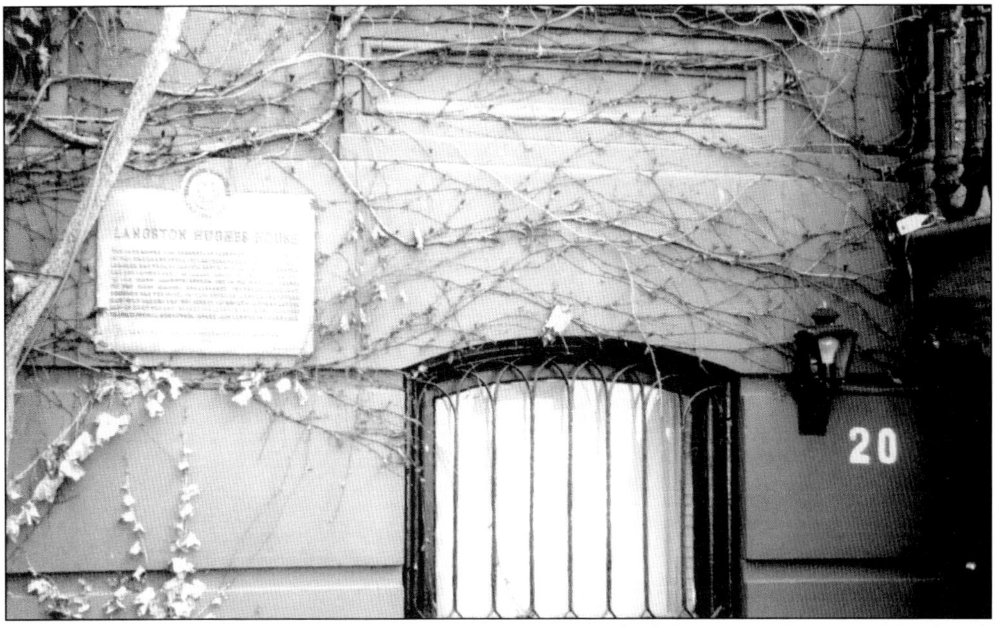


The plaque commemorates the Langston Hughes House, which became a designated landmark by the New York City Landmarks Preservation Committee in 1989. (Author's collection.)

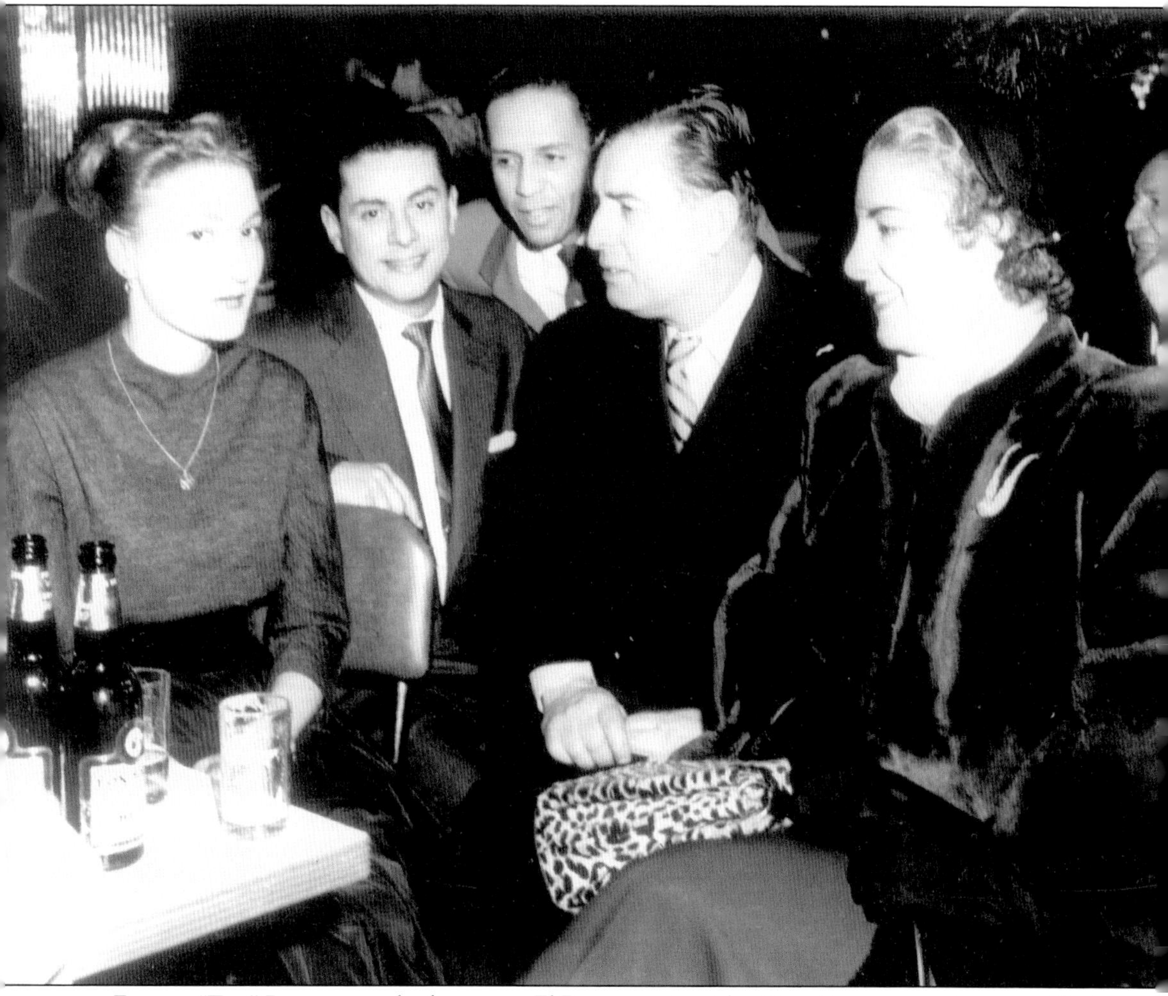

Ernesto "Tito" Puente was also known as El Rey, meaning "the King." Puente was born on 110th Street and Madison Avenue. After serving a stint in the navy in World War II, Puente attended the Julliard School to study music. Puente made over 100 albums in his career. "Oye Como Va," recorded by Puente in 1962, became a rock classic when Carlos Santana remade the song 10 years later. Here, Puente is pictured with friends at the Palladium in the 1950s. (Courtesy the Center for Puerto Rican Studies, Hunter College, City University of New York.)

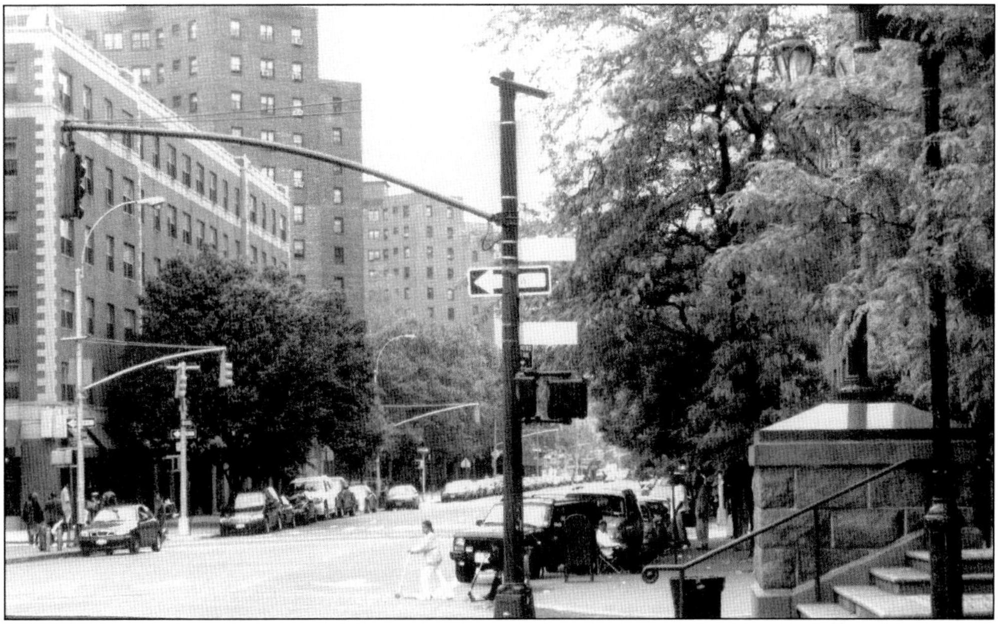

Tito Puente Way is located at 110th Street from Fifth to First Avenues. It was named in honor of El Rey, in 2001, after Puente's death the previous year. (Author's collection.)

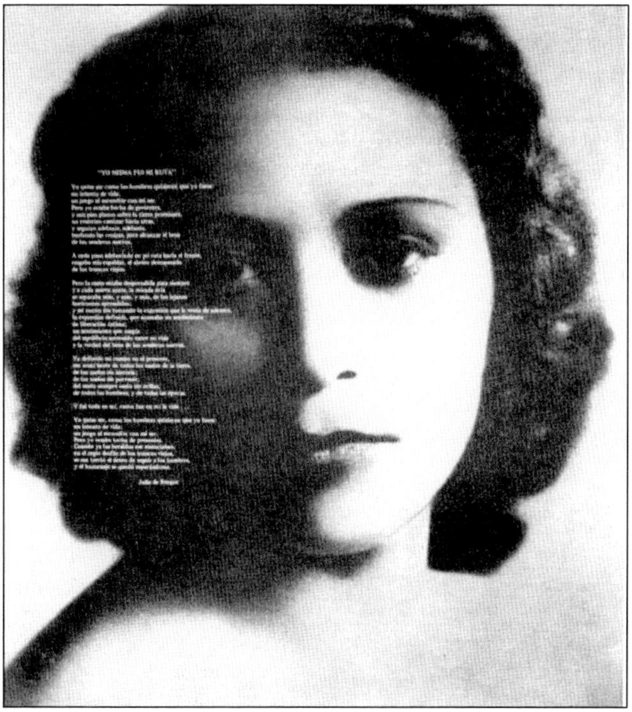

Julia de Burgos, a journalist, poet, and teacher, resided in East Harlem until her untimely death on 105th Street in 1953. Her poems include "El Mar y Tu" (The Sea and You). (Courtesy Fernando Sallicrup, director of the Julia de Burgos Cultural Center.)

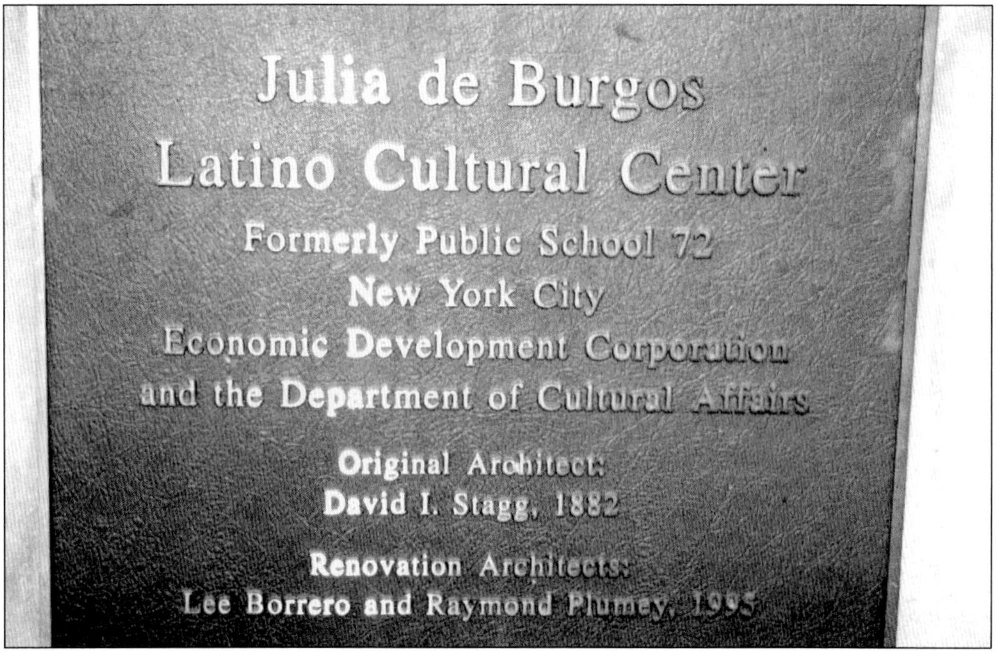

Seen here is the plaque of the Julia de Burgos Cultural Center, formerly Public School 72, located on Lexington Avenue and 106th Street. (Author's collection.)

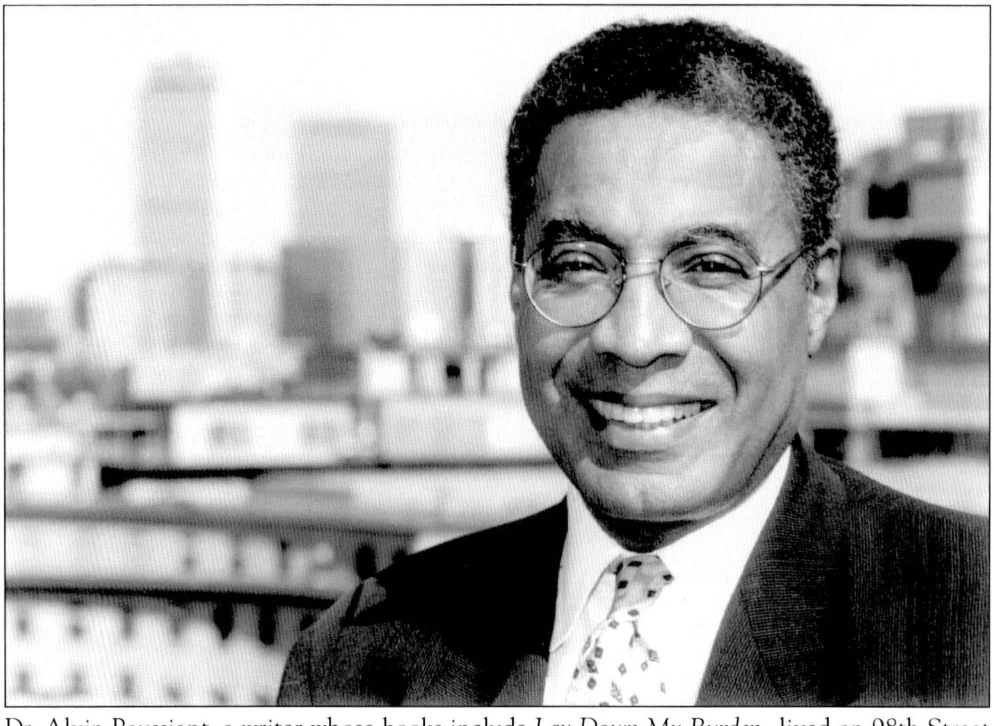
Dr. Alvin Poussiant, a writer whose books include *Lay Down My Burden*, lived on 98th Street and 102nd Street. Poussiant earned his bachelor of arts degree from Columbia University and then earned his medical degree from Cornell University. In the 1980s and early 1990s, he was an advisor for the successful Bill Cosby television show. (Photograph by Liza Green.)

This is a 1976 photograph of Michael Peter Pascale. A lifelong resident of East Harlem, Pascale served the community as a social worker and civic leader. Pascale often gave tours of the East Harlem neighborhood and ran Haarlem House, later renamed the La Guardia Memorial House. The portrait in the background shows Edward Corsi, who immigrated to New York from Italy in 1907. Corsi served under Pres. Herbert Hoover and Pres. Dwight D. Eisenhower. He was also director of Haarlem House. (Photograph by Herb Wiley; courtesy the Pascale-Evans Photograph Archives.)

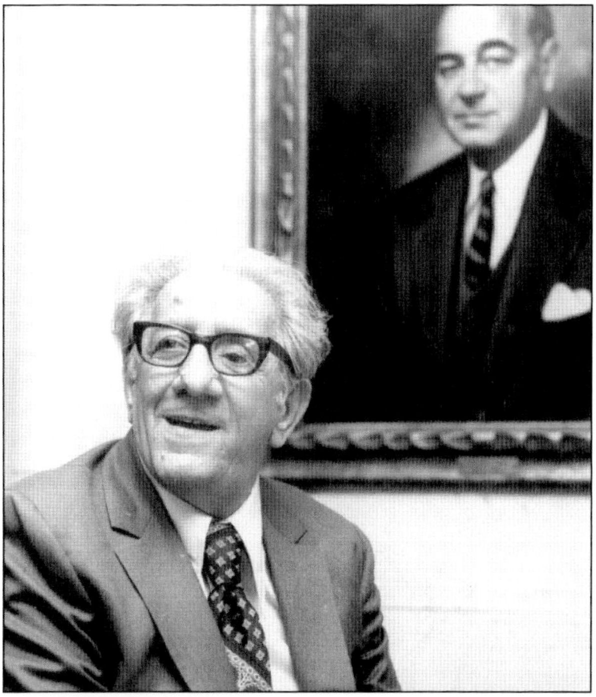

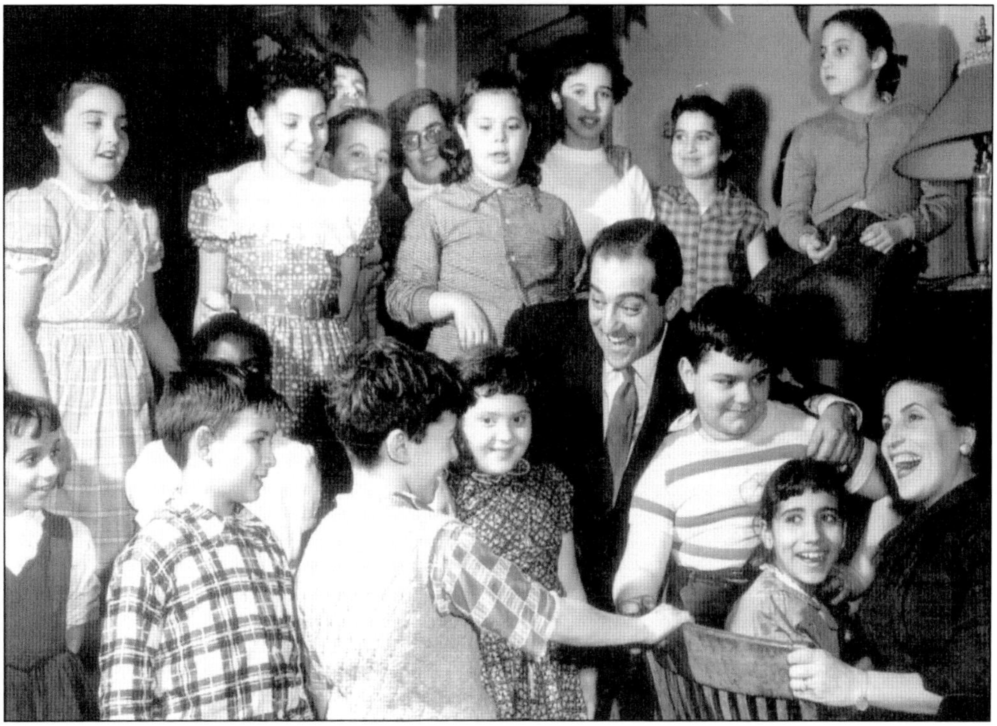

Opera singers Robert Merrill and Licia Albanese of the Metropolitan Opera are seen with the children of Haarlem House in 1952. In the bottom left is Lois Pascale Evans (the daughter of Rose and Pete Pascale), who still lives in East Harlem. (Courtesy the Pascale-Evans Photograph Archives.)

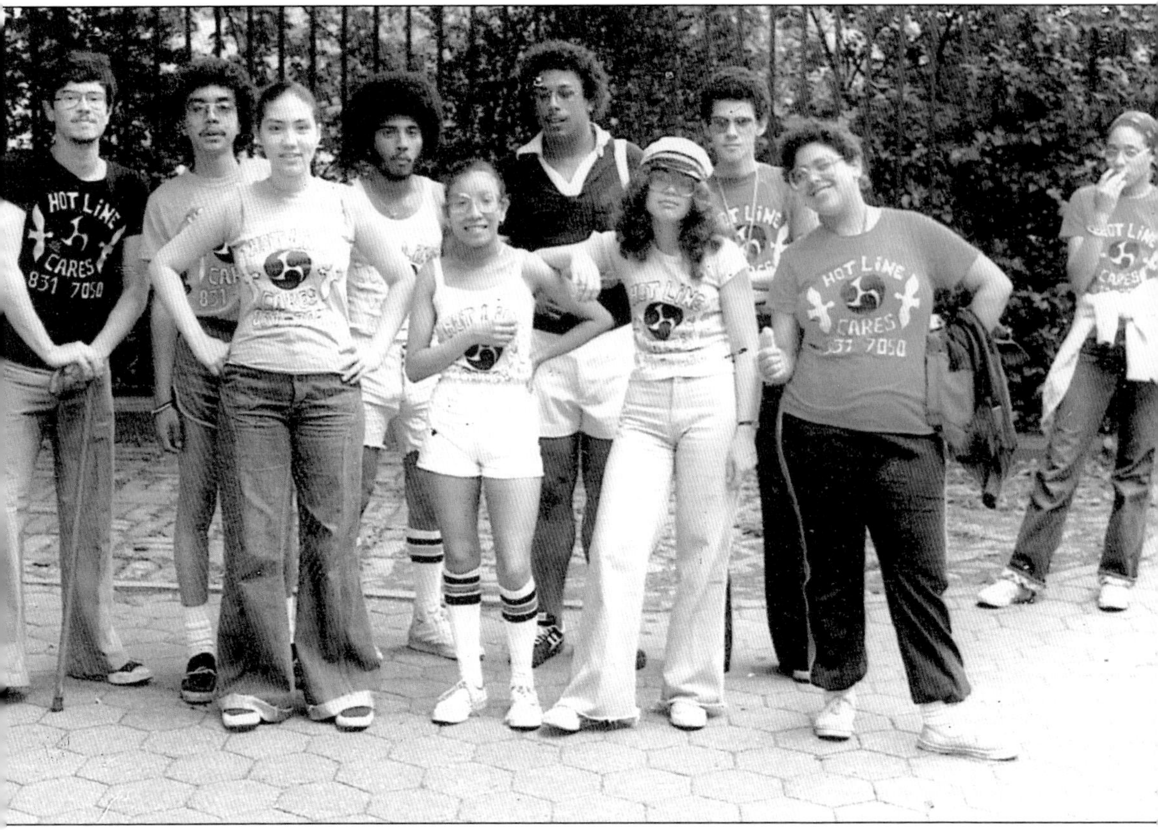


Raphael Antonio Flores (center) is surrounded by Hotline Cares volunteers at 110th Street inside Central Park in 1979. From left to right are Miguel ?, Emilio Bernard, Ileana Rodriguez, Freddy Carballo, Iris Carballo, Marlene Perez, Edwin "Spoony" Carballo, unidentified, and Rita Campos. For over 25 years, Raphael Flores ran Hotline Cares, the first and only youth crisis center in East Harlem. Through his efforts, many adolescents and adults in East Harlem and throughout New York City found a friend who was willing to help when society turned a deaf ear. The cases ranged from AIDS patients to the homeless to people with drug addictions. (Photograph by Raymond Carballo; courtesy Monique Flores.)

Harlem's courthouse, located on 121st Street between Lexington and Third Avenues, was built in 1892. Today, the courthouse serves the East Harlem neighborhood as the Harlem Community Justice Center. (Author's collection.)

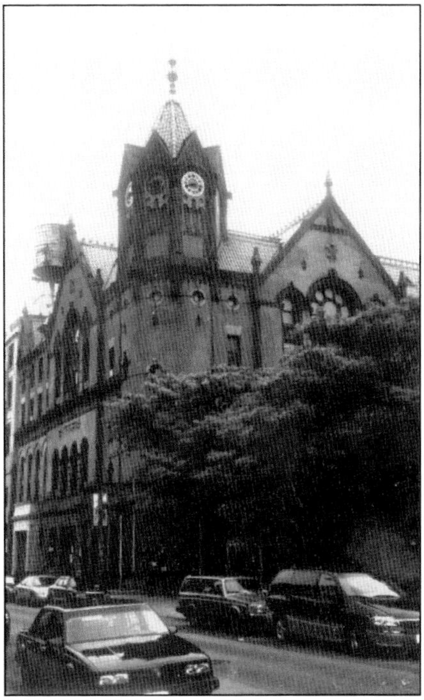

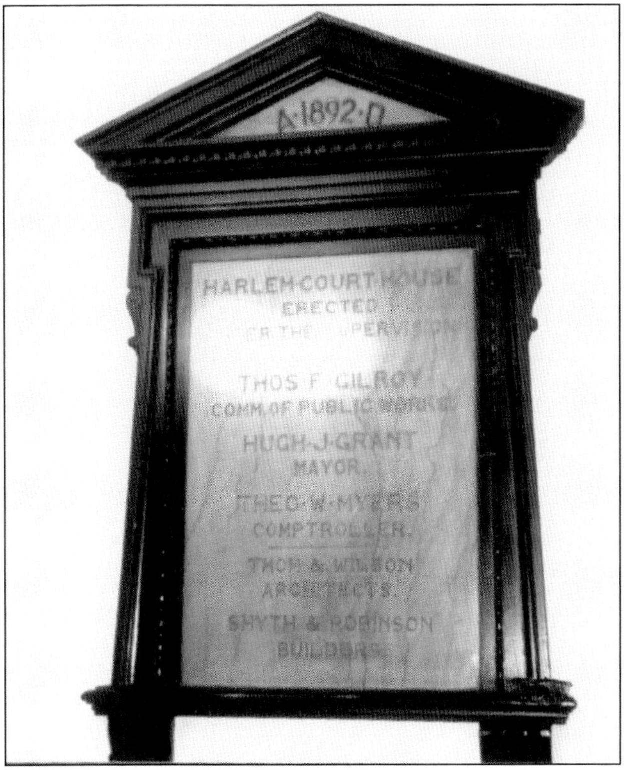


This plaque commemorates the erection of the courthouse in 1892. (Author's collection.)

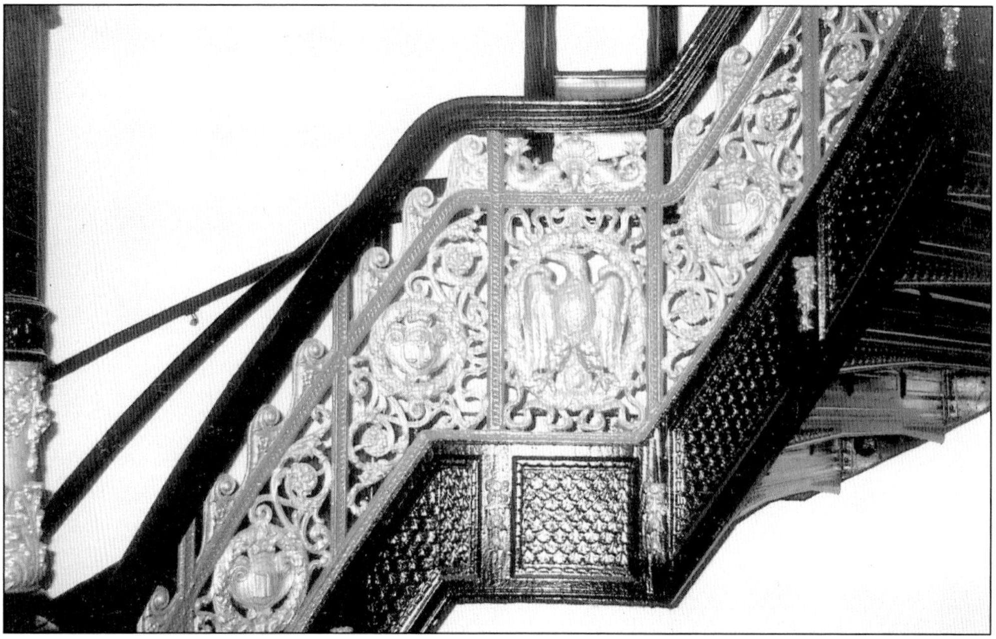

This refurbished banister, with the eagle in the center, denotes the Romanesque style of the courthouse. (Author's collection.)

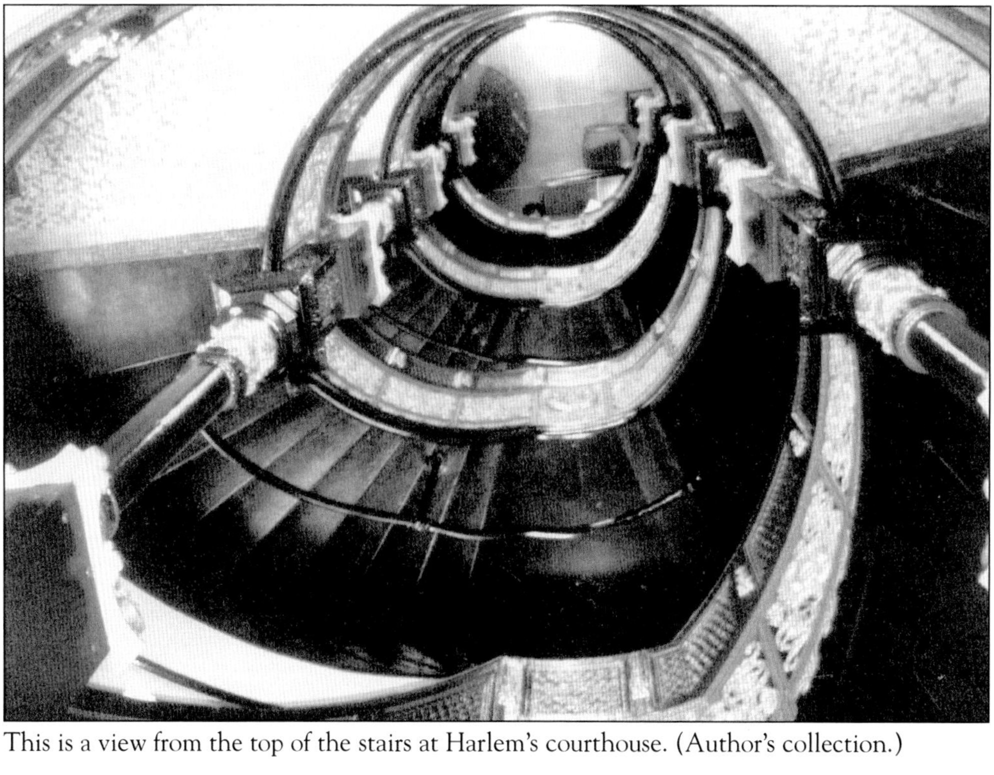

This is a view from the top of the stairs at Harlem's courthouse. (Author's collection.)

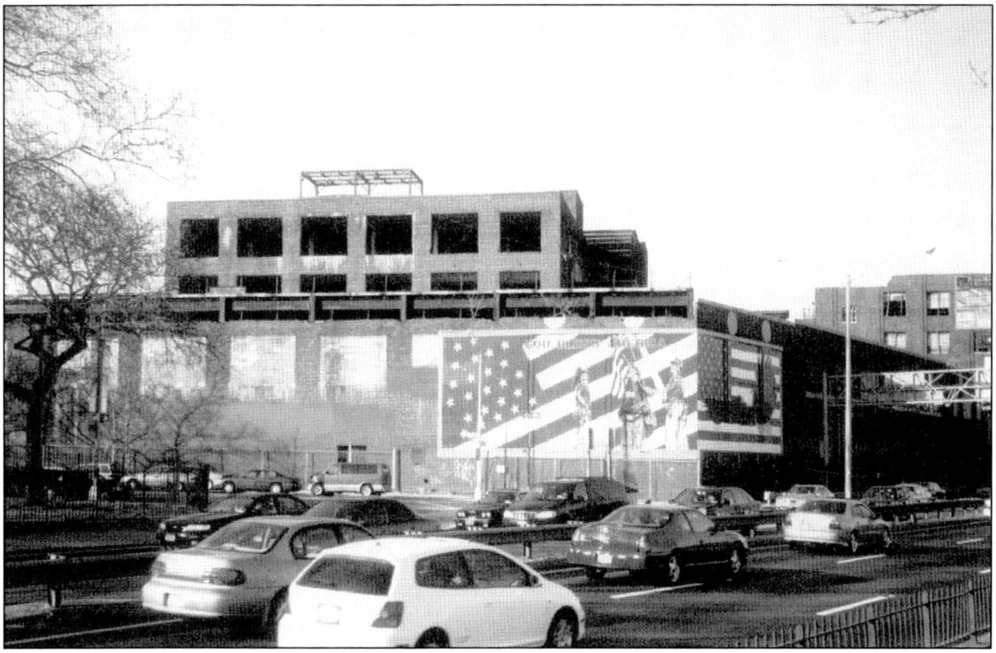

The former warehouse of the Washburn Wire factory, once located between 116th and 119th Streets along the East River. It closed in 1976 and was demolished in 2003. In the heyday of the factory, some 1,200 people were employed there. Clothes hangers and springs used to make pianos, phonographs, clocks, and motors were just some of the items produced at the wire factory. (Author's collection.)

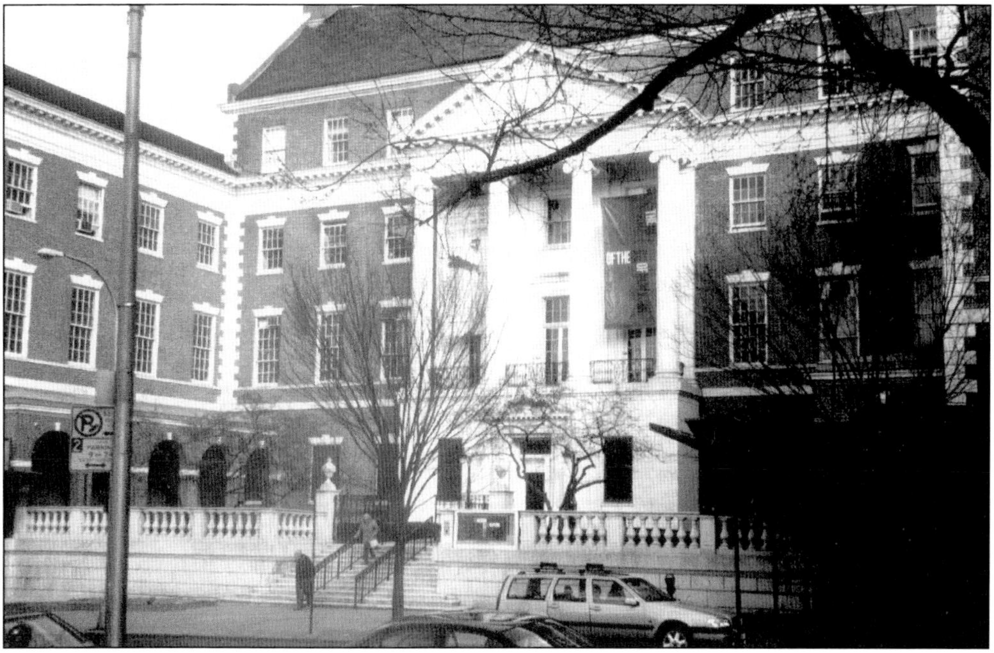

The Museum of the City of New York was built in 1934. It is located on 103rd to 104th Streets and Fifth Avenue. (Author's collection.)

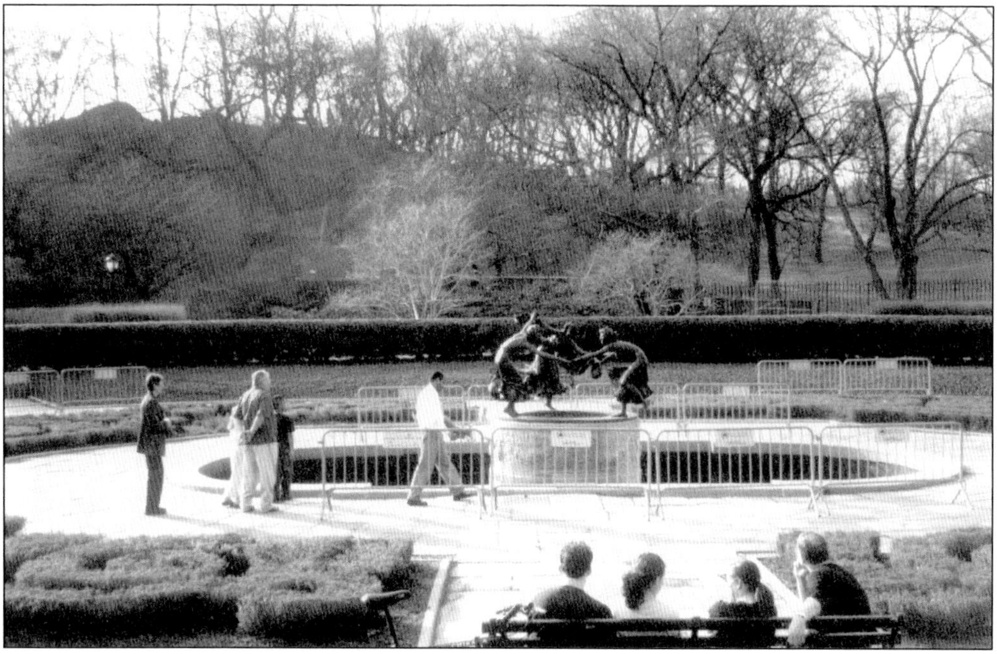

East Harlemites and other New Yorkers enjoy a warm spring day at the Conservatory Garden, located at 105th Street to 106th Streets and Fifth Avenue. (Author's collection.)

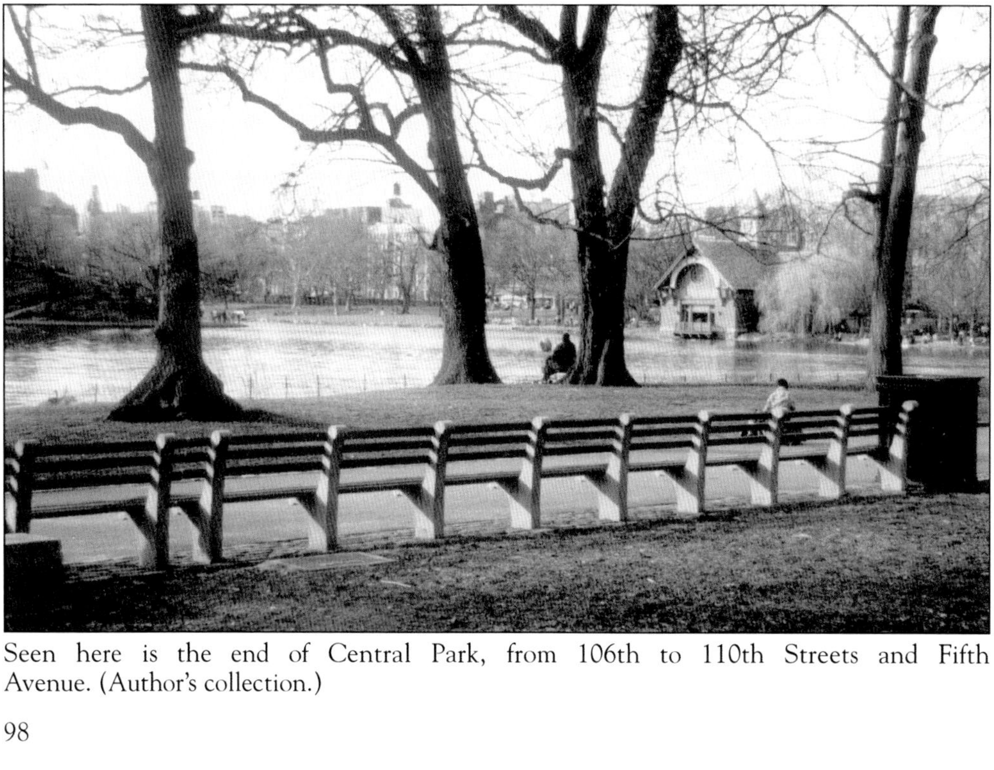

Seen here is the end of Central Park, from 106th to 110th Streets and Fifth Avenue. (Author's collection.)

*Seven*

# Parades, Ceremonies, and Then Some

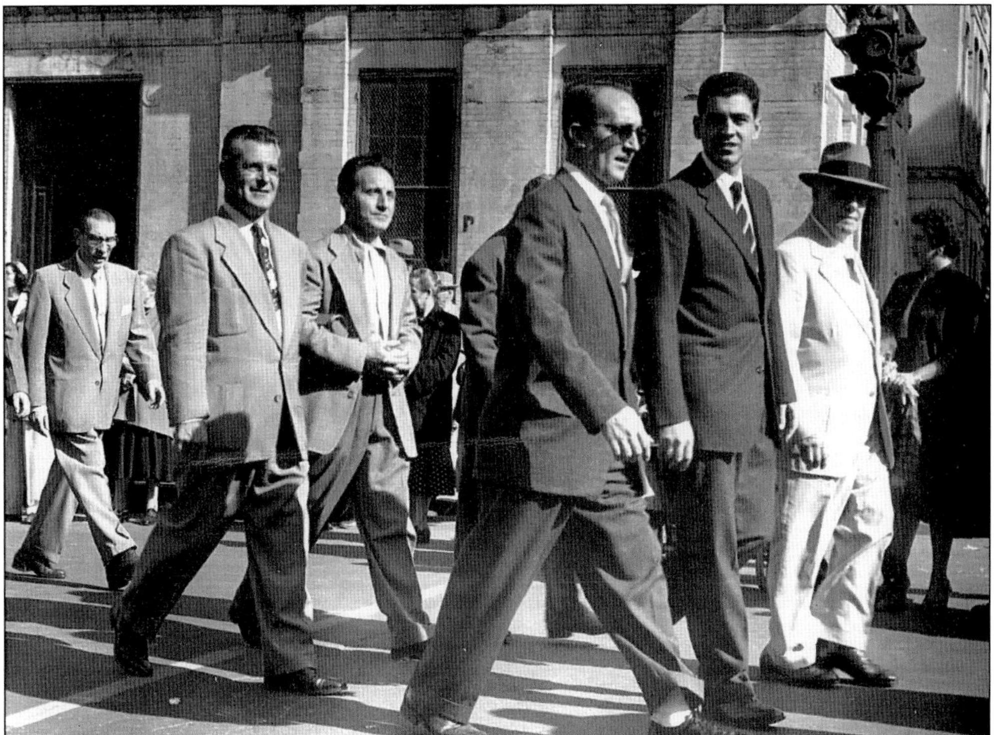

The 1952 Holy Rosary Church procession traveled along 115th Street between First and Pleasant Avenues. (Courtesy Fr. Alfred D'Incecco.)

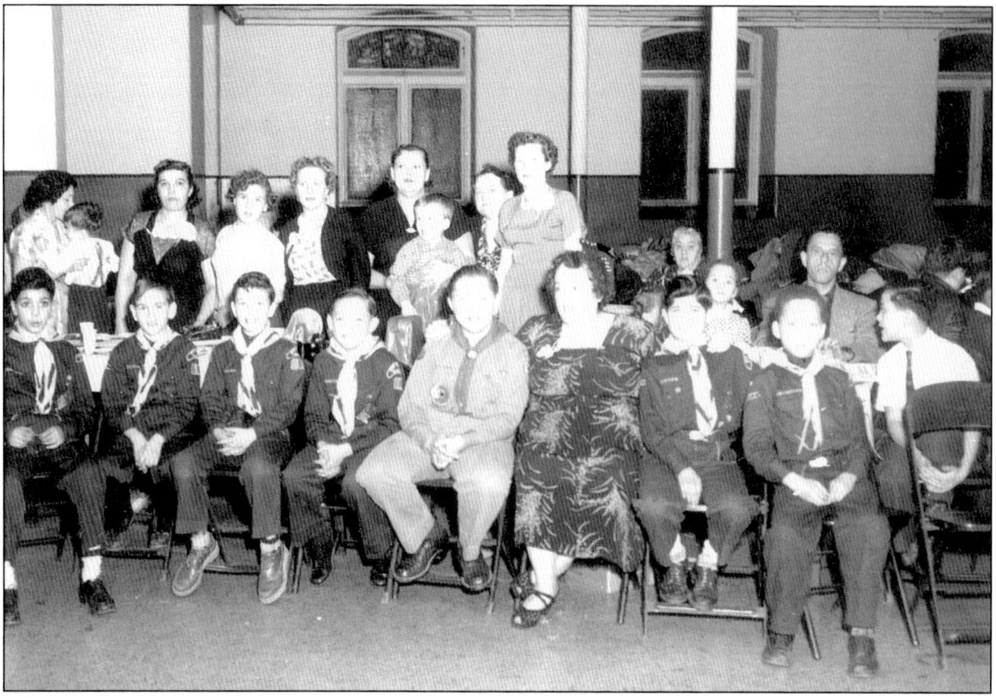

This 1952 photograph shows a Holy Rosary Church Cub Scout meeting. The year is 1952. (Courtesy Fr. Alfred D'Incecco.)

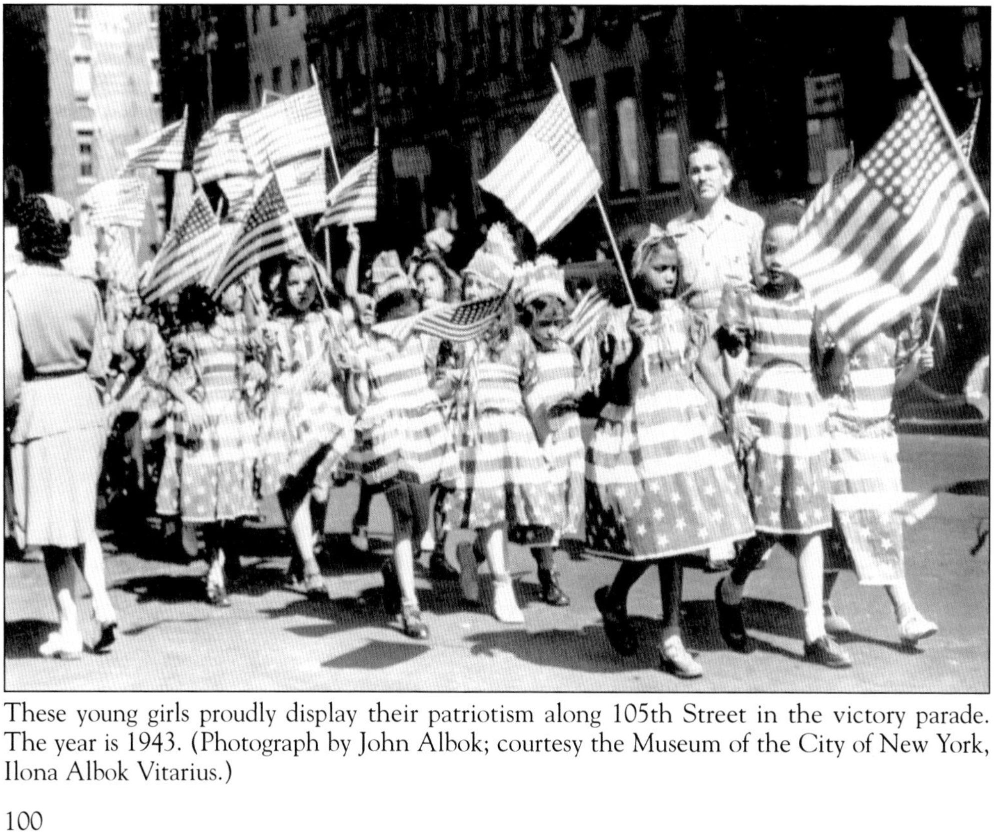

These young girls proudly display their patriotism along 105th Street in the victory parade. The year is 1943. (Photograph by John Albok; courtesy the Museum of the City of New York, Ilona Albok Vitarius.)

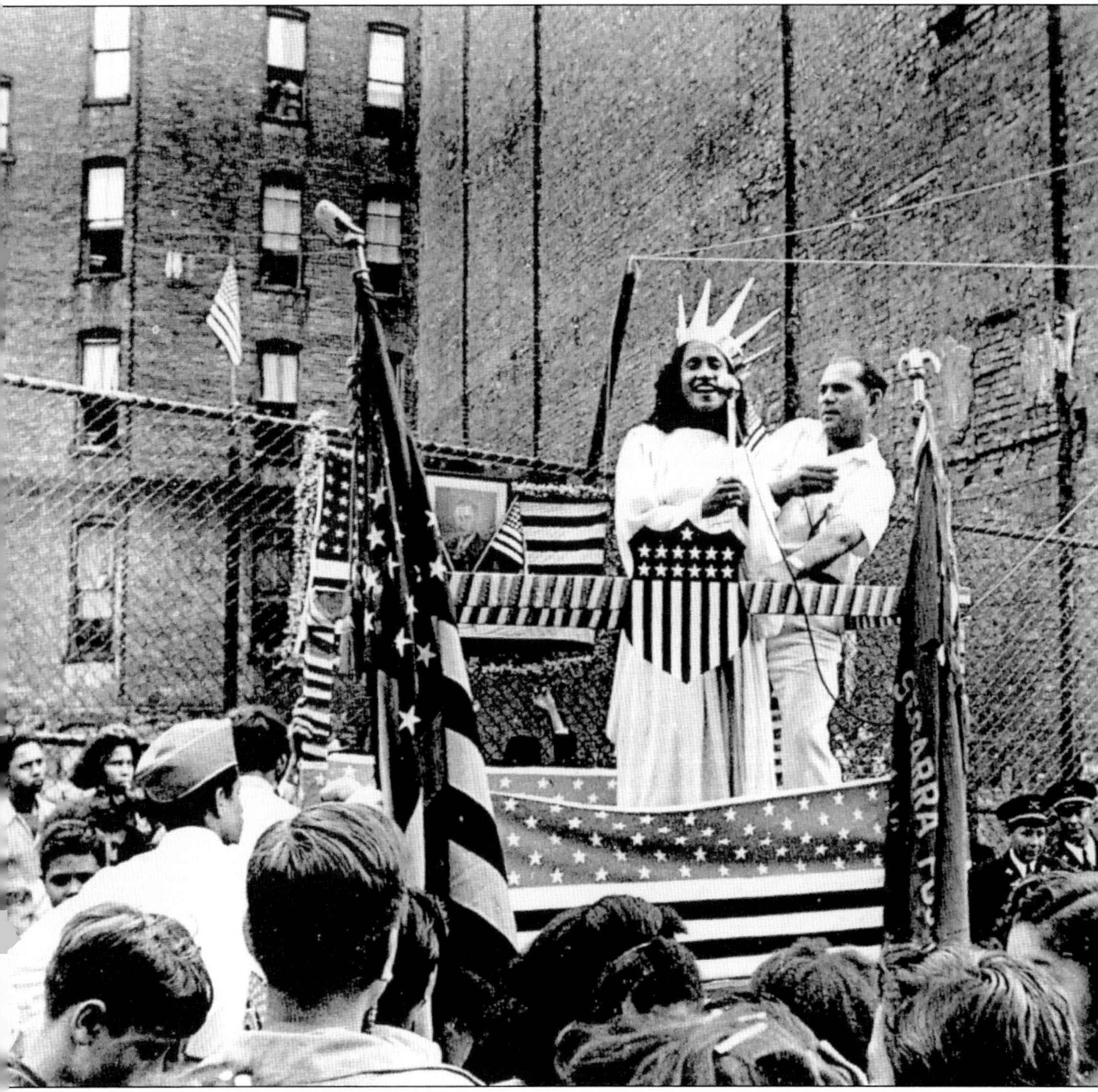

John Albok took this 1943 photograph of a young girl addressing East Harlemites on 105th Street during the World War II victory celebrations. (Courtesy the Museum of the City of New York, Ilona Albok Vitarius.)

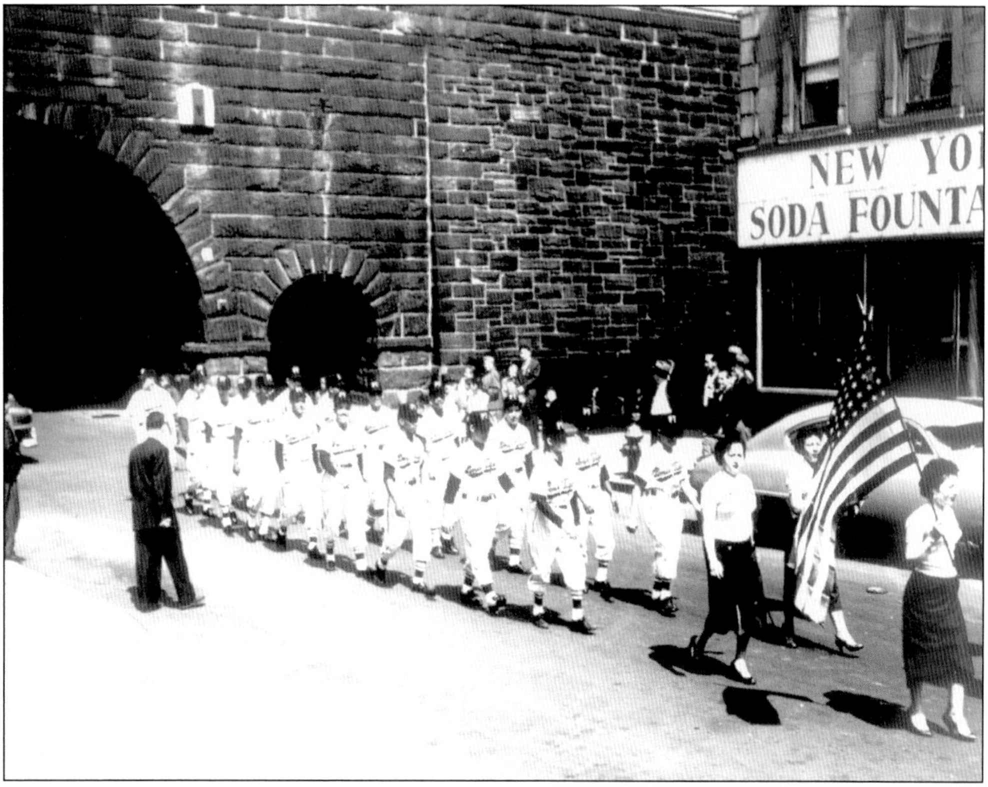


Here, 105th Street continues to be a rite of passage. This time, the participants are the Ponce Tigers baseball team. Ponce is a town in Puerto Rico. (Courtesy the Center for Puerto Rican Studies, Hunter College, City University of New York, Justo A. Marti collection.)

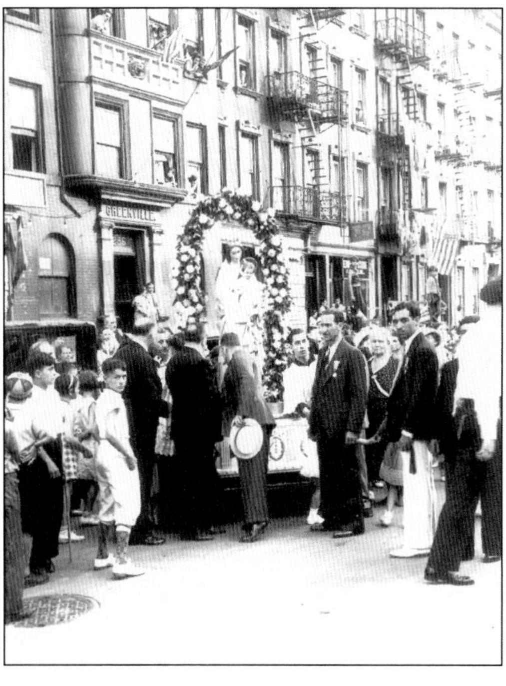

Italian Americans gather in front of the statue of Our Lady of Mount Carmel in 1936 during the annual feast in her honor. The festival takes place in front of Our Lady of Mount Carmel Church, on 115th Street between First and Second Avenues. (Courtesy the New York Public Library.)

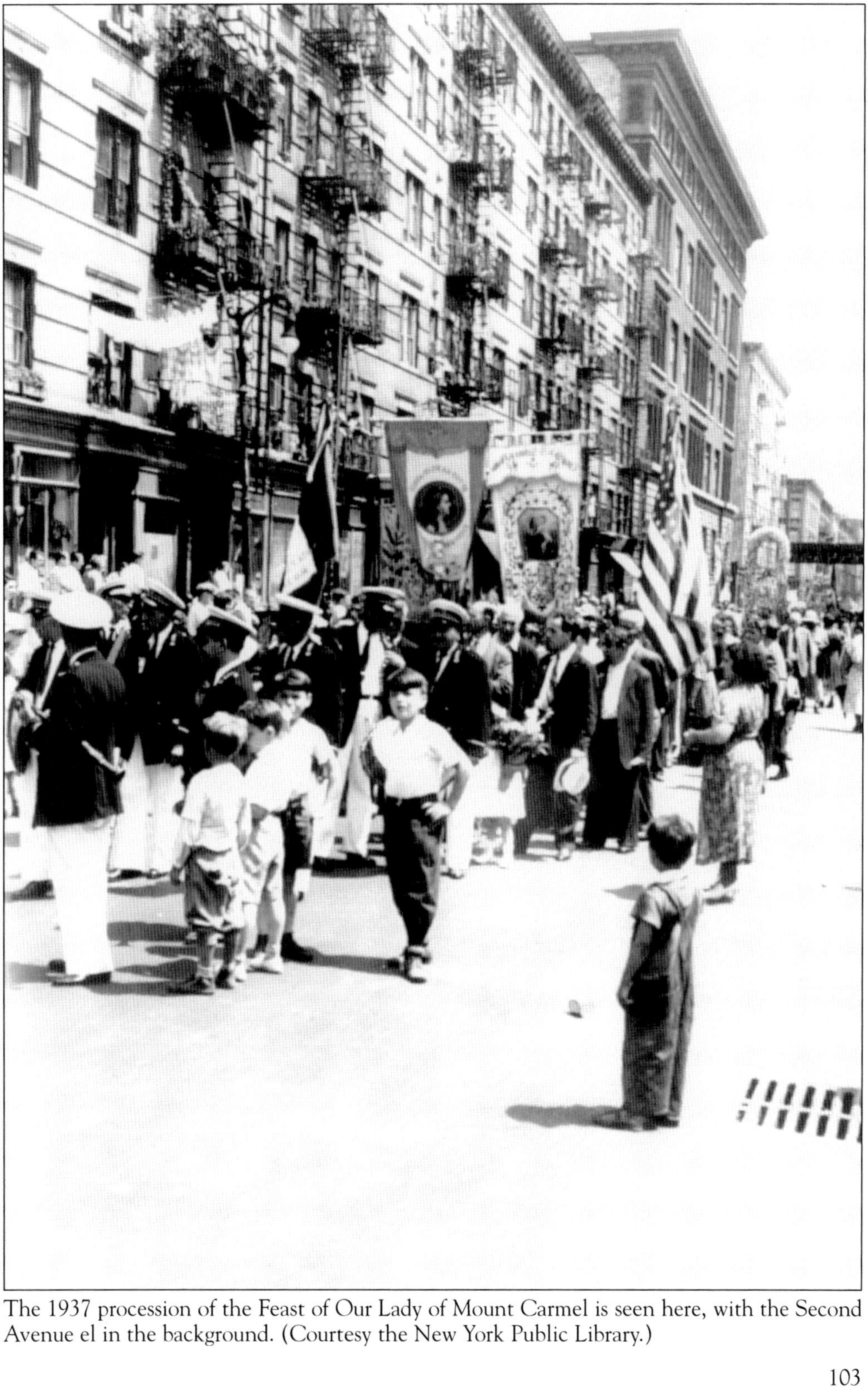

The 1937 procession of the Feast of Our Lady of Mount Carmel is seen here, with the Second Avenue el in the background. (Courtesy the New York Public Library.)

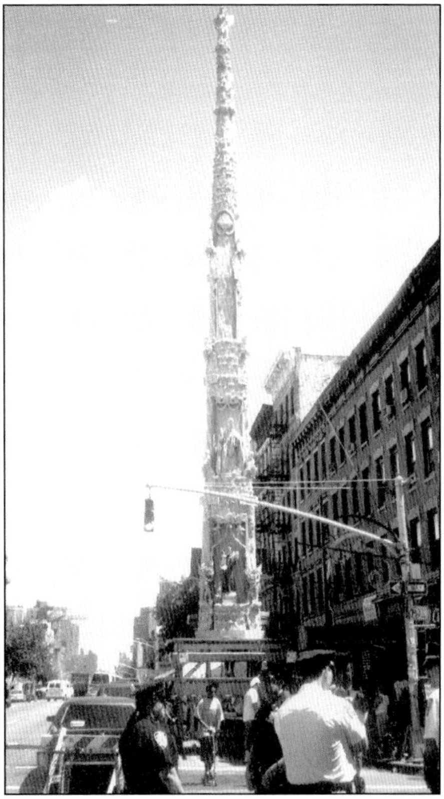

In 1986, the Feast of Our Lady of Mount Carmel, which had ceased for a number of years, returned to its roots with the help of Fr. Peter Rofrano and the Giglio Society of East Harlem. This photograph, taken a few days before the 1999 festivities began, shows police personnel guarding the 80-foot statue of the Virgin Mary, at 115th Street and First Avenue. (Courtesy Jerry and Eleanor Koffler.)

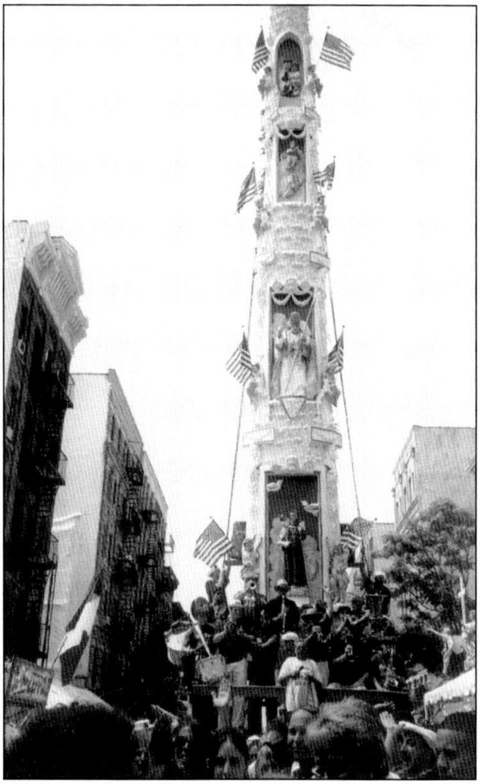

The statue of the Virgin Mary is shown being lifted by at least 100 men. Today, many nationalities celebrate the occasion, from Italian Americans to Latinos to Haitian Americans. This photograph was taken in 1999. (Courtesy Jerry and Eleanor Koffler.)

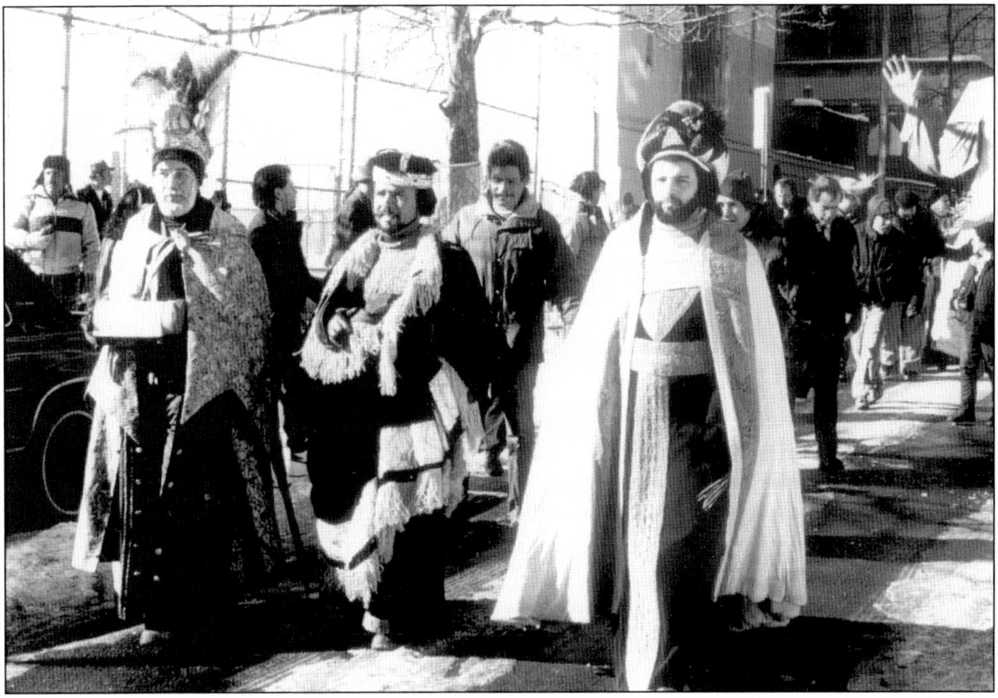

Los Tres Reyes De Magos (Three Kings Day) is an East Harlem tradition celebrated every January 6. It is sponsored by El Museo Del Barrio, located on 103rd Street and Fifth Avenue. In this 1987 photograph, the three kings are walking along 104th Street between Fifth and Madison Avenues. (Courtesy Jerry and Eleanor Koffler.)

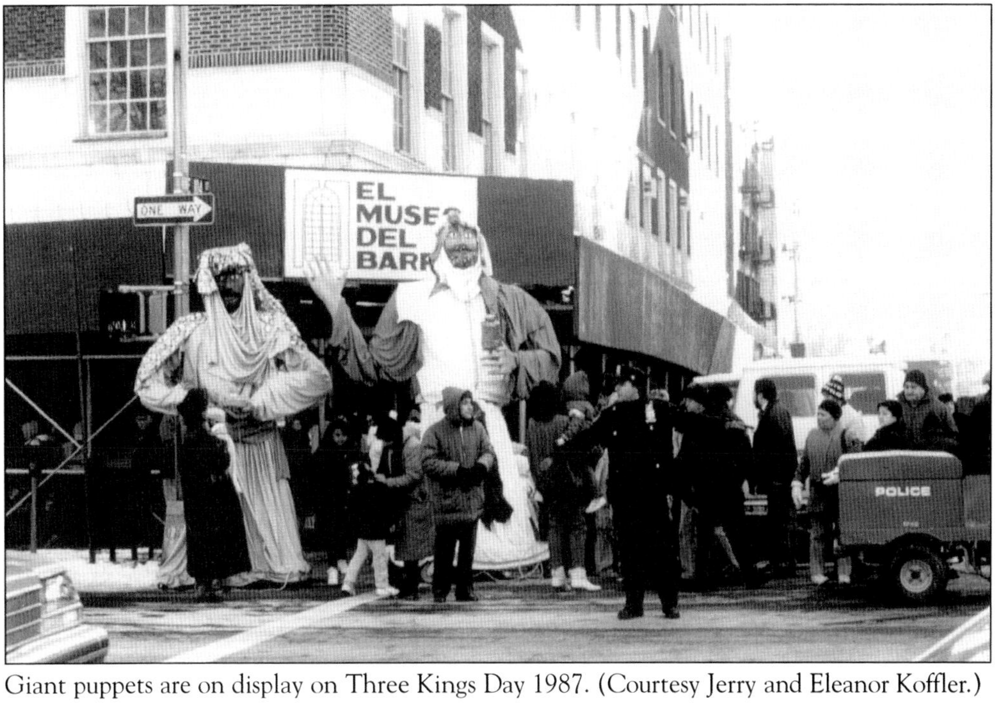


Giant puppets are on display on Three Kings Day 1987. (Courtesy Jerry and Eleanor Koffler.)

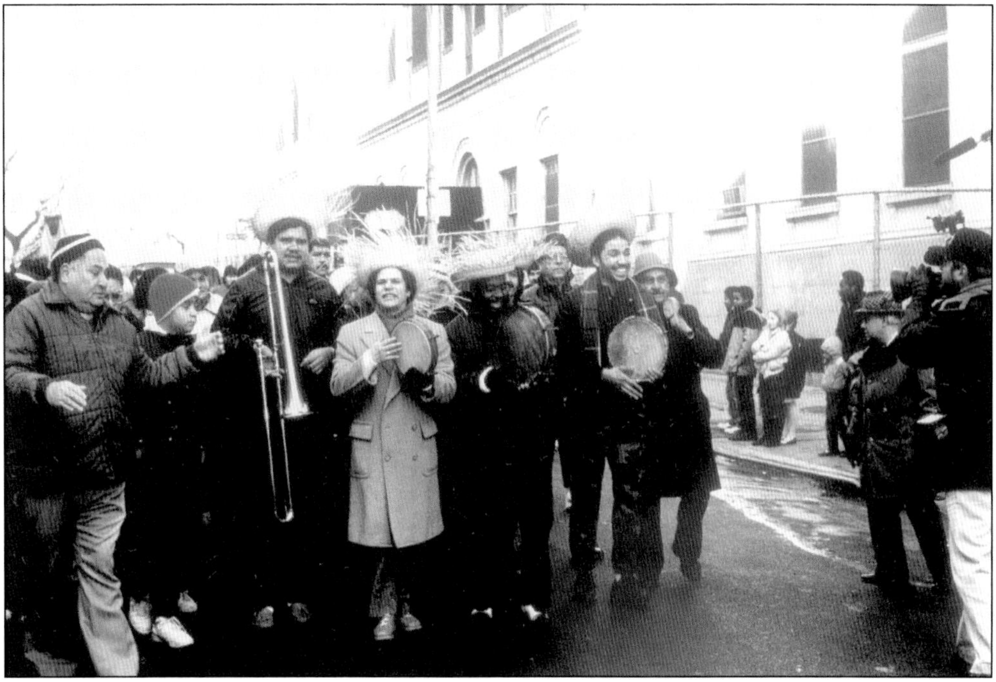

Musicians participate in the Three Kings Day procession in 1987. The hats are traditional headgear worn in Puerto Rico. The media, including local television stations, throughout New York City covers this annual event. (Courtesy Jerry and Eleanor Koffler.)

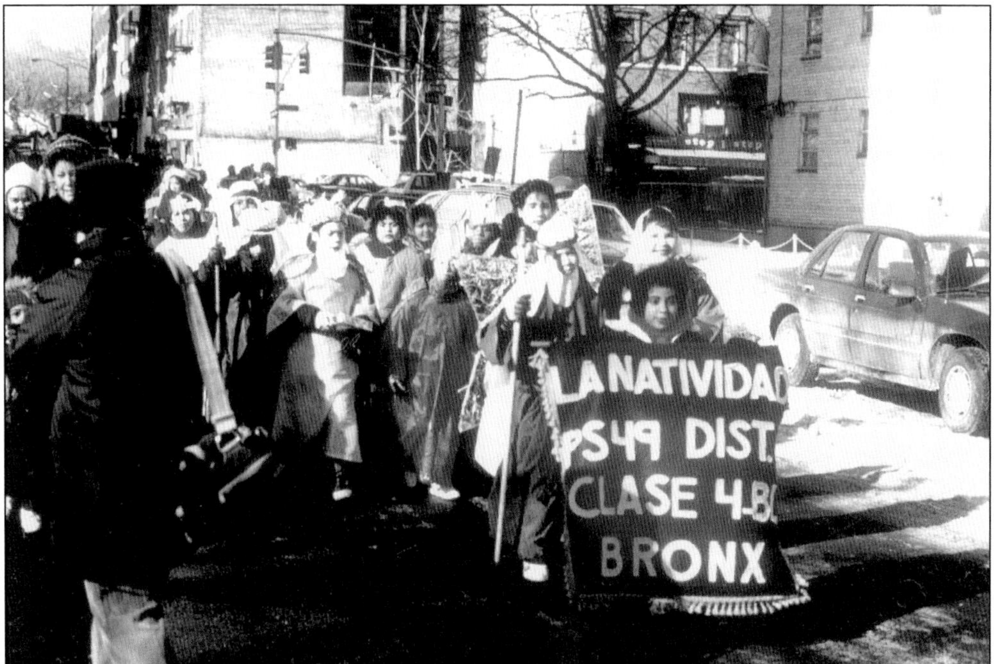


Future kings and monks march in the Three Kings Day march in 1987. Although the school nativity is from the Bronx, people throughout New York City participate in this annual event. (Courtesy Jerry and Eleanor Koffler.)

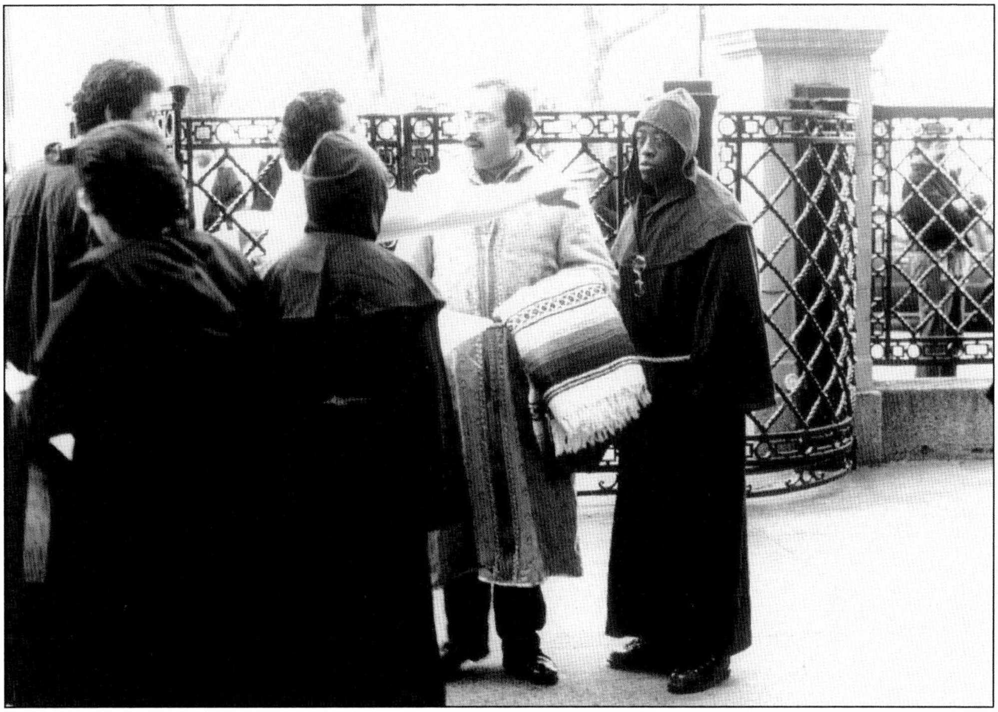

These monks are receiving their marching instructions at the start of Three Kings Day in 1987. (Courtesy Jerry and Eleanor Koffler.)

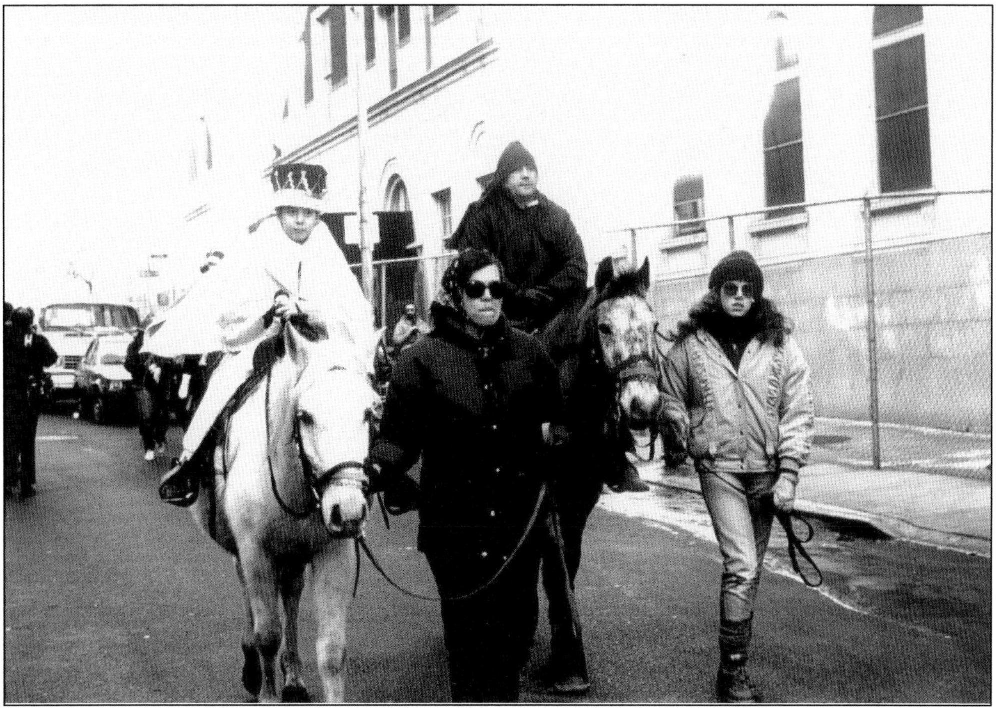

Young kings and monks are on horseback in the Three Kings Day march. (Courtesy Jerry and Koffler.)

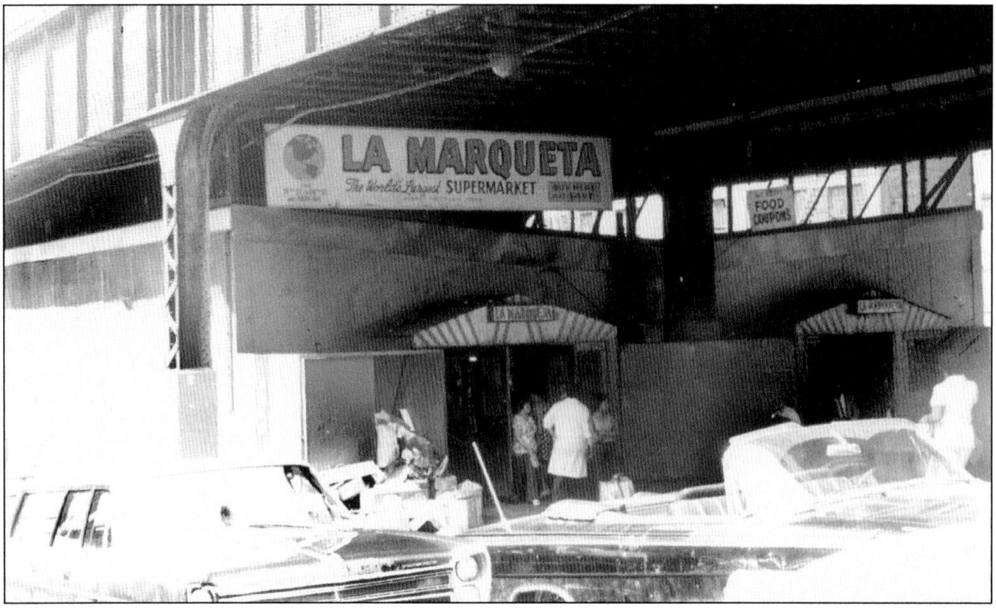


Seen in this 1973 photograph is the entrance to La Marqueta (the Market), located between 112th and 115th Street and Park Avenue under the Metro North, formerly the New York Central Railroad. Prior to this establishment, pushcart vendors would peddle their products on the streets of Park Avenue. Later, Mayor Fiorello La Guardia created this shopping center. Originally called Park Avenue, the center was renamed La Marqueta when East Harlem's clientele changed from Italians to predominantly Puerto Ricans and African Americans. (Courtesy Jerry and Eleanor Koffler.)

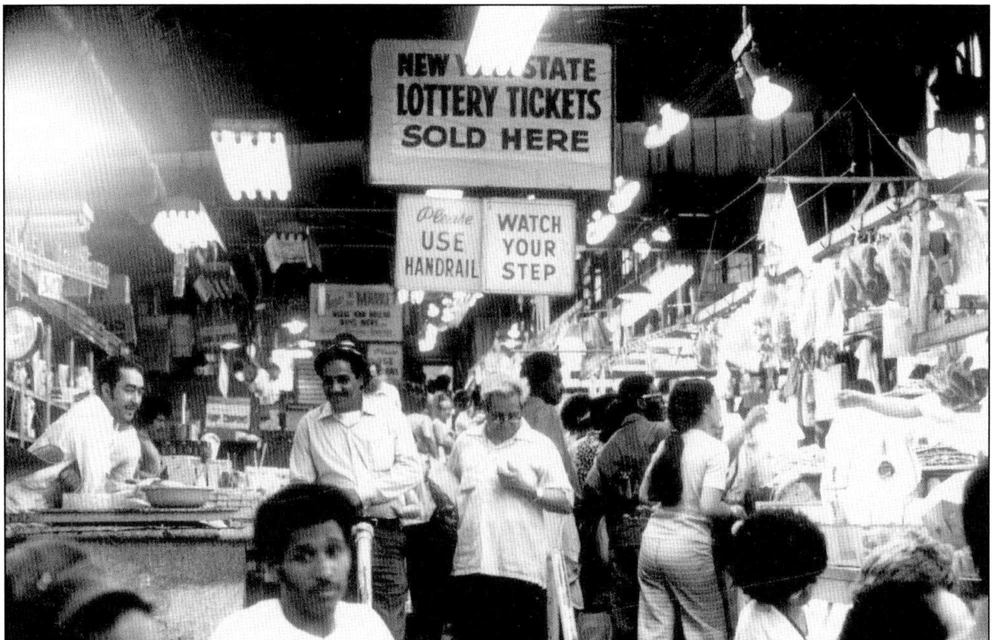


Inside La Marqueta, customers are at the meat market. The sign reads, "New York State lottery tickets sold here." This photograph was taken in 1973. (Courtesy Jerry and Eleanor Koffler.)

A butcher listens to his customers at La Marqueta in 1973. (Courtesy Jerry and Eleanor Koffler.)

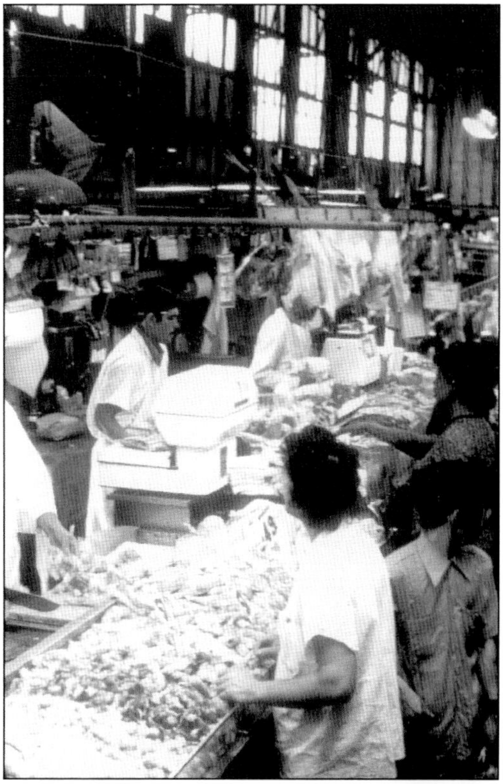

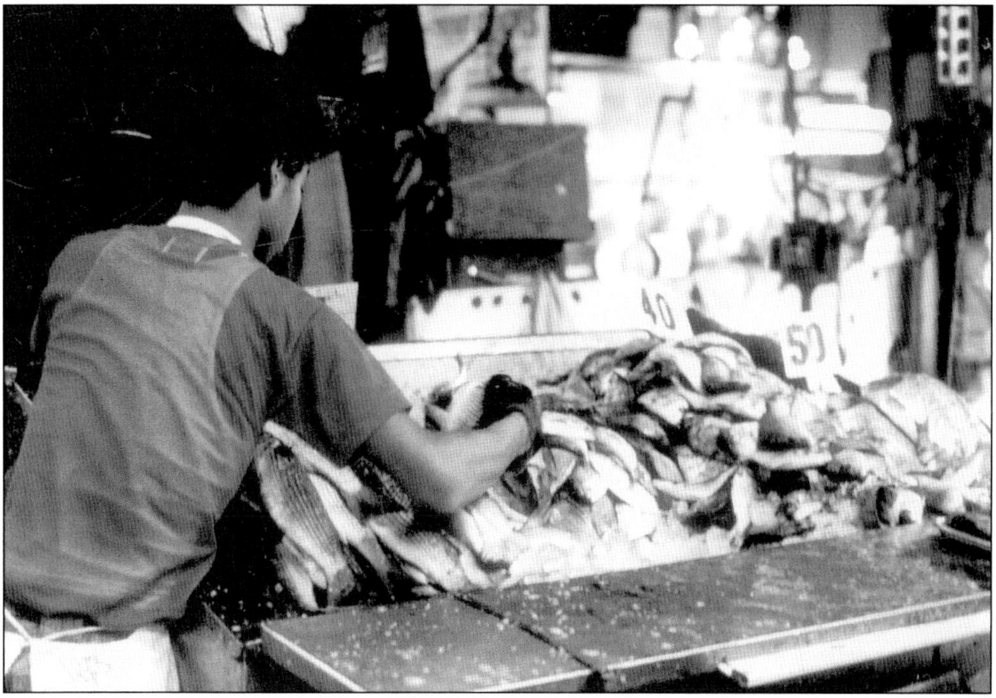


This vendor is gathering his fish, priced at 40¢ and 50¢ a pound, in this 1973 photograph. (Courtesy Jerry and Eleanor Koffler.)

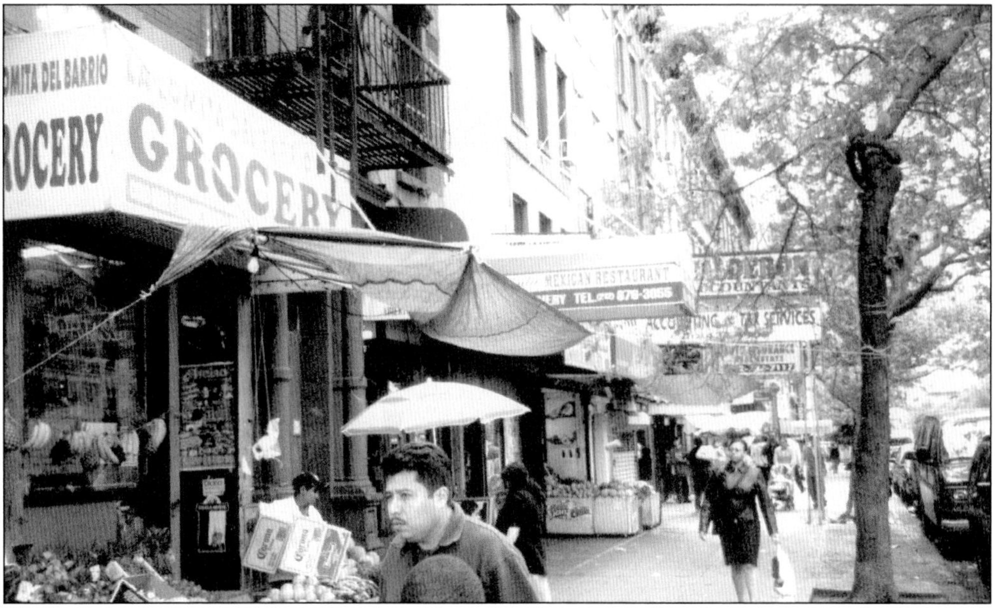


During the mid-1990s, many Mexican Americans settled in East Harlem and opened up stores and restaurants. Seen here is a worker placing his produce outside on 116th Street between Second and First Avenues. (Author's collection.)

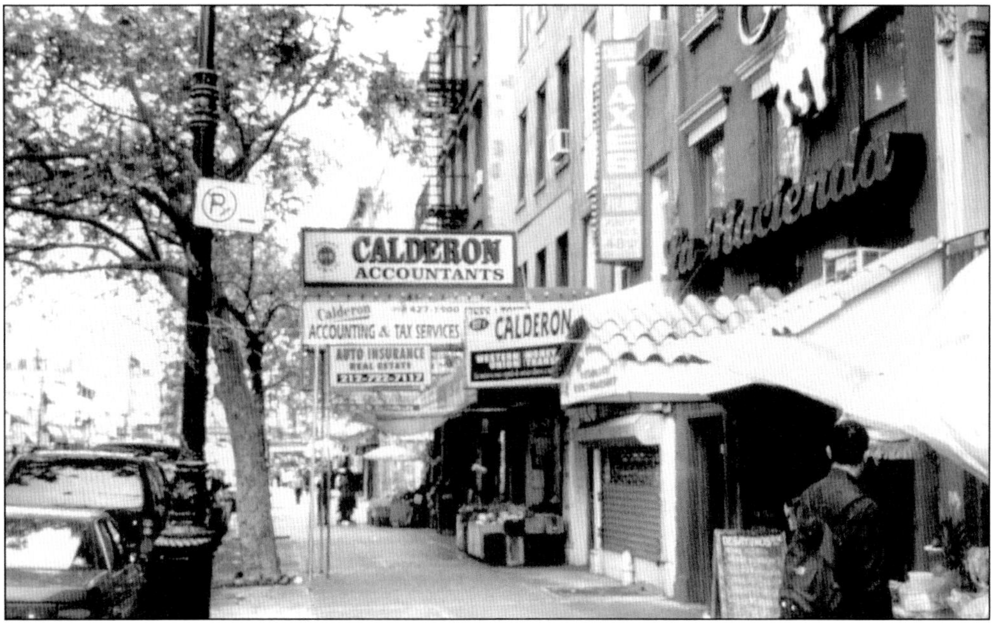


Farther down the block is La Hacienda, which serves breakfast daily. (Author's collection.)

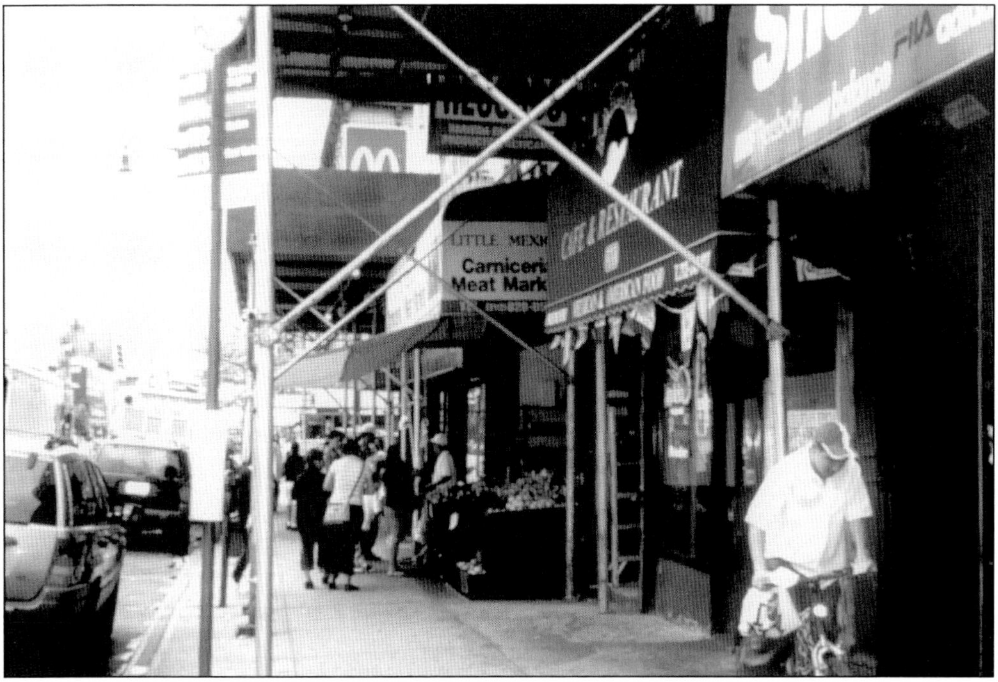

On 116th Street and Third Avenue, East Harlemites can eat at the Mexican restaurant or buy groceries at the Little Mexico Carnicieria, a meat market. This photograph was taken in 2003. (Author's collection.)

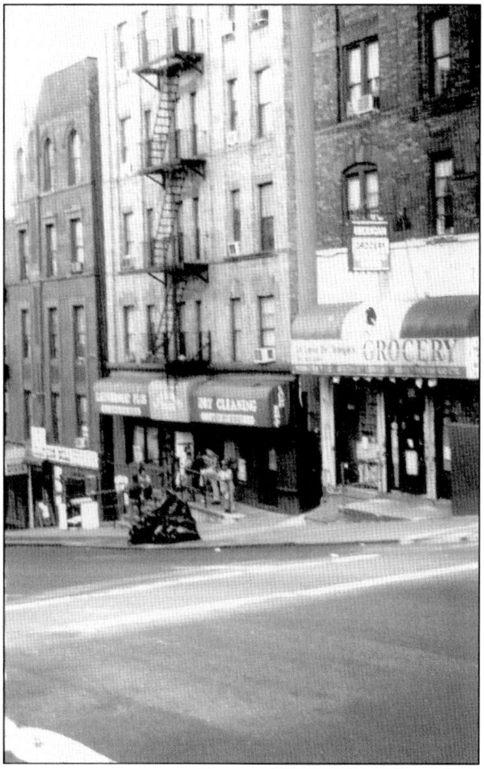


Seen in this recent photograph is another Mexican restaurant, located between 102nd and 103rd Streets and Lexington Avenue. (Author's collection.)

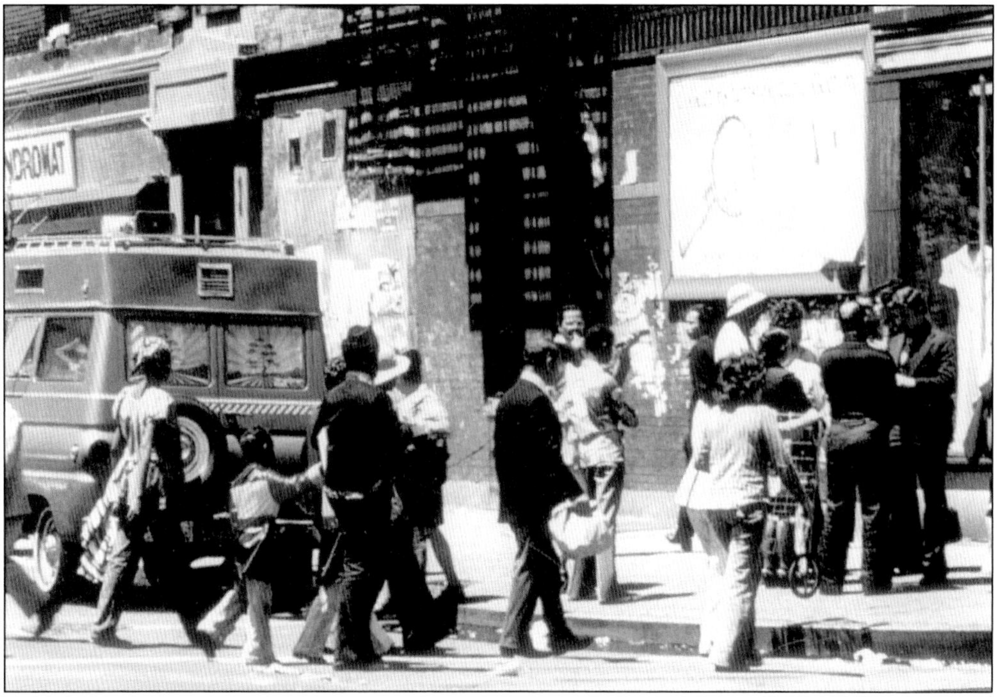

A street preacher speaks to hopeful converts on 105th Street and Third Avenue in 1973. (Courtesy Jerry and Eleanor Koffler.)

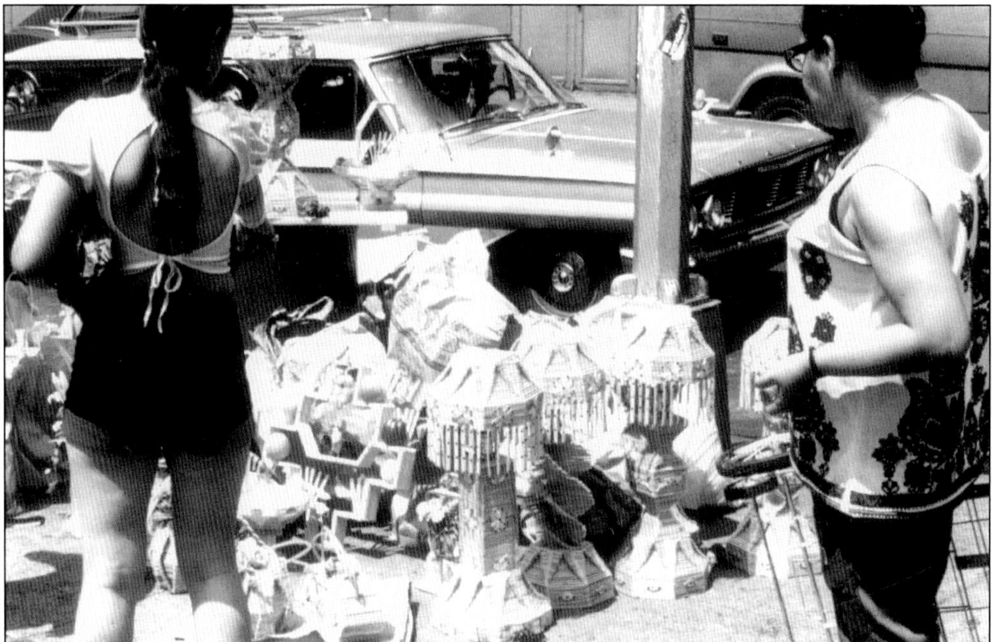

These ladies are looking at the elaborate lamps and other materials made out of matchsticks across the street from La Marqueta in this 1973 photograph. (Courtesy Jerry and Eleanor Koffler.)

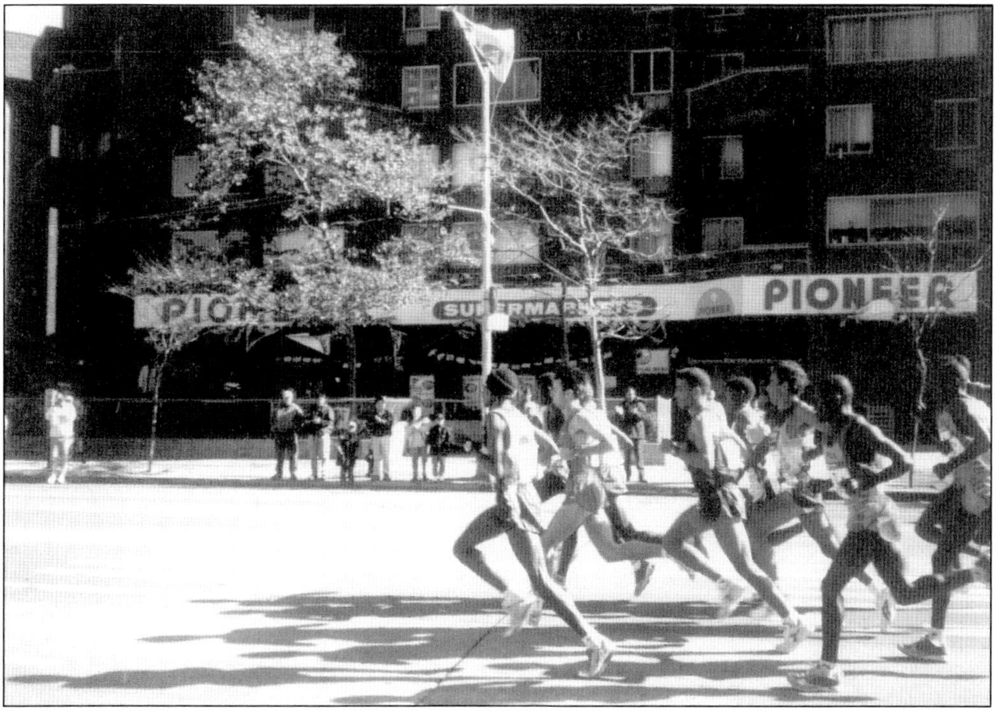


The New York City Marathon, which began in 1970, was at first a 26-mile race that runners would participate in by circling around Central Park five times. In 1976, the route was expanded to cover all five boroughs. Here, the runners are entering the 20th mile on 108th Street and First Avenue in the 1990s. (Courtesy Jerry and Eleanor Koffler.)

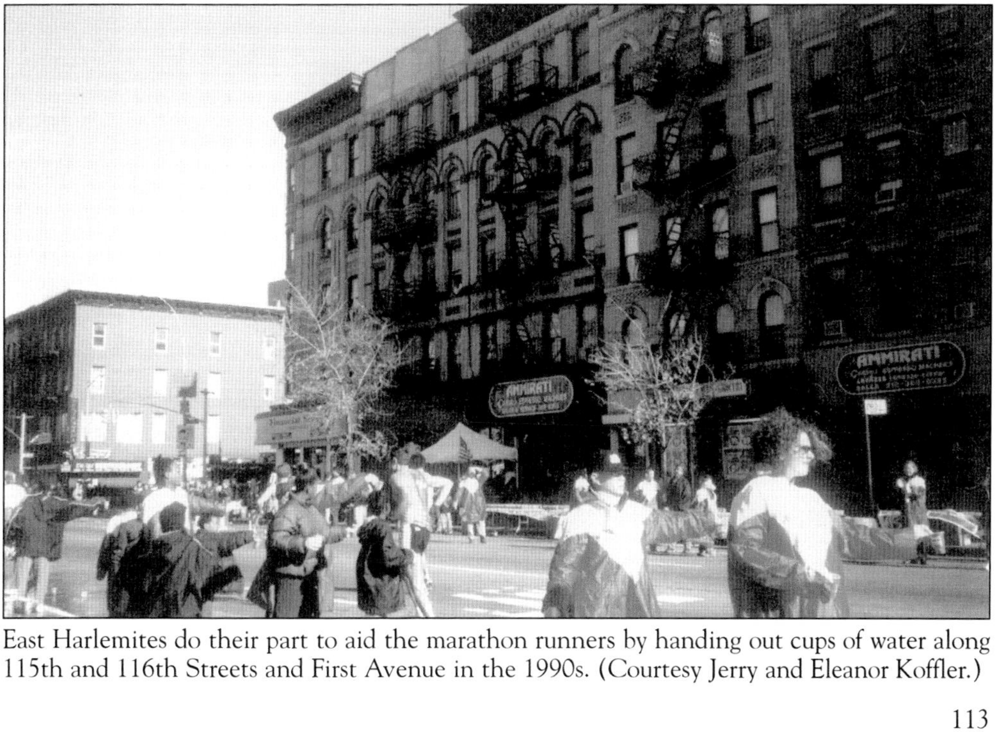


East Harlemites do their part to aid the marathon runners by handing out cups of water along 115th and 116th Streets and First Avenue in the 1990s. (Courtesy Jerry and Eleanor Koffler.)

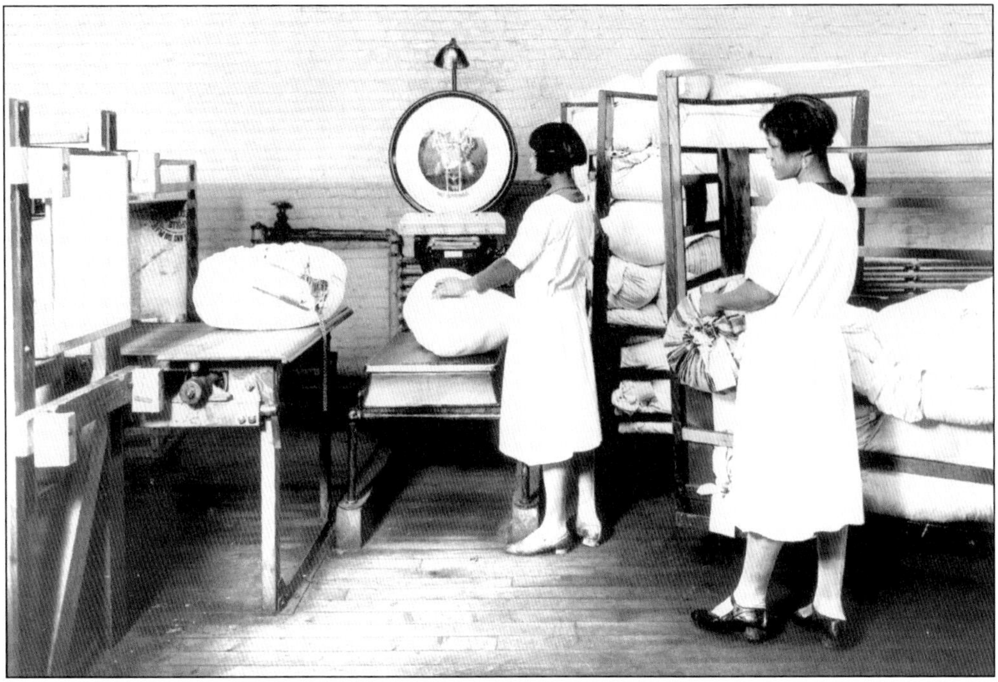

These women are weighing bags of laundry at the Carolyn Laundry in 1928. The laundry house was once located on 129th Street and Park Avenue. (Courtesy the Museum of the City of New York, Byron collection.)

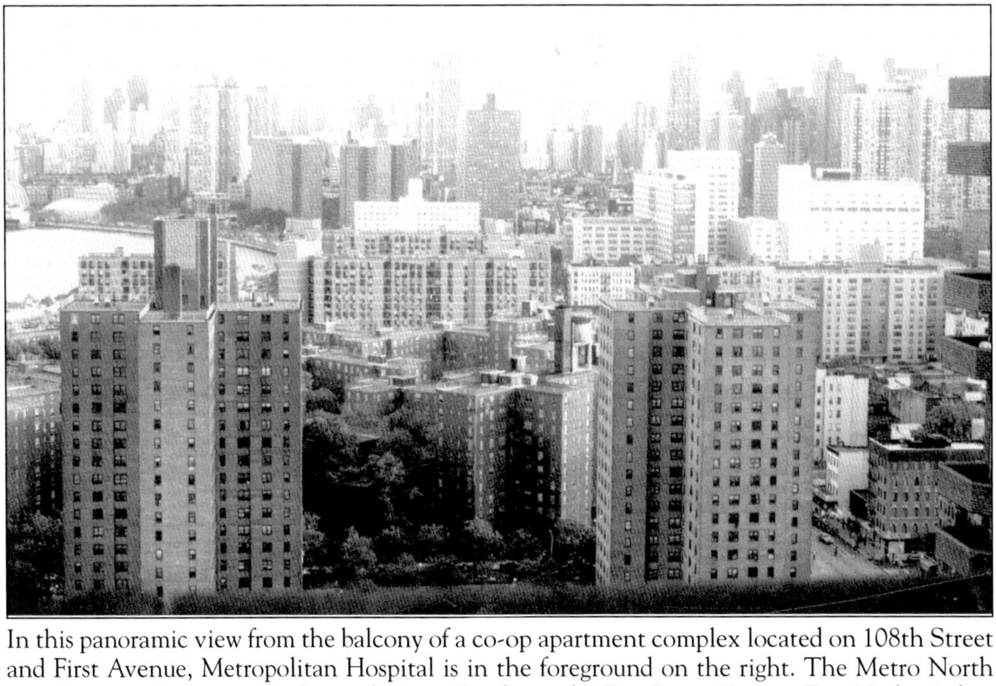

In this panoramic view from the balcony of a co-op apartment complex located on 108th Street and First Avenue, Metropolitan Hospital is in the foreground on the right. The Metro North complex is in the center. In front of Metro North are the East River Houses, East Harlem's first housing projects, built in 1940. The tall housing projects on the left and right are the Woodrow Wilson Houses. (Courtesy Raymond Rodriquez.)

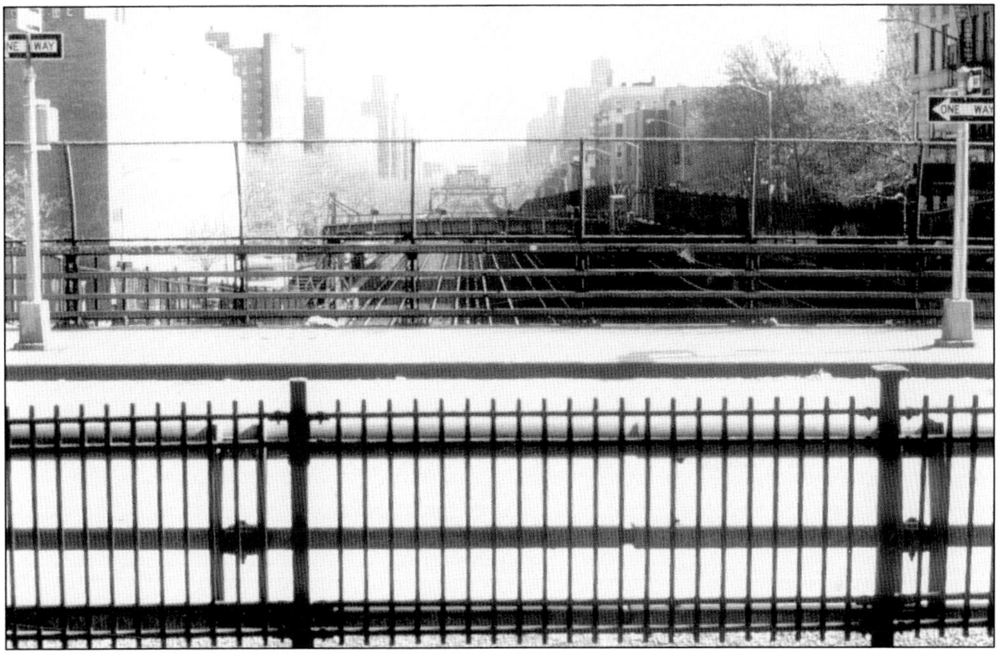

This 1973 view, looking north in front of the Metro North tracks, shows East 97th Street and Park Avenue. (Courtesy Jerry and Eleanor Koffler.)

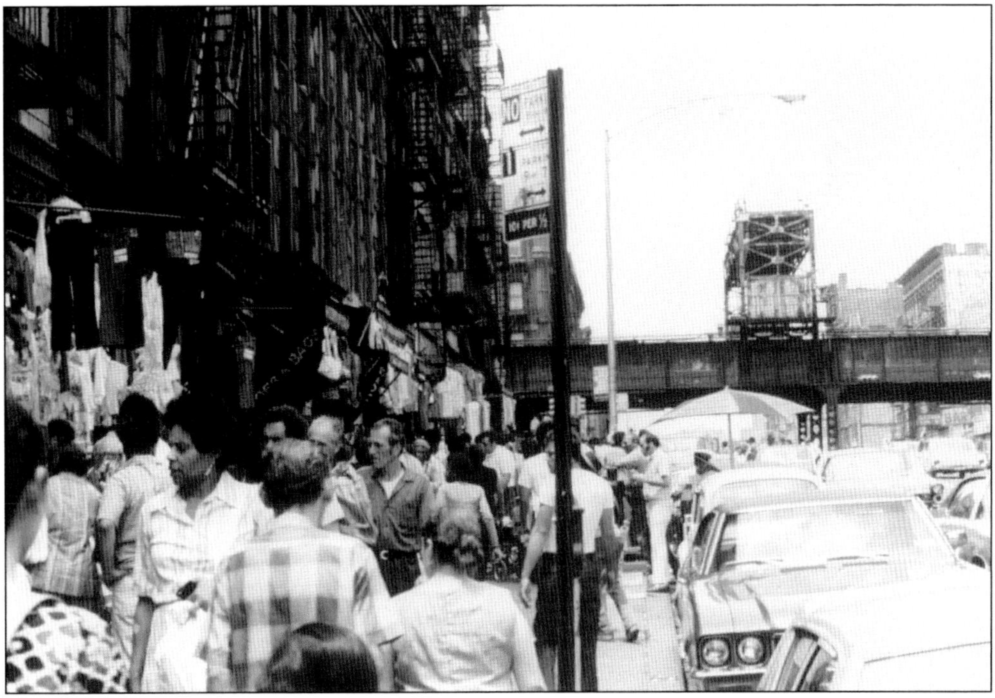

East Harlemites could still buy quality clothes at discount prices at 116th Street between Park and Lexington Avenues. This photograph was taken in 1973. (Courtesy Jerry and Eleanor Koffler.)

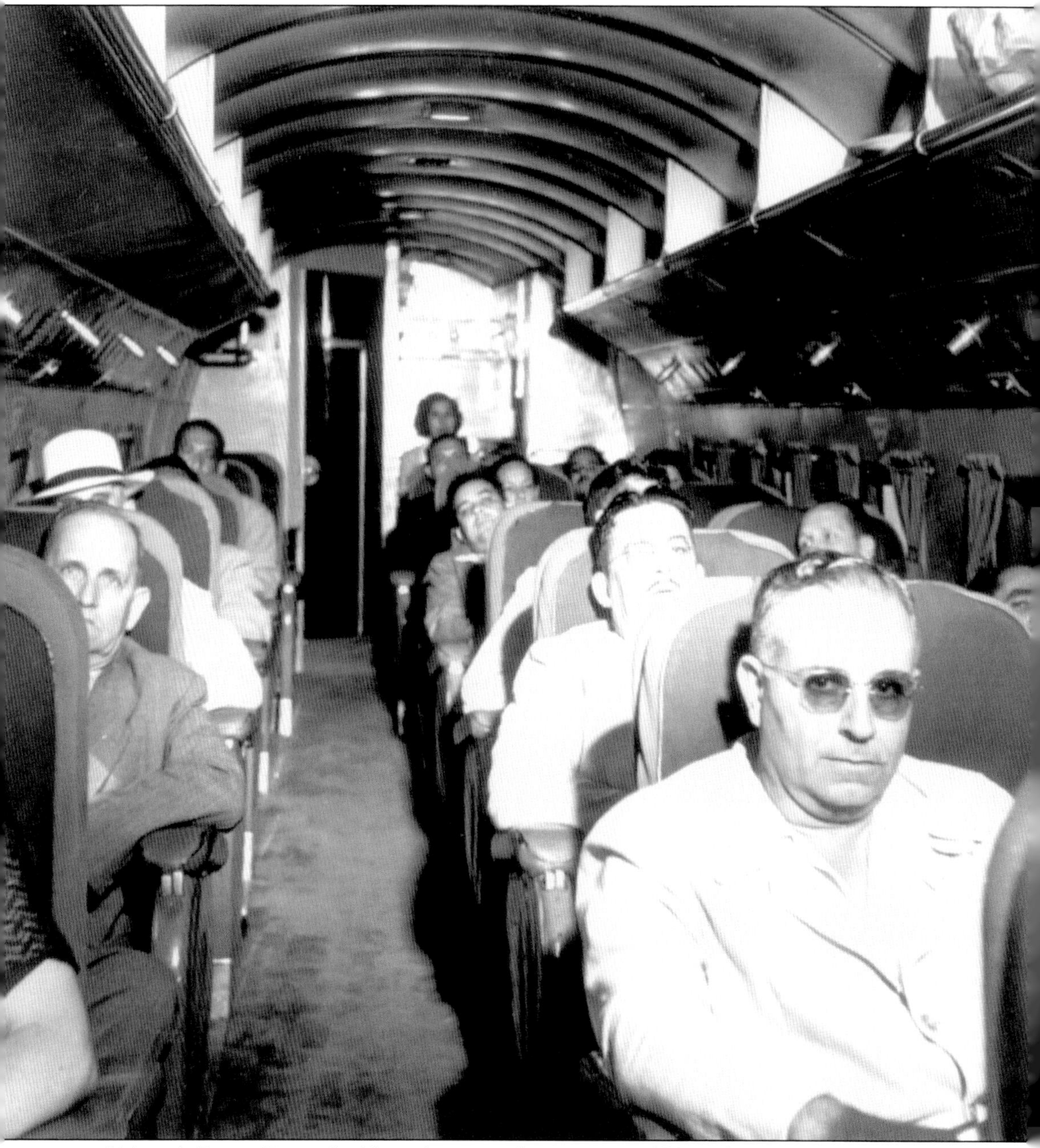

Although Puerto Ricans had been living in the continental United States since the mid-19th century, many arrived after World War II. This photograph shows Puerto Rican passengers traveling on an airplane in 1946. (Courtesy the Center for Puerto Rican Studies, Hunter College, City University of New York.)

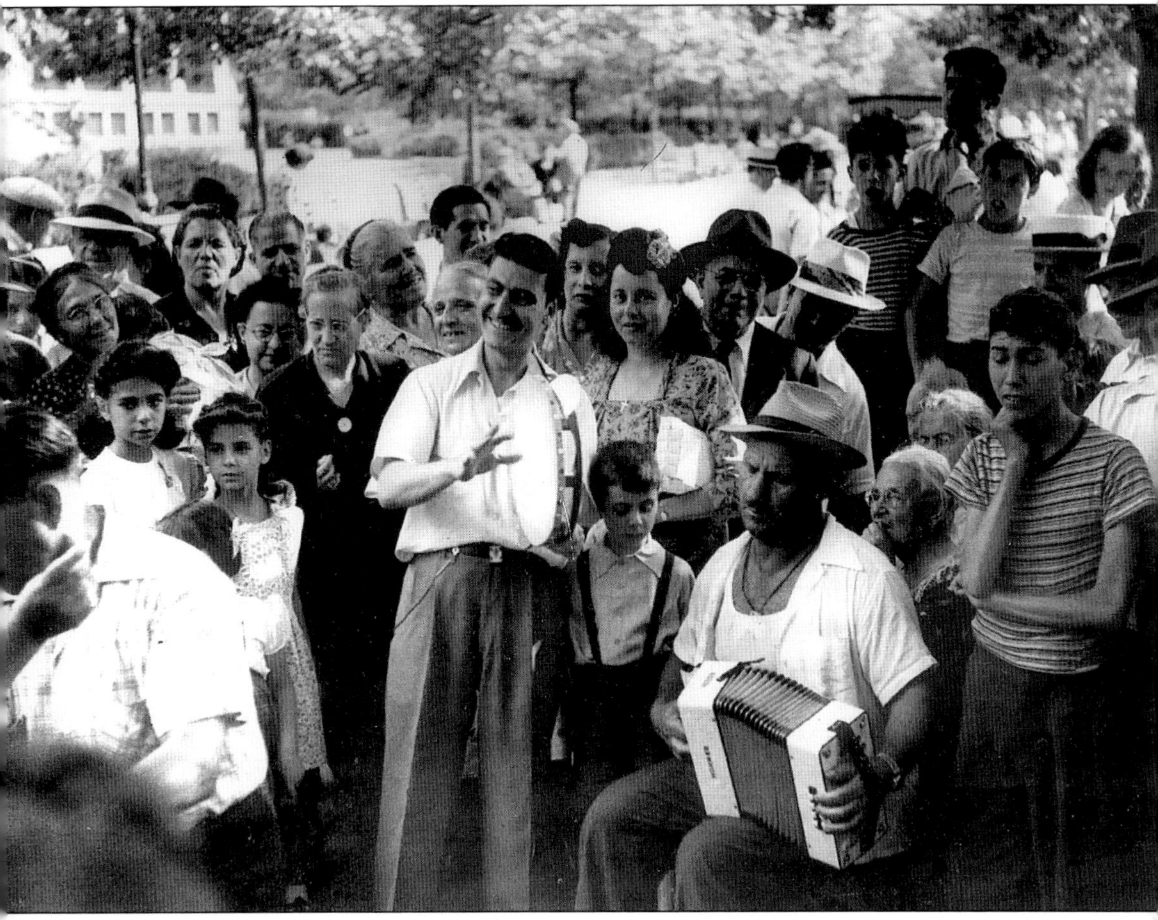

East Harlemites gather at Thomas Jefferson Park to celebrate the boys coming home after World War II. (Photograph by John Albok; courtesy the Museum of the City of New York, Ilona Albok Vitarius.)

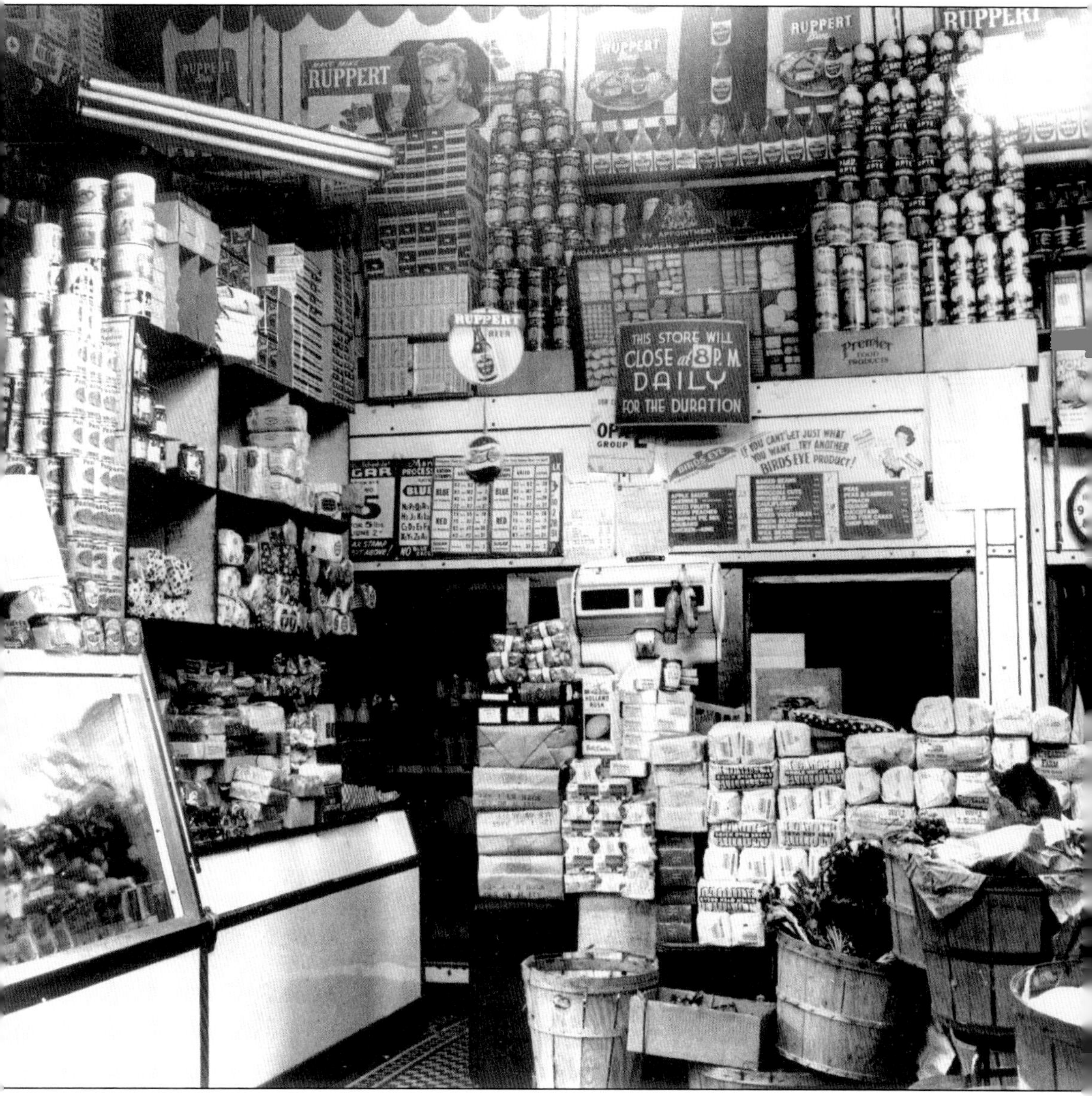


Before the advent of the mega-supermarkets such as Pathmark and Wal-Mart, the local grocery store in the neighborhood provided produce for the community. In this 1940 view, we see the Interior Celentano, located on Madison Avenue between 96th and 97th Streets. (Photograph by John Albok; courtesy the Museum of the City of New York, Ilona Albok Vitarius.)

Today, an East Harlemite can still purchase produce at Sammy's Gourmet. (Author's collection.)

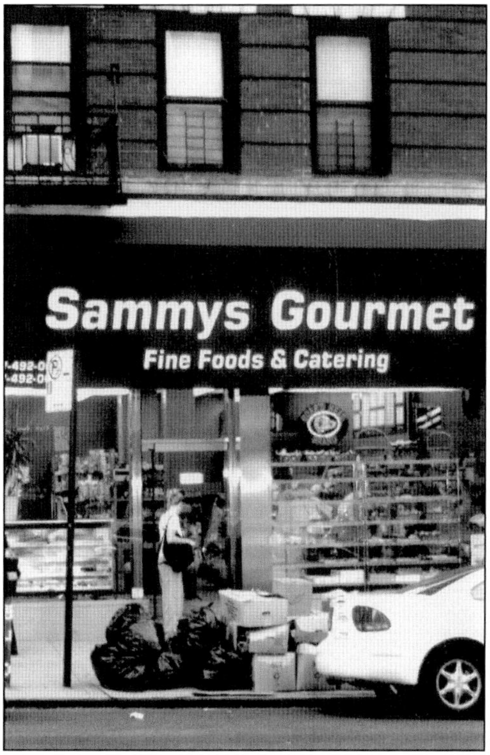


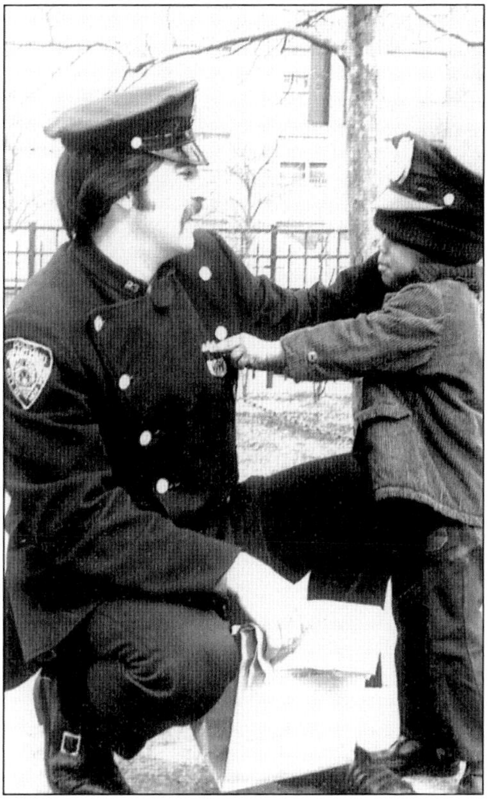

Seen here are an unidentified policeman and a young child in the early 1960s. Notice the number on the collar of the police uniform, indicating the 23rd Precinct, located on East 104th Street between Lexington and Third Avenues.

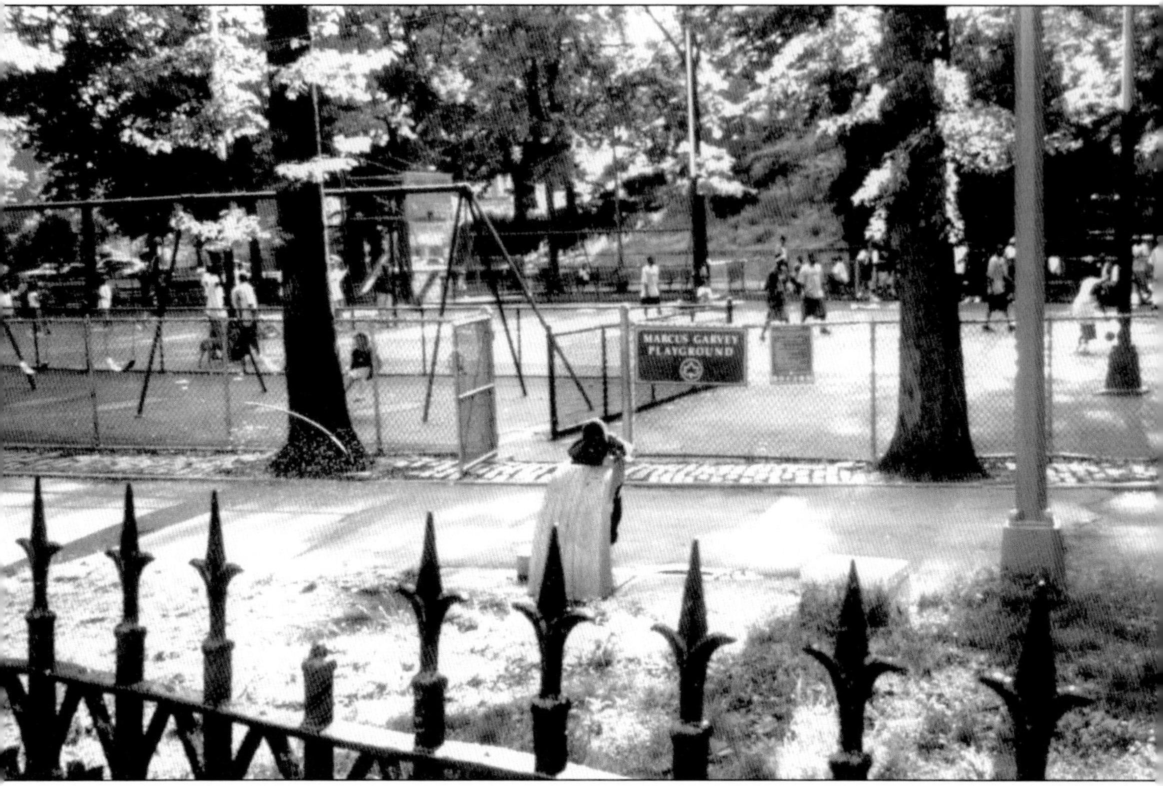


East Harlemites enjoy themselves at Marcus Garvey Park (formerly Mount Morris Park), located between 120th and 123rd Streets in 2003.

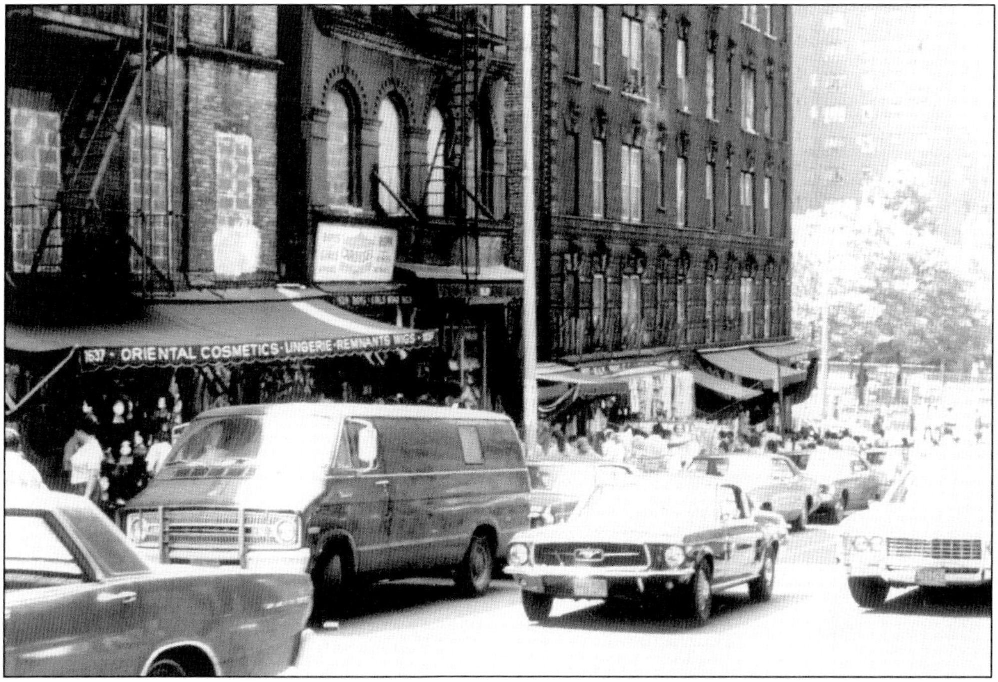


Cars stream up a small hill on 116th Street between Madison and Fifth Avenues in 1973. (Courtesy Jerry and Eleanor Koffler.)

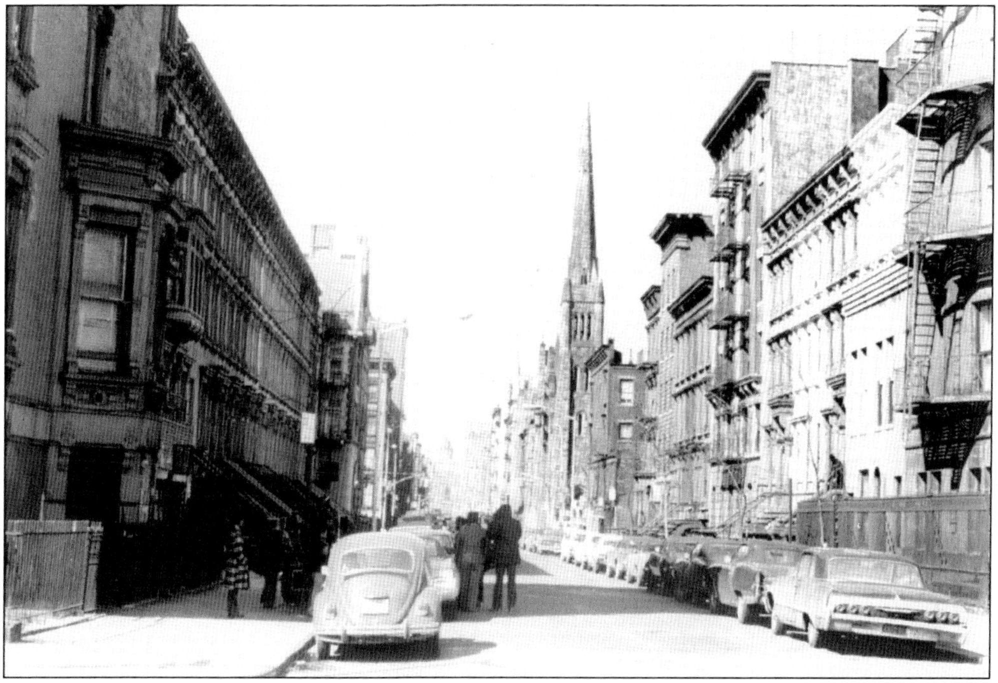

This view, looking west on Fifth Avenue in 1973, shows 123rd Street. (Courtesy Jerry and Eleanor Koffler.)

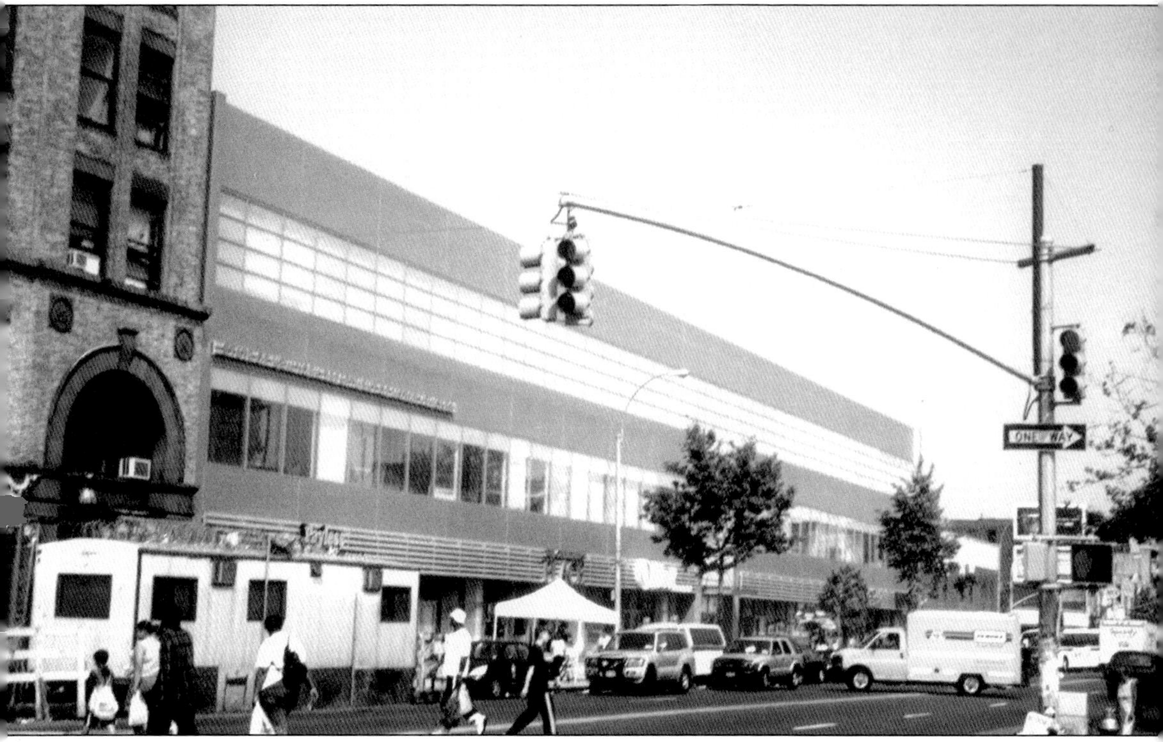


Recently, major businesses have moved in and provided many jobs and services to East Harlem. Here, on 125th Street between Lexington and Third Avenues, a McDonald's, a Payless Shoe Source, Children's Palace, and a Fleet bank have settled. (Author's collection.)

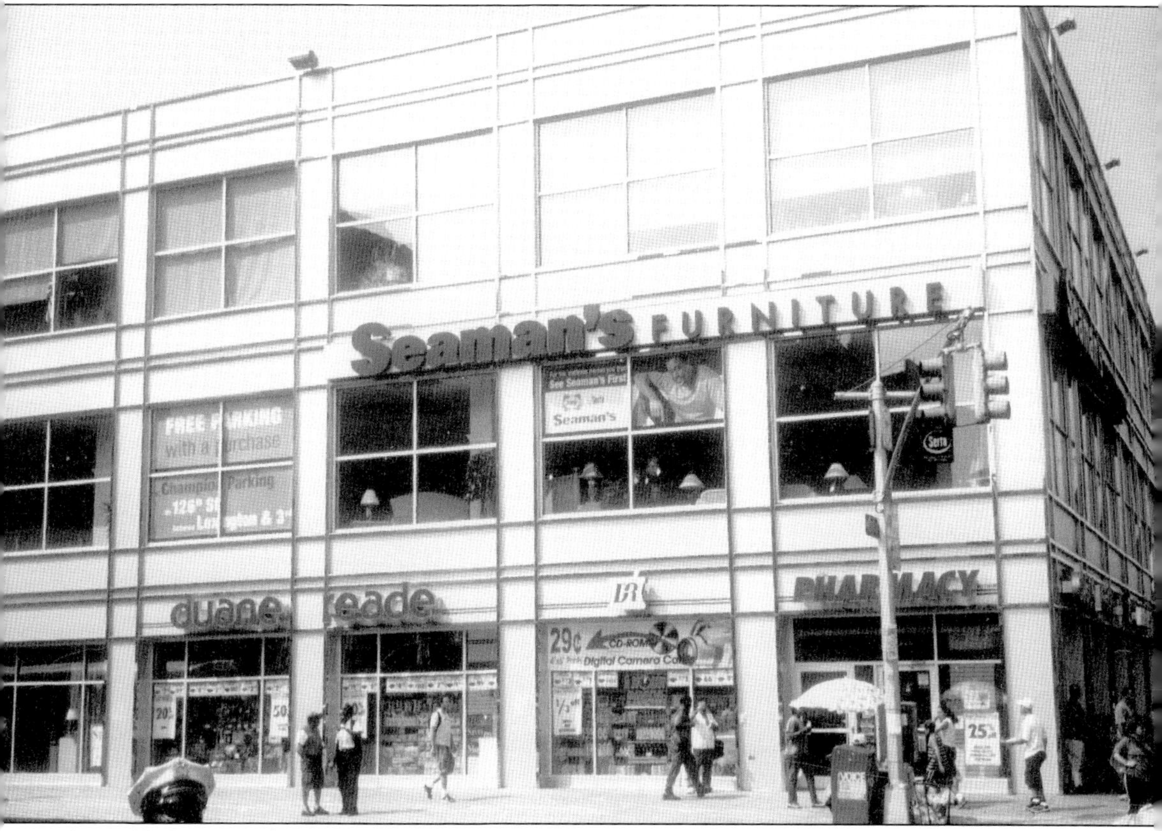

At 125th Street and Lexington Avenue today are Seaman's and the Duane Reade pharmacy.

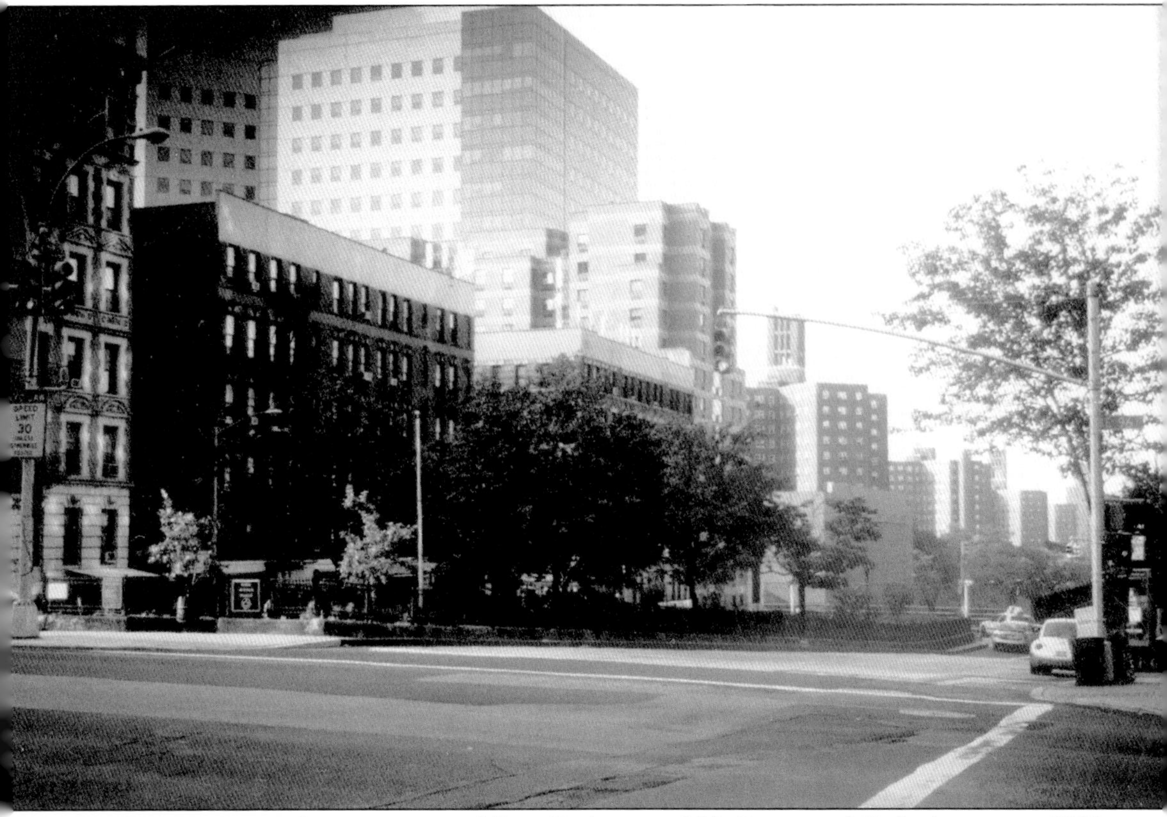


Seen is the southernmost part of East Harlem on 96th Street and Park Avenue in 2003. (Author's collection.)

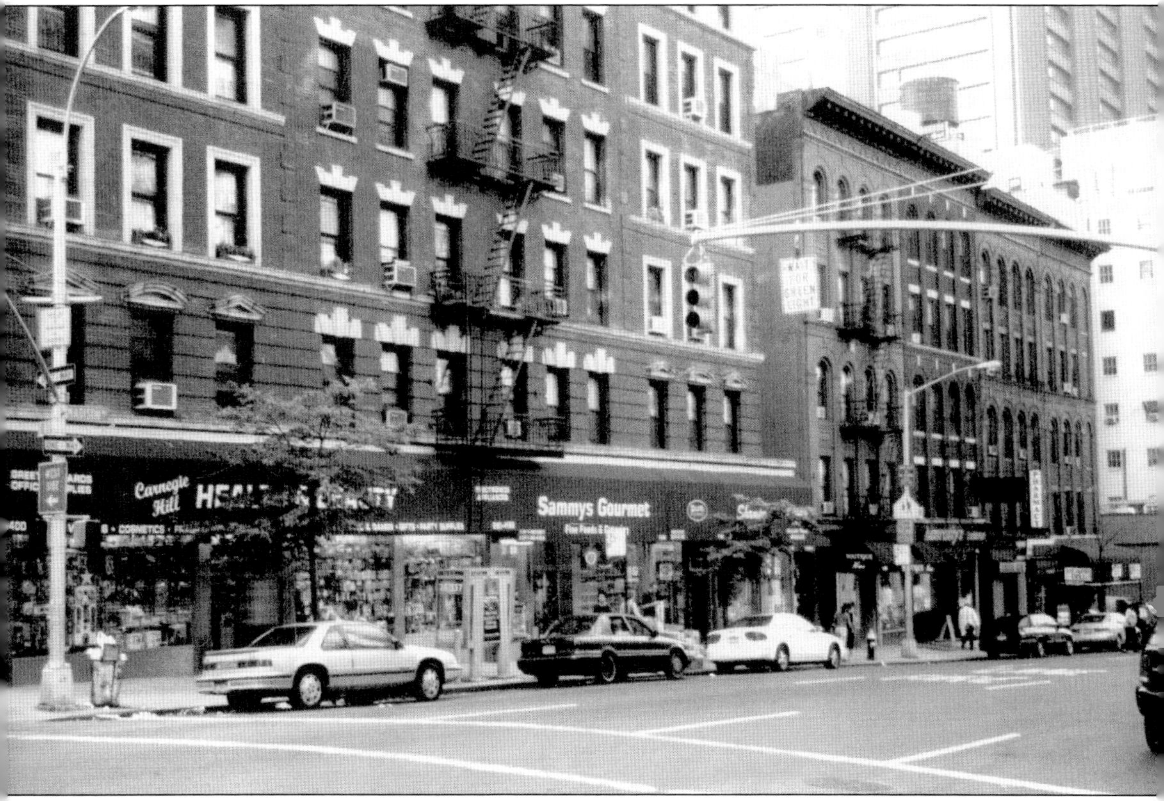

This view looks north on East Harlem on 97th Street and Madison Avenue. (Author's collection.)

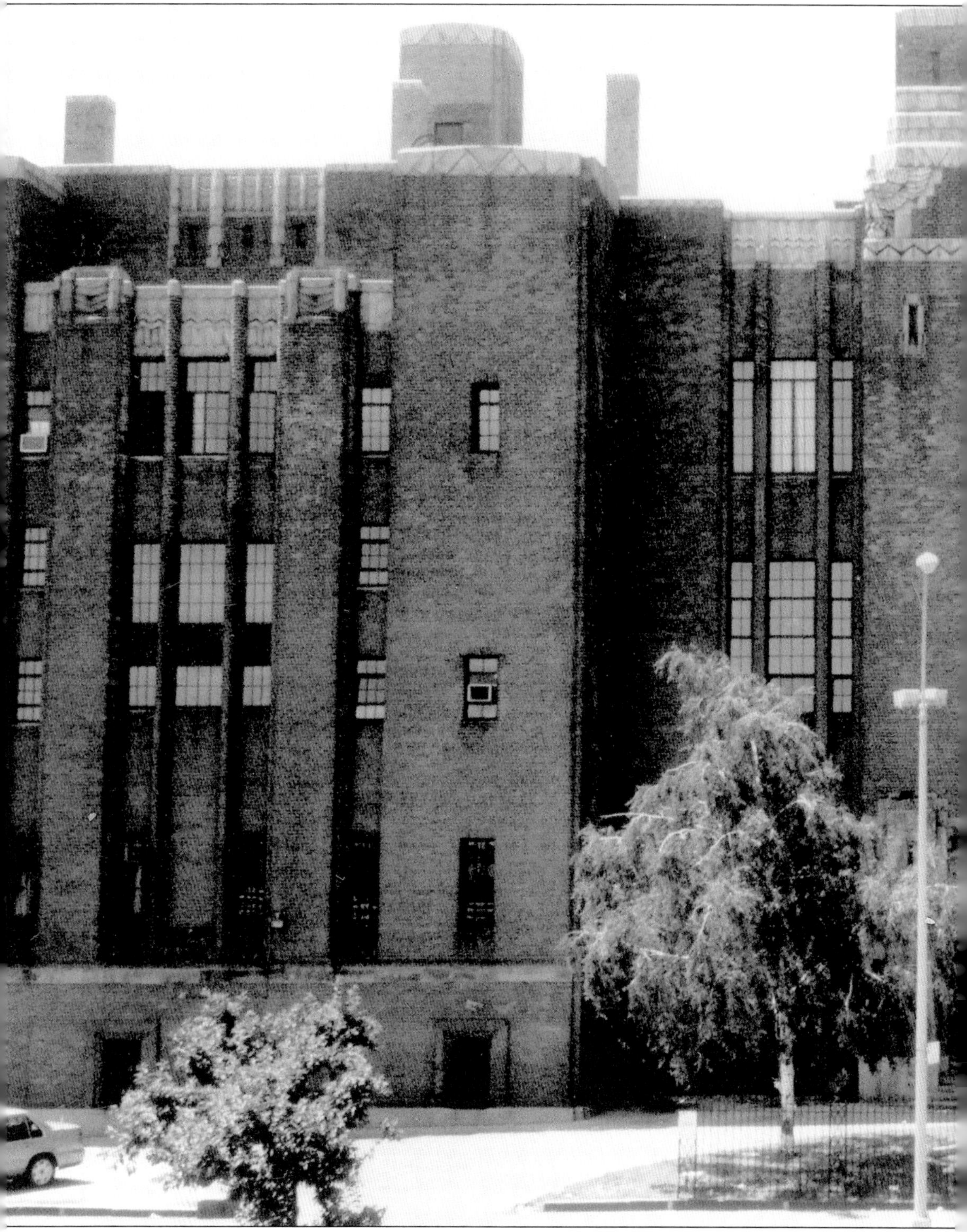

We have come to the northernmost end of East Harlem. In this photograph is the 369th Armory, located on 142nd Street and Fifth Avenue. The armory is home to the Famous Harlem

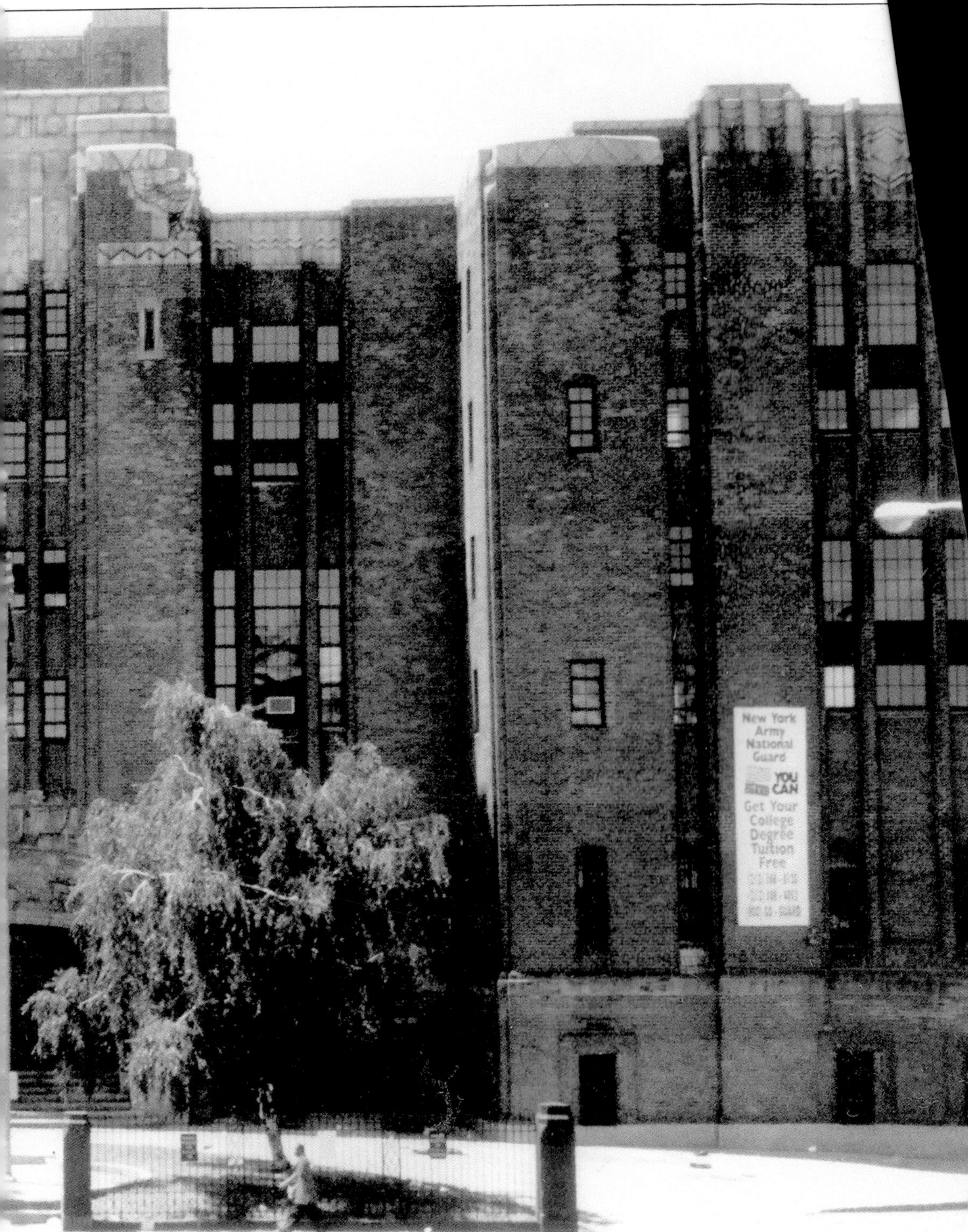


Hell Fighters, an African American unit that distinguished itself in World War I.

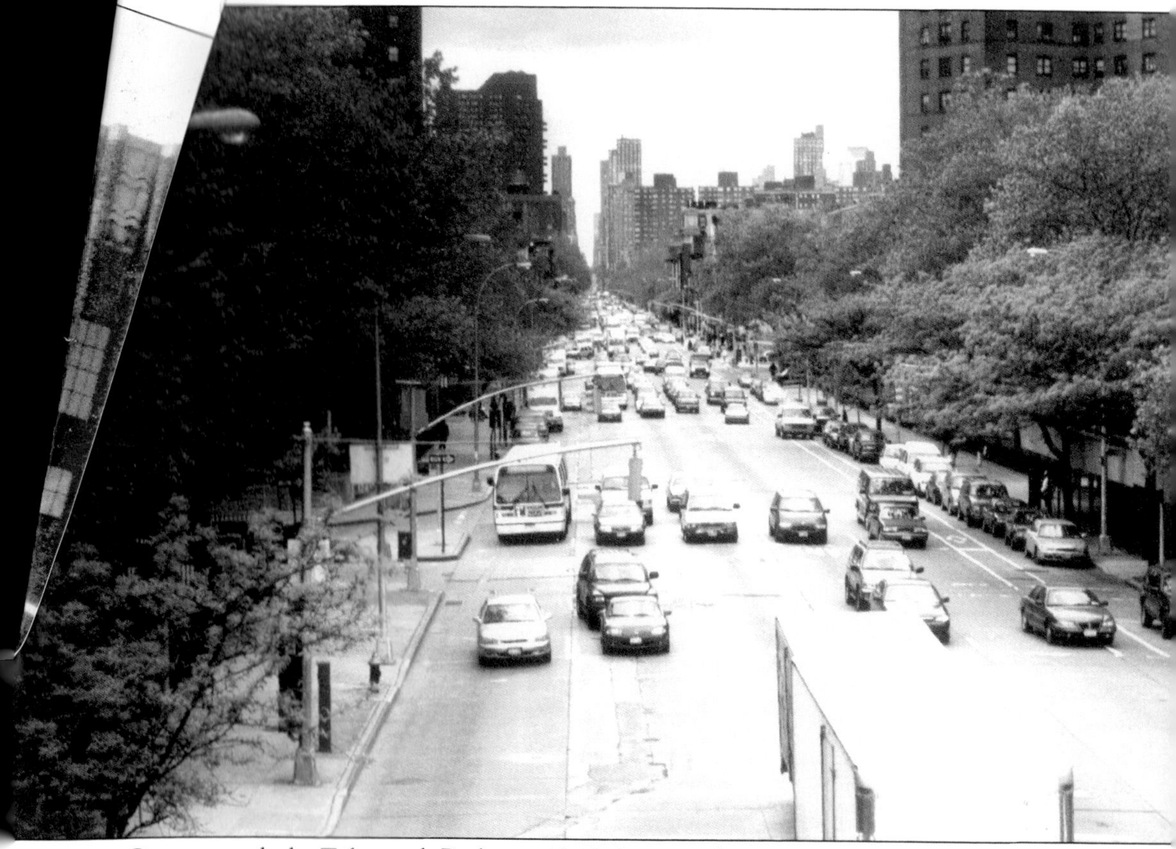

Cars approach the Triborough Bridge on 124th Street and First Avenue. (Author's collection.)

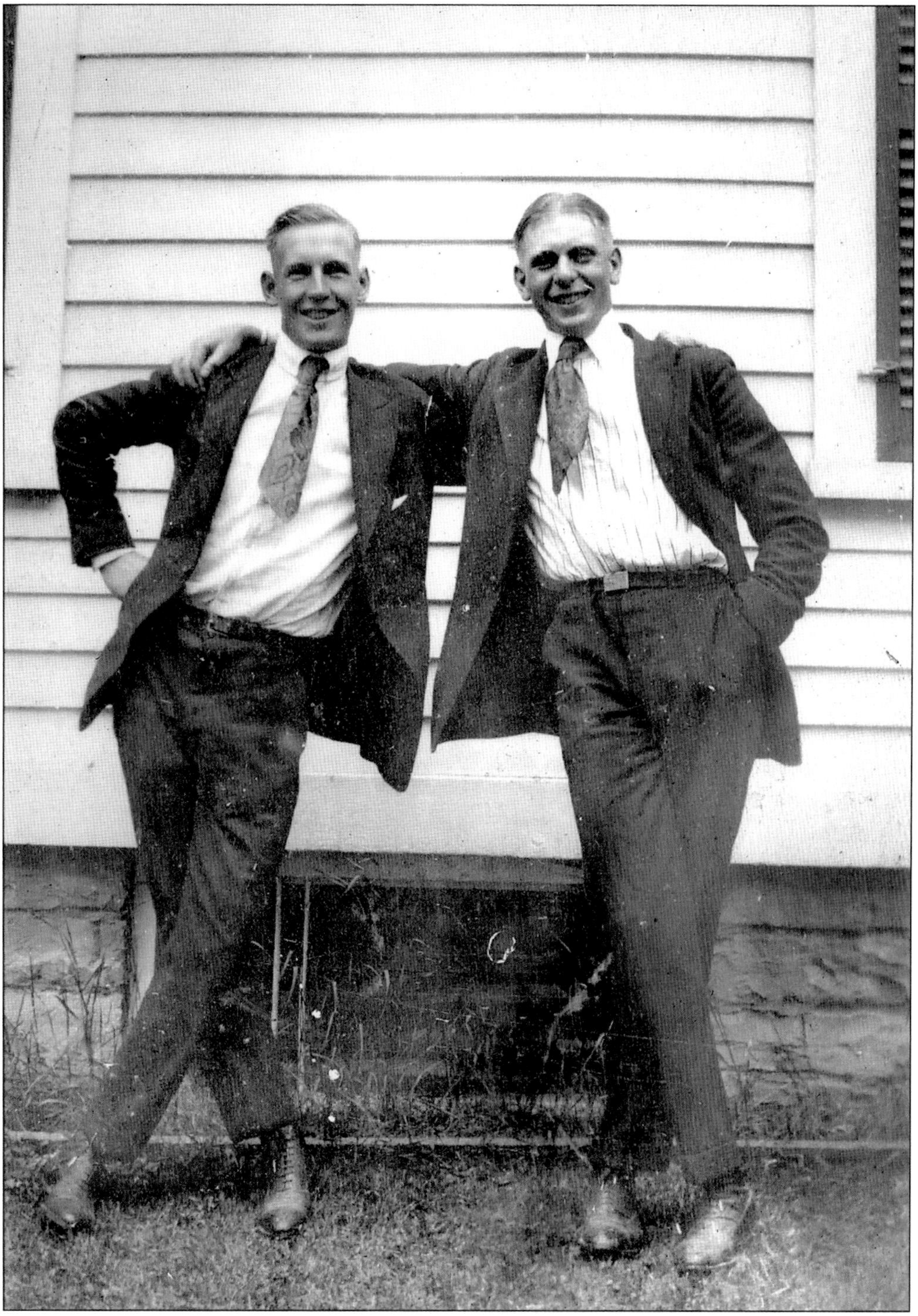

Good friends Stacy Wilson (left) and John Stiles pose before Stiles went off to fight in France in 1918. Stiles was killed in France, and his body was brought back home for burial as a hero. Before the war, Stiles was a teller at the bank in Cooperstown, and a plaque still commemorates him at the Key Bank branch in Cooperstown.

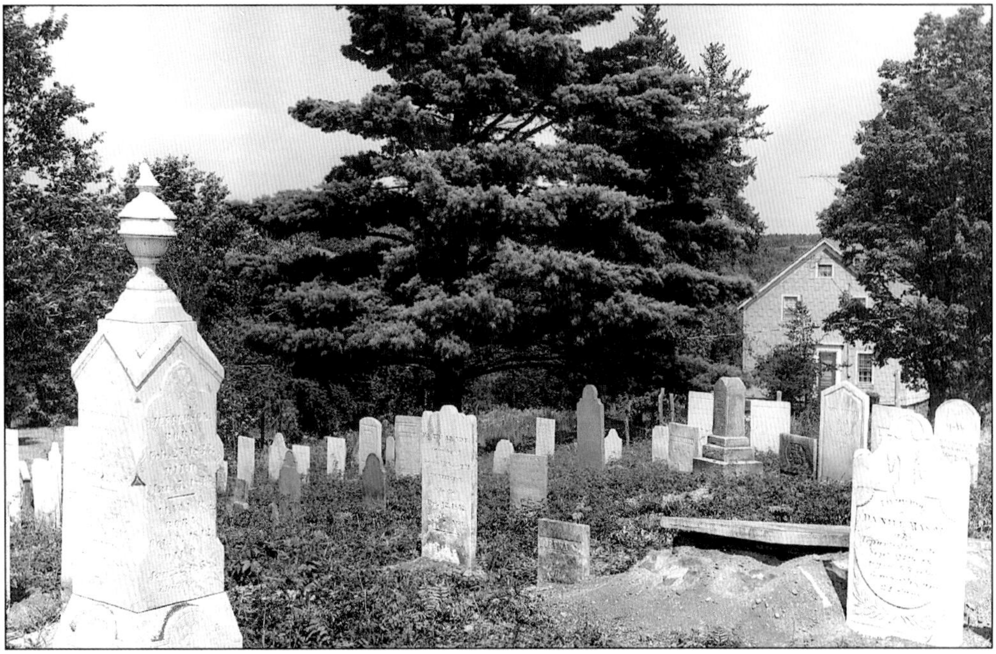

The Old Middlefield Center Cemetery was restored in 1969. Many stones had to be reset. (Courtesy TMHA.)

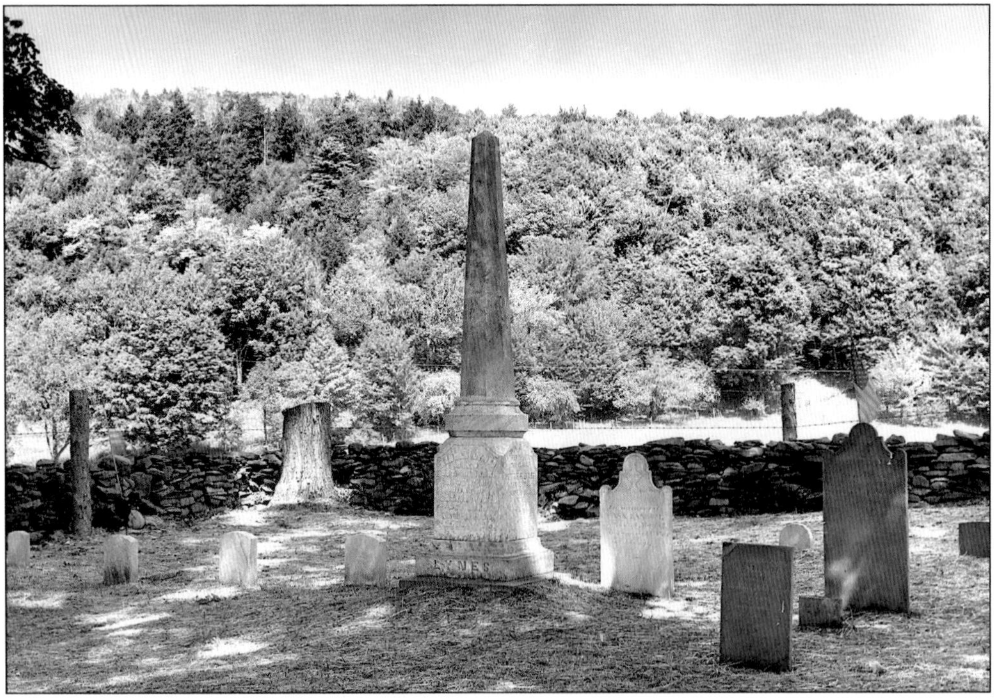


The Lynes Family Cemetery on River Road was restored in 1969. It was common for a family to erect a fine obelisk to mark its burying ground if the family means could support such an undertaking. (Courtesy TMHA.)